Coptales:

From the Penthouse to the Basement

Also by Steven Lowell-Martin

Moses' Chisel

Coptales:
From the Penthouse to the Basement

by

Detective-Sergeant Steven Lowell-Martin (Ret.)

Everlasting Publishing
Yakima, Washington
USA

Coptales:
From the Penthouse to the Basement

By Detective-Sergeant Steven Lowell-Martin (Ret.)

ISBN: 0-9852739-7-6
ISBN 13: 978-0-9852739-7-2

Cover photo: Caitlin Leahy Photograph
"Spritle Leahy Photograph"

Photos from author's personal collection
unless otherwise noted.

First Edition
Everlasting Publishing
PO Box 1061
Yakima, Washington 98907
USA

This book is dedicated to anyone whom has ever affixed a gun belt and headed out onto the streets... uncertain if they would ever return home.

Contents

Introduction
Day One — Hour One
"The Real World."

The young man sat behind the wheel of a 6,000-pound blue and white piece of metal, as the powerful engine idled passively. He hoped that his nervous shaking would be mistaken for the regular car machinations, as the police radio crackled routine business that so often entailed daytime "second-watch" police business. A burglary report, a car accident, a shoplifter detained by store security were all mentioned. To his right slouched a uniformed man twice his age. The senior officer was all-American athletically built, looking like he should have been playing in the NBA, rather than folded into a patrol car seat. He was singing inane jingles from local commercials, "Time for milk... Any time is the right time for milk..." paging through a Sports Illustrated, and yawning. His name was Mark Sabourin, and he would serve the purpose of training the "day one rookie" as a Field Training Officer, or FTO for short. In doing so, he would be empowered with the responsibility of ensuring that the kid would live a long and interesting life. (If the kid passed the muster.)

The sun shone unusually bright and warm through the driver's window for early March in Seattle, known for rain showers to prevail for many more weeks. The young man found the sunlight reassuring as he sat. He found himself wondering how he could be wearing such a strange ensemble — the all blue wool uniform; the stiff and squeaky black leather gun belt cutting miserably into his hip; and the strange fibrous under- garment wrapped around his extremely tall/thin frame like a combination plastic wrap and cardboard. The bulletproof vest was designed to save his life. Yet, the vest served a second, comic purpose. It jutted outward from the sides of his beanpole body, beneath the blue shirt. The older officers at the station had joked that at least it made him look three-dimensional. He felt a sense of awe and empowerment with the revolver at his side and shiny eagle-shaped badge on his chest.

A mere youth at 21 years of age, the young man had chosen the most serious line of work. He did so mostly out of the need to make a real living and impress his young wife, but also out of earnest interest in a profession that had often intrigued him. He had always thought that he would end up a writer some-how, or at least a teacher of literature. He dreamed of pitching in the big leagues, but reality and a torn shoulder had ended that dream abruptly. He loved to write poetry and short stories and was thus nicknamed "John Boy" by his family years ago, in comparison to a writer/character of a popular TV series. But writing wouldn't pay the bills, or build a future house. A serious kid needed a serious job in the real world.

He reviewed in his mind all the controls of the vehicle. The up toggle, for blue and red flashing lights, the down for flashing red "wig-wags" and the twist knob to engage a siren. He thought of how to unlock and remove the shotgun pointed upward at the car roof, and the portable radio jammed into a console, making scratchy conversation.

"Two-Boy-6 going on traffic" spoke the radio. A monotone dispatcher responded, "Two-Boy-6." The cop's voice continued, "55th and Greenwood, Washington License..." Mark righted himself in the seat and turned to the rookie. "You know what to do?"

The rookie answered "I should go back him up," searching desperately his recollection for how to find 55th and Greenwood.

With all the maps provided in training, with quartered "precincts, sectors, and beats" blurring into a jumbled mass, he prayed his memory would not fail him.

He placed the powerful vehicle into gear and the engine responded immediately. He liked the feeling of obvious speed beneath him and thought how it beat driving the little Japanese import he and his wife were sharing. He turned left, eastbound, down a busy arterial, and drove a half block. He then took another left northbound on a residential street and traveled several blocks. He saw the waiting patrol car, lights flashing overhead. The other patrol car was parked at a diagonal angle to a stopped vehicle at the curb. The local zoo entrance stood 50 yards ahead. School children poured from yellow buses and followed teachers toward their field trip destination. It was a perfect spring day.

The waiting officer nodded acknowledgment of the arrival of his backup in front of his mirror and placed his eight-point hat upon his head. A muscular mustachioed Hawaiian man of about 28, the "older" cop exited his vehicle. He had the gentle face and deep voice of a man who could be trusted immediately, in any situation. The rookie and his trainer exited in unison to join the other. They moved toward the passenger side of the offending red coupe, while the Hawaiian officer walked cautiously toward the driver's door.

A non-distinct "pop" came from within the vehicle, much like the sound of a wadded plastic bag poked to exhale. Instantly, all the windows of the vehicle turned crimson, and nothing within could be seen. The Hawaiian grabbed for his gun and crouched, while the training officer merely placed his hand upon his holster, slowing his approach. The rookie sought to imitate his trainer, a half step behind the senior officer.

Mark reached for his portable radio while turning to the rookie, "Do you know what just happened?!"

"I THINK so," uttered the rookie, more confident in sound than in reality.

3

"What?" asked the trainer.

"I think he just shot himself, Mark," responded the rookie.

As the trainer turned the portable radio sideways to his mouth, the long antenna wobbling to his every syllable, the rookie and Hawaiian officer cautiously approached the driver's door of the vehicle. The rookie opened the door as the other officer pulled a slumping body by one arm, seemingly lifeless from the vehicle. A rifle fell sideways to the floor of the vehicle in a splash upon the blood. The rookie grabbed the other arm as the man hung heavily, facedown toward the pavement. They dragged him to a sidewalk and rolled him over.

The man's entire face was gone, save for a few lower teeth. His upper palate no longer existed, nor did his eyes or much forehead. All that existed was what seemed like gallons of blood, pouring out of the cavity that once was a face, and squirting minutely elsewhere from the injured head. The lifeless man began to convulse and a deep and tortured moan gurgled from his throat. The sound immediately reminded the rookie of roars from Godzilla in old 60's movies.

The rookie thought to himself, "My God, he's alive!" as the two of them rolled the monster to his side. The blood poured freely from the remaining throat, and the coughing, gurgling, and moaning continued without end.

The trainer bent over the two attending officers, now converted to helpless medics. He spoke over the shoulder of the rookie, "Welcome to the real world." And the sirens approached...

What you have just read is a true story, as complete and accurate as one may recall of a defining incident, now some 33 years ago. The incident was concluded by riding in the passenger seat of a patrol car as the trainer took control of the "blood run" — the hurrying of a blood sample taken by paramedics to be typed at the blood bank, and rushed to the

Harborview Medical Center operating room. The speed topped 100 miles per hour, as the all-America athlete was clearly an all-America driver as well. The incident was my first day on the job as a Seattle Police officer. As this author would one day pen in a poem, "The Poet Died Today" was true to a vast extent of that date. Yet, the adventure into that unique and remarkable line of work within the Seattle Police Department was an education of incomparable dimensions. This education has provided insight into humankind beyond what most Americans could ever dream.

***

What you are about to read is true, partially true, or maybe even totally contrived. You make up your mind. Yet, I would assure the audience of one absolute. That truth is stranger than fiction. The asterisked names shall indicate altered names to protect the innocent, the not so innocent, and those in the gray areas. I tried to select names that would, nonetheless, convey the tenor of those individuals. I do not claim to be the star player in each story related herein. Still, at the very least, I was overwhelmingly involved, either primarily or secondarily. Were I not directly involved, my sources are trusted peers whom were indeed the primary players, and gracious enough to share all insight. I back up their insight with documentation and evidence.

The following will encompass all of mankind's dimensions. I would caution the reader to steel the mind for the prospect of the morbid, the tragic, and the disheartening, as well as the inspirational and hopeful. Humankind would seem to embody every emotion imaginable, and I will seek to capture all emotions fairly and accurately. Some of what is depicted will be graphic, some will be profane.

I do not claim to have seen it all. And I would be remiss to claim to have had experiences surpassing that of the everyday officer on the streets. However, your author is one of scant few in SPD whom have worked every patrol district in that beautiful, but bizarre city. Few assignments to department special units have escaped being cursed by my presence as well. In addition, I have met three presidents and the Queen of England. To repeat, I am not so arrogant as to claim to have seen it all, but I know there is nothing in this world that remains to shock me.

***

In a follow-up to the above, readers may be amazed to know that the man whom attempted to kill himself actually survived the 30/30-caliber bullet through his mouth and face. To the best of my knowledge, he remains in a nursing home, cared for by the taxpayers of the State of Washington. He was said to have had numerous plastic surgeries following miraculous life-saving work by the extraordinary doctors, nurses, and surgeons at Seattle's Harborview Medical Center, about whom I will often rave in subsequent chapters. He is said to possess artificial eyes, reconstructed cheek bones and teeth, and can feed himself soft foods. His brain suffered little damage, and his reasoning eventually returned. I can only imagine what torture led to his horrific choice, and what suffering he has endured as a result thereof.

Your author returned to the station at the day's end of that initial "tour of duty" to be greeted by numerous veteran officers and curious fellow rookies. While sick to my stomach, I ratcheted as much bravado as I could find and joked to the gathering, "Well, that's what you get for shooting your mouth off." The veteran officers, then clad in only uniform pants and sweaty t-shirts roared their approval. Meanwhile, the rookies nervously joined, and acknowledged the points scored with peers by myself.

My nausea increased exponentially, to the point of secret vomiting deep within a bathroom stall. I waited for the nausea to totally abate, yet the feeling returned for 32 years at the beginning of each shift.

Moreover, the shooter wasn't the only party to suffer. To this day, the gentle Hawaiian officer remains in patrol. And, to this day, he remains greatly apprehensive to approach a vehicle on a traffic stop. Supervisors in the past have sometimes been critical of his reluctance to enforcement traffic laws. Yet he has never related to them the reason behind such. And I had no right to intervene, only respecting him all the more, haunted myself by the sound of those tormented moans.

***

Chapter 1: The Adam Family

Circa summer of 1985 the Seattle Police Department formed specialized street narcotics units for each of the 4 precincts. They were named "Anti-Crime-Teams" or "ACT" units. Selected patrol officers were teamed up in 12 person cadres to combat the epidemic of "rock" (crack) cocaine and rock-houses. The existing major Narcotics Unit was otherwise burdened with high-level trafficking investigations. They were totally understaffed to handle the exploding numbers of drug dealers plaguing Seattle's streets and neighborhoods. The ACT teams would fill that void. The first thing that struck the ever-sarcastic chosen officers as odd about the concept was the unit name. After all, we felt, wasn't *everybody* in the department "anti-crime?" We knew of no "Pro-Crime Unit" in existence at the time. Our suggested re-naming included, "Doper Doomsday," "Rock Rollers" "The Crack Attack" et al, but to no avail with department command. What could you expect of a politically crafty Police Chief whom had previously changed SWAT to "Emergency Response Team," and Police Dog "Chopper" to "Topper?" The unit would be known officially as the "Adam Sector", as were teams formed during a previous narcotics crisis.

Years earlier a precursor to the unit had been tasked with combating newly arrived "Marielito" marijuana and hashish dealers. During that era the Marielitos cursed the historic and vital Pike Place Market area with a bravado and brutality never previously seen. Many in the community cursed Jimmy Carter for allowing the worst of the worst in Cuban prisons to come to the country as "refugees." The precision with which the Marielitos could group-stab a competitor scores of times toward each necessary organ was astounding even to local coroners. It was later discovered that the federal government merely re-located those arrested for drug sales to other "refugee" housing units in the U.S., in apparent avoidance of prosecution. Our current team had nonetheless gained invaluable experience in street level drug enforcement that would serve well on the war on crack.

The naming rights hurdle overcome, the elite ACT teams sought to form innovative strategies to combat tremendous numbers of street level cocaine dealers and the resultant violence. Our unit would be tasked with orchestrating innumerable undercover rock cocaine buy operations on the street level and subsequent search warrants in downtown drug- den hotels and apartments.

On the first day of logging onto police radio as a new unit, the team Sergeant advised my partner, Tony Jensen, and I to invent a new call sign number for use. For those familiar with a hugely successful 70's police TV series, our choice to use "One-Adam-Twelve" that first day shall strike a comic nerve. The radio dispatcher hesitated slightly when hearing, "One Adam 12 is in service," and quickly responded, "Last unit?"

Seasoned and respected veterans from the previous era of street narcotics operations were combined with young and promising officers to set up undercover ACT purchases and subsequent arrests known as "buy-busts." Hundreds of search warrants of drug dens would also be served. The West Precinct ACT team was the first in the city to be formally created. Involving primarily, the downtown corridor of the city, the drug dealing was deemed most prevalent, most visible, and most apt to ruin a thriving business community. Sergeant

Steve Butler was chosen to head the unit. A twenty-seven year veteran at the time, Sergeant Butler could easily pass for a B-movie cowboy picture actor. His feathery red hair and bushy mustache showed few flecks of grey to betray his 52 years. His piercing blue eyes, good nature, and quick wit still garnered attention from passing females.

Sergeant Butler was respected greatly for having led a patrol squad of inexperienced young kids to gain citywide respect for tenacity and loyalty. The former squad was ultimately nicknamed "The Killer Bees" for their aggressive, swarming approach to the criminals.

Sergeant Butler drafted numerous members of the Killer Bees for his new narcotics responsibilities, inclusive of myself. The work would be dangerous. Several hundred narcotics search warrants would be served in notorious drug dens. Sometimes, several of these high-risk forced entries were to be made in a single day. Such a task is easily the most dangerous aspect of police-work. Training and experience taught the officers to fear entry into such doorways, with scant knowledge of what lay on the other side. For that reason, the doorways were known as "the funnel of death." Officers faced booby-trap attacks, pit-bull dog attacks, and confrontations with heavily armed suspects. On one such occasion, an entry team officer faced a .357 magnum revolver in his face, as he burst through the door. The suspect pulled the trigger. By an act of God, the bullet in the chamber was defective. Each member of the unit tempted fate on a daily basis.

On the streets, "Buy Bust" operations were usually devised to involve the younger officers making undercover street purchases of drugs, while observed by "spotter" and "cover officers." These purchases by the younger officers were no less dangerous in nature than search warrant activities.

Indeed, the purchasing officers performed such a task singly, often unarmed, and thus very much exposed.

Spotter officers joined the Sergeant at the windows of the office building command post settings, often joined by intrigued county prosecutors. They served to observe, film, and narrate the purchases below by radio to the nearby plain clothes cover officers on the street level. The cover officers ultimately served to provide protection to the UC (undercover). Were the UC to make the universal gesture of help needed — raising both hands in the air — the cover officers were expected to quickly approach and take the seller down. Their second task was that of making the arrest of the sellers as they would walk away from the purchase site to count their profits and inventory. Several cover officers dotted a given block while operations were conducted. Cover and UC officers, et al, were expected to dress in such a manner as to blend in with the local street environment. UC's were further tasked with resembling local drug buyers. Danger notwithstanding, the assignment provided clear opportunities for enjoyment. Some creativity certainly surfaced. It is with this overview in mind that the following story should be viewed.

***

The pimp vs. the priest

Officer Alvin "Big Daddy" Little was paired for the night with Officer Rob Bolling to function as cover officers. "Big Daddy" was an enormously muscular black man of 28 years of age at some six feet two inches and nearly 260 pounds of muscle. He was five years experienced within the department. He was known for his profound strength, reliability, aggressiveness, and, above all, for his stand-up comic style of humor. He was often quoted as saying, "Aint nothin' scarier than a black man with authority." He chose to adorn himself in a ridiculous all black leather outfit, spiked shiny boots, and a black velvet fedora, complete with purple feather atop. "Big Daddy be pimpin'," he was proud to announce at the command/observation post. In actuality, he was a highly articulate individual. Not to be outdone, Officer Bolling made his grand entrance. While never overtly stated, 20-year veteran Rob was clearly the most obviously gay officer in recorded history. He was known for his propensity for effeminate pink sunglasses, a red convertible corvette with pinkish seats, and flamboyant off-duty fashion ensembles. Yet, he was also known and respected as one hard-nosed and dependable cop. Rob presented himself tastefully adorned in a vintage priest outfit — albeit with his trademark pinkish hue, complete with the collar, crucifix, and Bible.

Already at ease with the flakiness of his troops to perform these unique missions, Sergeant Butler barely batted an eye.

Operations proceeded throughout the night with profound success. Officers found it amazing how they could pursue and tackle scores of drug dealers a mere block away from their fellow entrepreneurs, without so much as slowing the sidewalk industry. The numbers of drug dealers were simply as thick as flies around a carcass. Each arrest seemed to go off without a hitch. UC's made the buy, gave a pre-determined signal to confirm the purchase of drugs, and cover officers would pursue and grab the unlucky offenders around the street corners. Drug dealers sat "on ice" in the nearby "penalty box"-- a very large converted utility van. The penalty box was not renowned for comfort or sanitary conditions in the rear thereof, yet the dealers sat patiently like stacked cord wood within. They really had no choice. They each added to the unique fragrance coming from inside the old van.

A glitch occurred eventually in the best drafted of plans. It would seem a crafty seller abdicated the traditional style of walking away from the place of his sale in a predictable direction. He stalled, and ultimately walked in an unexpected direction. Indeed, he proceeded up an escalator, into a nearby skyscraper and out the backside beyond any cover teams. It was thus incumbent upon some team to close the distance in a hurry, and not lose sight of the individual with department "buy money" and his stash of narcotics.

Big Daddy and Rob were the first to gain a visual of the suspect, a block and a half away to the north on a sidewalk. The suspect was walking nonchalantly past dining patrons of local sidewalk cafes, oblivious to the spectacle to follow. He was distancing himself further from cops he did not see. A tall and wiry man of 45, Officer Rob broke into a sprint. Rob quickly outdistanced the panting, but determined Big Daddy. He eventually gained ground on the distant suspect. The drug dealer took notice of the approaching undercovers and "the chase was on." The suspect, no tortoise in his own right, motivated his legs to resemble sewing machine needles. He deftly maneuvered through the vast sidewalk crowds of wine glass-toting diners without spilling a drop or crumb of the fine local fares. Similarly, Rob wound his way through the crowd of yuppies like a world-class maître-d.

Big Daddy approached in his own unique, but effective style. Like a Brahma bull he charged, the sweat flying from his face and mucous dripping from his nose. Amazingly, his stylish hat remained atop his head. Big Daddy navigated the crowd, much like a fullback seeking pay-dirt in the Super Bowl. Diners and tables, chairs and dishes alike, all went airborne in a cacophonous din. Yet, Big Daddy forged doggedly onward, clearly inspired by the scent of bad guy.

The trio of players then flew out of sight of any command post positions, and concerns for officer safety grew. Fortunately, neither the nervous silence of the command post, nor frenetic running searches by other approaching teams were to span for painfully long.

The scanner on the police radios quickly locked onto the downtown frequency, as the West Dispatcher began to orate animatedly. "All units be advised...we are receiving dozens of calls from witnesses stating that a huge black pimp has pulled out a large gun and is chasing a priest down an alley." The dozens of relayed 9-1-1 calls provided a consistent play-by-play narration of the location of the starring cast, and the suspect was quickly apprehended by responding patrol units and undercover officers. The suspect was even quoted later as stating to arresting officers, "Oh thank God, the *real* police....get me away from those f---ing lunatics!"

A slightly vomiting Big Daddy drew a respect-driven pat on his sweaty back from the priestly presence, as the two officers sat laughing on the sidewalk.

"I think I need a beer," Big Daddy was later quoted as saying.

"I think you need some Tic Tacs," was the appropriate response of Rob, with a slight lisp.

A few days later Sergeant Butler re-played for the squad recordings of the 9-1-1 calls of the event in question. Great humor was generated by hearing of the tale of the poor priest seeking to save a drug dealer's soul, only to be nearly killed by an out- of -control pimp. I thought to myself at the time, "Someday I've gotta write a book about this."

***

The reader may already be recognizing within the above text that it is the personalities, both within and beyond the Seattle Police Department, that are the real story. It is my hope that I may capture the essence of these remarkable men and women in blue, both the heroic and the highly disappointing. Hopefully, those whom the cops serve may be described very similarly. In meeting three presidents, the Queen of England, Hollywood stars, and every caste upon the city streets, one principle has remained constant — they were all just people.

***

Chapter side note: Officer Nicholas Carnovale #1343

Officer Nick Carnovale was the most intelligent human being I have ever known. With all due respect to my chosen profession, it was always baffling as to why he chose to wear a uniform and not don a NASA engineer outfit, or a college professor's attire. Nick would serve the Seattle Police Department for nearly 40 years, and his name would become legendary. I spent many a fascinating hour visiting with Nick, marveling at his genius, and hearing portions of his tragic life story.

Nick was the only child of an Italian immigrant couple. His father was a restaraunteur in downtown Seattle in the late 1940's, and his mother sought to raise her prodigy son. She would spend hours acting as his personal tutor, as she conveyed a profound love for literature, history, and the arts. Yet, she would die of unknown causes when Nick was very young. His overworked father was relegated to raising a son and running the downtown establishment. Nick was thus assigned to chores within the restaurant and entertaining himself in the back kitchen for hours. His father was a decent, but demanding man, and the relationship never neared the closeness of mother to son.

Nick held fond memories of the visitors to the restaurant. Local Mafioso's often enjoyed the Italian food and wine and had interesting stories of the Chicago mob days, before organized crime became "pansies" in Seattle. He particularly enjoyed the many Seattle Police Officers whom loved to frequent the business. He had always found the dichotomy to be ironic. But, it seemed, the mafia knew when not to appear, and the cops knew when not to ask questions. Nick's dad lavished the cops with under-priced heaping meals of delicious pastas, and the conversation would last well into late hours. Nick was always treated with respect and affection by the officers, who would throw him some coins and pat the back of his head. While kids in school would call Nick "retard" for his total lack of social skills, the cops always told him he was a "good kid." They marveled at how Nick could complete complex puzzles in mere minutes, and knew the kid was "special."

Apparently, Nick's father knew that he was dying, as Nick approached 18 years of age. It was believed that the ailment was a cancer, yet the father shared little information. The father would ultimately implore the policemen to find Nick a job with the city before he died. He worried that his son would not be able to care for himself, and any dream of attending college was lost. The policemen soon spoke for Nick to those in power, apparently not long after the funeral of his father.

On March 31, 1952 the genius Nicholas Carnovale became appointed a uniformed Seattle policeman. He was assigned to a myriad of locations within the city. They tried him at directing traffic full-time at first and Pike, years before streetlights would prevail. They tried coupling him with other policemen in patrol cars. But Nick could not relate with the others to a vast extent. Finally, out of respect for Nick's father and deference to the many police friends, young Officer Carnovale was assigned as downtown precinct clerk. He, and two other officers would staff a front desk at the combined West and East Precincts in the Public Safety Building. Nick would handle the filing of reams of police reports, prepare the Sergeants for roll call presentations, and answer phones. Above all, he would handle the countless walk-in complaints from the public. And the "public" that populated the lines at the desk would make the local circus seem tame.

Few will ever forget Nick's profanity-laced tirade in response to an irate woman, many years later. The woman was berating Nick for the "defective" emergency telephone system. After all, how could she dial nine-eleven when she had no eleven button on her phone?! Veteran officers even now can imitate Nick's furious response.

It was thus, 34 years after the beginning of Nick's career, that a young 23 year-old know-it-all officer would first have the pleasure of conversing with Nick. He was a sight to behold. Nick's black and grey hair would fall about his head as per the laws of gravity and no other known rules. His thick black glasses appeared to have been purchased at an 88 Cents Store, but seemed to function well. Nick's blue uniform shirt was neatly tucked into his belt in the front, but did not conform so neatly in the rear. His shirt pocket was stained with multi colors of ink that created a rainbow spotting effect beneath the stuffed clump of pens. His giant 8 inch .357 magnum revolver was maintained haphazardly upon the desktop before him. Yet, with each and every complainant coming to the desk, Nick could provide the answer to any question. He was simply a walking encyclopedia *and* dictionary.

Your author, fresh out of college, fashioned himself quite a wordsmith, boasting of an unparalleled vocabulary. Yet, it quickly became a humbling experience with Nick. It would eventually become readily apparent that Nick's vocabulary totaled in the hundreds of thousands. Nick literally corrected the dictionary! Not in a boastful manner, but as a means of expressing exasperation with Mirriam Webster, Nick would display to me correspondences he had with the dictionary's author. Nick would write critical letters to Webster, demanding that he correct his dictionary. Mr. Webster often expressed his appreciation in return correspondences and promised to correct his mistakes. I wish now that I asked for a copy of one such letter.

Nick also spoke an estimated 21 languages. He would simply review tapes, read the books, and "pick up" another language. He seemed to enjoy Hungarian, Russian, and Arabic especially. He was also very quick with a retort. This was evidenced one morning when an obnoxious defense attorney (redundant) spouted, as he read the precinct directory mentioning the Intelligence Unit, "Huh, that's an oxymoron—POLICE Intelligence?" Without a second's hesitation, Nick responded, "Yeah, buddy, kinda like LEGAL ethics."

I sat down with Nick in the West Precinct break room after one daytime shift many years ago. Jeopardy had just begun on the television as Nick began his dinner. My jaw dropped as Nick screamed at the television at how childish the questions were. He answered every single question with ease, and was angered at the simplicity thereof. "The dumb bastards!" he would announce. Veteran motorcycle officers merely nodded at Nick and made eye contact with one another.

One afternoon, as I was walking past the clerk's counter, I grabbed the ringing phone before the other clerks of the "hole crew" could rise. A strangely familiar voice was on the phone. He simply stated, "Uh, yeah, this is John....can ya tell Nick I'm callin' for him?" Nick slowly ambled over, pulled his sagging pants up, and took the receiver off of hold. He said, "Hey John. Yeah. Kinda busy here too. Sure. Rook to Queen's 3….yeah, you too. OK. Bye." I watched Nick walk to a nearby back office and move a piece upon a chessboard.

I looked at the two other clerks, each 30-year plus veterans in a quizzical manner. Officer Gordy Olson, a 33-year veteran was puffing on his famous pipe, with his feet propped atop the counter top and smirked. "You know who that was?" he grinned. He let me pace in circles trying to place the voice. I could still not identify the voice. Finally Gordy answered, "That's John Wayne, kid." Instantly it made sense! Yet, my quizzical look immediately returned and the other clerk, a fuzzy-mustachioed red-haired "younger officer" of only 30 years named Patrick "Red-Eye" Wallace chimed in. "Yeah, I guess they've been playing chess in person or over the phone ever since Mc-Q." The two renowned clerks explained that Nick and John Wayne had become instant friends when "The Duke" had filmed the movie "Mc-Q" in 1974 in the very spaces we then occupied.

While the public was never aware, John Wayne was a quasi-world class chest master and obsessed upon the game. Somehow, in between scenes, the legendary actor and the precinct clerk took to playing the game. Nick beat him. And then beat him. And then beat him again. The two would play epic battles, and John Wayne would win a few. When years later the most famous actor- ever died, only family and Nick were invited to his funeral. Or so the story is told.

On any given Sunday morning before roll-call, Nick could be seen with two crossword puzzles spread across the clerk's office counter top. To his left would lie the New York Times Sunday crosswords, and to his right the Los Angeles Times counterpart. In each hand Nick held an ink pen, and he would delve into the formidable tasks. In fewer than ten minutes, while writing simultaneously with each hand, Nick would complete the two crosswords.

(Note: I once related this story to a reporter from a local newspaper while on a department-mandated ride-along with me in my patrol car. The reporter scoffed at the ridiculousness of my claims of Nick's grandeur. I thus instantly typed a message on our newly installed in-car computer to every on-duty patrol officer in the West-downtown Precinct..."Can anybody tell this know-it-all reporter about Nick Carnovale and the crosswords?" Within seconds I received scores of accounts of the amazing events..."New York Times... L.A. Times... Pen in each hand... Ten minutes, max!... Damnedest thing I ever saw." The reporter was quickly humbled and the ride-along took a much more pleasant turn.)

The succeeding generations of cops all loved Nick as much as their predecessors, as he was an institution in the West Precinct. They enjoyed taking Nick to Reno with them. They would have preferred to travel to Las Vegas, but Nick was ultimately prohibited from the Vegas casinos. It would seem, he became persona non grata in Vegas casinos for vocally expressing that they were cheating on the cards... because, of course, he could memorize all the cards! The dealers in Reno were more honest and Nick enjoyed many a trip on junkets with the boys, his pockets ridiculously full of coins that he spilled everywhere.

Not that Nick was at all eccentric, but there were just a few 9-1-1 calls about Nick over the years. It became commonplace to hear alert tones over the radio reporting a probable armed robbery in progress at the Tradewell grocery store a few blocks uphill from the station. As the suspect description of a disheveled white male with crooked glasses, laying a huge revolver upon the checkout stand counter came out, it was obvious. We would all slow down and advise radio that we were sure it was Nick, plopping the gun on the counter to dig out some change. We would greet Nick warmly within the store, and remind him to stuff the huge revolver back down his sagging pants pocket. Eventually, even radio and the store clerks knew to expect this of Nick.

For years I visited with Nick and heard his knowledge pour forth about any given subject—the Chilean economy, military history, the arts or politics, etc. I loved to banter about words and sought to stump Nick on a definition or concept just *once*. One quiet Sunday morning before heading out to patrol, I threw out to Nick a prospect. "Nick, we all know that one whom hates women is a misogynist, right? " A nod and grunt. "But, Nick, there is no term in the English dictionary for one whom hates men." Nick went quiet for a moment, and I headed out to patrol and waiting calls triumphantly. After handling a petty parking complaint a voice came over the police radio, "West Precinct." Radio would respond to the radio call... The voice then stated, "Would you have Queen 6 return to the precinct ASAP?" I acknowledged and soon returned. Nick waited at the desk and merely stated, "Misandrynic." He produced his legendary 400,000-word dictionary and pointed out the word. "This is the only dictionary that has it…that dumb boob Webster hasn't added it yet."

With that, the legend grew. Knowing how I loved words, Nick gave me a gift for my future thirty years of police-work. The gift was the word, "stercoraceous." Once again, only the oldest and most in-depth dictionary contained the full definition or spelling. While the little books define the word as, "of or pertaining to dung," the big book cites the meaning as, literally, "full of shit." I often used Nick's gift word for Internal Affairs statements, and in response to annoying defense attorneys in courtrooms. Whatever annoying audience it is that receives the gift word, they are all forced to scramble toward a dictionary to seek the genesis thereof.

Nick Carnovale suffered from acute respiratory problems all of his life. Doctors could never quite quantify nor completely treat the ailment. His coughing would continue without end nearly all of his life. Ultimately, Nick was hospitalized for the affliction and doctors remained stumped. Scores of uniformed patrol officers and detectives in suits would come to visit Nick. Doctors and nurses were confounded regarding his visitors. They eventually asked why we had all taken such an interest in the "derelict" in the bed. We informed them that Nick was no derelict, and was the revered character described above. Nick stayed for considerable time in the hospital with little improvement. We ultimately purchased Nick the most high-tech computerized chess game on the market for his entertainment. While Nick greatly appreciated the gift, he quickly became annoyed at the ease at which he could defeat the ingenious computer.

While making his rounds, the staff physician observed Nick playing the chess game. The doctor thought he would display his mental superiority to the old man by sitting down to win in a couple of minutes. He was rather quickly humbled by a decisive defeat and sat dumbfounded. After the good doctor regained his composure Nick advised him, "Oh, and by the way you have me misdiagnosed. If you had read the New England Journal of Medicine and some French publications, you'd know I have two afflictions…"

In another ironic and cruel twist of fate, Nick had two children. Both were highly mentally challenged and relegated to institutions for life. Nick's beloved wife much resembled his mother, and for that, it would seem, she suffered the same fate. It was my understanding that she died very young.

Nick lived a quiet and very lonely life. Yet, he was enveloped by his only real family — the men and women of SPD, and his enormous caches of books that filled his large and cluttered home. Many years later, a new precinct Captain deemed Nick to be a disgrace to the department. The highly disdained commander re-assigned him to patrol duties, after nearly forty years behind the desk. Nick immediately retired from service on January 13, 1990 and was rarely seen again. He died four and a half years later. Nick had amassed a relative fortune via brilliant investments. Yet every dime of this cache was devoted to the lifetime care of his children and the compassionate institution that was their permanent home.

The men and women of the Seattle Police Department actually paid for Nick's gravestone and he will be forever remembered as a friend, policeman, and genius. May he rest in peace, and enjoy correcting God.

Chapter 2: Babyface goes undercover

As stated previously, beginning street narcotics enforcement in Seattle was an evolutionary work-in-progress in the early 1980's. The department sought to respond appropriately to each apparent wave of new drugs, new drug peddlers, and ever-increasing related violence.   Department commanders and supervisors quickly made notice of your author, then 21 years of age, and looking to be all of seventeen. *Nobody* would suspect me of being a cop. In fact, on two occasions as a rookie patrolman, 9-1-1 callers re-contacted dispatch in order to confirm that the boy standing at the doorstep was indeed the real police. Thus, an obvious usefulness was noted.

In early 1982 Cuban "Marielito" drug dealers sought to take over the Pike Place Market area of downtown Seattle. It became apparent that one of the most scenic tourist settings in the world was becoming home to bloody conflicts, filth, and intimidation. Once teeming crowds seeking to enjoy the local restaurants, open air fish markets, and many artisans and performers in the unique locale, shrunk to a mere trickle. Unsolved brutal stabbings of known traditional local drug dealers became commonplace at the time. Often the victim would suffer dozens of stiletto stab-wounds to vital organs, with the precision of surgeons. While most of the murders could not be solved, it was readily apparent that the Marielitos were flexing their muscles. Broad daylight did not dissuade them in the slightest from selling incomparably high-grade marijuana and hashish.

The Marielitos were readily identifiable. They bore distinct and heavy tattooing from their native Cuban prisons, spoke a loud and staccato Spanish, and had no desire to hide their bold street intentions. They were extremely athletically built, with hair either heavily greased backward or with oiled shaved heads. They evoked caution in even the toughest and most experienced of downtown "David Sector" beat cops.

The David Sector patrol Sergeant responsible for most of downtown during daylight hours was 27-year veteran Bernie Miller. A former Vietnam war hero in the Army, and 14-year veteran from the homicide unit, Bernie was the epitome of toughness and resourcefulness. Standing a mere five foot eight and no more than 155 pounds, every square centimeter of his body appeared to have been carved out of concrete. Not a single grey hair of his short-cropped style was out of place. No one ever knew if his exposed teeth sufficed for a smile or a mere grimace that added to his bulldog demeanor. He could twirl a hand-crafted rose-wood night stick like a circus juggler, and would often receive comments from passersby by that he looked "intimidating." He always responded by tipping his hat and stating, "Thank you very much." Bernie Miller was the perfect choice to direct a street operation.

The first "buy-busts" thus began. A rag-tag group of patrol officers coupled with a few former narcotics detectives were assembled. Legendary beat cop Fred Ibuki was drafted to assist with planning and intelligence. Fred had long ago made his name during 1970's riots, Black Panther shootings, and numerous downtown narcotics arrests. He was physically capable, yet his legend lay with his memory. Fred had an absolute photographic memory. Peer officers sought Fred in lieu of any existing computer technologies at the time. He could remember names, dates of birth, addresses, license plates, accomplices, et al without hesitation. He knew all of the Marielito gangs as if they were his closest family members.

Command post observation rooms were quickly established from the upper Pike Place Market area with a clear view of 1st Avenue and Pike Street, both North-South and East from the vista. Businesses were highly enthusiastic to assist in any way, especially if the owners could gawk at the operation from the command post. Young and convincing officers were drafted from within and without the precinct to act as drug purchasers. Your author was told that he would be happy to assist.

The operation, while low-tech in scope, was well-conceived and orchestrated. The Sergeant and command post summoned the purchasers into the secure and hidden room to first observe the drug dealing. The operations were viewed occurring on the sidewalk across the street through binoculars. Cameras were set up to record the purchases. Officer Ibuki would point out the drug dealers, their leaders, and their characteristics. The most violent of enforcers for the gang would be pointed out as individuals to be avoided, if possible. The purchaser was under *no* circumstances to be lured out of sight of the command post. Cover officers in plain-clothes would hover in nearby alleys and doorways with radio earplugs narrating events. Were there to come a need to rescue the purchaser, the onus was upon them. The purchaser was ordered to approach the gang unarmed and without recording devices. It was known that the Marielitos would conduct a thorough body search of any prospective buyer. A few basics on how to protect oneself during a drug buy followed and one quiet Hail-Mary was given by Sergeant Miller. And away your author went.

The first thing that came to my very nervous mind was that I could not *look* nervous. Firstly, I was being filmed and watched by my senior peers above, and secondly, I surely did not wish to tip the Marielitos. I thought to myself of the one positive to the assignment. I could suddenly stop cutting my hair in such a way as to reveal ears that had been safely covered since the 1960's. I even thought at the time, "I'll write a book about this job someday."

With the long hair and jeans, ratty tee shirt and tennis shoes, I ambled out of the command post and onto the streets. Hands in pockets, I slowed my walk toward 1st and Pike into the malaise of evening-time humanity. Cabs honked past, music droned rhythmically outward from local sleazy "live girls" cabarets, and the colors of the big city were apparent. Before I could even get down the block, a dark Cadillac with tinted windows slowed beside me. A window rolled slowly downward. An elderly affluent man of about sixty called out, "Hey baby, I'm lookin' for some." I nearly vomited, as I sought to chase the man away without tipping my cover. He persisted in following for several yards before giving up and driving further forward, in search of prevalent "boy whores" in the area. A nearby pair of cover officers hiding in a doorway could not conceal their laughter.

My heart raced as I approached three Marielitos loitering in front of Ship's Tavern—a total dive that they considered home. I kept my hands in pockets while they checked me with their eyes. I let out a deep, slow breath, and voiced, "Hey man, you got some?" Stupidly, I tried to fake some hybrid Hispanic and black accent, and came out sounding ridiculous. The Marielitos uttered rapid Spanish to one another. Little did they know that I spoke fluent Spanish and understood them to be discussing if I were real or the police.

Ultimately, a leader of some sort emerged from within the tavern. It was obvious that he was packing a handgun beneath his belt. He was huge, and muscular, shaved head, and oily. He smelled of marijuana, and was clearly halfway high. He finally ordered his minions to search me and sell to me, and returned to the smoky noisy bar to continue his game of pool. Strange, but wonderful Latin music was playing loudly from a jukebox.

Two of the Marielitos would perform a very thorough search of my body, as I held my hands outward. I felt sickened at the thought of these filthy and stinking druggies putting their hands all over me, yet I remained conscious of not raising my hands too high upward. Were my hands to be raised well above my head, that would be a gesture to the command post that I was imperiled. Cover officers would come running, guns drawn and ready for business. Finally, the large baggies of hash were presented by the individual who did not search me.

I asked, "How much?" to which he replied, "Hundred dollar." I quickly responded as taught in the command post, "Too much," and started to walk away. Immediately, the trust was gained and the seller jumped in front of me. "OK, eighty dollar." I asked him, "This good shit?" and the response came, "Da best." I produced the 80 dollars from my pocket while looking around nervously, seemingly afraid of the cops. Yet I ensured that the handing of the cash happened to be observable from across and above my location.

Free enterprise had been conducted on Seattle's streets and the dealers, believing themselves to be clever, never had a clue. Little did they know that the "policia tonto" (dumb cops) had photo-copied every bill used in the purchases. Serial numbers had been recorded, and the purchases of drugs were all videotaped. The undercover purchaser would amble behind and back into the command post as soon as possible. The drugs were immediately placed into evidence, and a detailed written statement by the purchaser would authenticate the video tape taken. Still photos of the sellers and transaction were also taken by Officer Ibuki. They were of extremely high quality, and Sergeant Miller would often comment, "If you want good photos taken, you need a good Jap."

Operations of this sort would continue for weeks. No arrests were made of the Marielito dealers, and they were seemingly getting rich from SPD taxpayer-provided dollars. Your author became very adept at the process of undercover work. Indeed, the art of scamming and lying became frighteningly easy as the weeks moved on. What I found amazing was that I could return to regular foot patrol duties the following day, work the same area in uniform, and never get recognized by the druggies. It would seem the only thing bad guys saw was the uniform. We were otherwise faceless robots to them. Ever mischievous, I did once approach a dealer in uniform and offer him forty dollars for some hash. He simply laughed at me, shook his hands in a "no-way" motion and began to walk away. But I persisted. I insisted that I had a habit, loved smoking dope, and couldn't buy any because people knew I was a cop. I even mentioned that it was getting tough to steal the hash from the evidence room.

My groveling ultimately paid off and the sale was made. I thus immediately placed the individual under arrest and booked him. Regrettably, when the case went to court, some two months later, the presiding judge could not bring himself to believe the story. He freed the man from the charges while rolling his eyes incredulously.

We were ultimately advised that a last day of the purchases operations would commence one summer evening, as ample evidence and documentation existed for arrests. I was thus sent forward for my very last buy. Feeling all too clever and experienced in the process at that point, I sought to make a bigger purchase. But I only possessed the standard hundred dollars of buy money and wasn't about to ask Sergeant Miller for more. I finally cut up some greenish paper from the copying machine to the dimensions of the currency and wrapped the true cash around such.

I commenced the approach of the dopers in the usual manner. But then I indicated that I wanted half a kilo (the standard for federal charges). He indicated that would not be possible, at which time I flashed my supposed money. I got cocky and tucked my "$500 dollars" into my pocket and advised him that the new dealers down the block would be happy to take my money. The individual finally summoned a substantial quantity of the hash from within the bar, but remained suspicious. I then pointed out one of the cover officers down the block and told him, "Hurry the f--- up, cops man!" I apparently was successful in harrying the man, as I tucked the money in his pocket and grabbed the large lunch-box sized bag of drugs.

Upon return to the command post, Sergeant Miller read my detailed statement. Steam seemed to come from his ears, and he calmly stated, "Kid, that's your last buy." I didn't dare to respond that it had been the last buy anyway. But I later realized how stupid my actions had been. I could have easily been stabbed by the dealer whom became furious when he unfurled his $100 and phony monies. Rescuing fellow officers could also have been placed in harm's way by my cockiness.

Months later, facing federal charges in US court, the dealer appeared for the proceedings neatly groomed in an expensive suit, and represented by a pricey attorney. He seemed smugly confident of his impending freedom, as his lawyer pleaded entrapment, racism, and "cultural misunderstanding," etc. However, he could not restrain his client from taking the stand, to show bravado and play the angel role. The defendant indeed had swayed the jury at one point, speaking of horrible conditions in Cuban prisons, and the new life he had in America. Yet, his temper would later be his undoing. As I bragged during my testimony of scamming him on the cost of drugs, he stood up from behind the defendant's table and screamed, "That's right... he f---ing ripped me off, man, I want *all* of my money!" One would hope he found American prisons more comfortable.

Ultimately, over fifty Marielito drug dealers would be arrested on arrest warrants and each would be convicted of drug trafficking. Search warrants were served by SWAT members upon their filthy residences, and much of the earlier buy money was recovered, with serial numbers matching that of photocopied bills.

Most, if not all of the dreaded Marielitos would leave our city, one way or the other after serious legal and physical clashes. Ironically, the owner of the bar whom they had once commandeered, wished to show his newfound bravery toward the gang. He hung a "No Cubans" sign prominently above his entrance door. An ACLU law-suit quickly motivated him to change the sign to "No trouble-makers." Other business owners hung signs in the area, "Illegal activity prohibited in this area." (We were never really sure where illegal activity was *not* prohibited.)

***

Chapter side note: Cop Culture—We are a different breed.

An exceptionally bright wife of an officer once wrote a PhD dissertation in Anthropology, citing police officers as a totally distinct cultural group. They are compared most closely to prison inmates in attitudes. Indeed, while police officers are arbiters of right and wrong and dictated social rules, they have their own strongly unique beliefs.

With few exceptions, police officers are, at best, harsh realists, and at worst, extreme pessimists. While your author's wife is an extreme optimist, I must claim, only half in jest, that the glass is half empty — and *tainted*. I would maintain that the overwhelming majority of my peers share the same attitude.

Police officers see humanity on a daily basis at its very worst. It is disheartening to observe how inherently corruptible and foolish humanity has become. While the vast majority of human beings are honest hard-working people, just trying to get by in life, there are way too many whom exist in stark contrast. Police officers have a term for such persons. They are known as "a---holes." It is remarkable to view how many people choose to lie, cheat, and steal. And it is exponentially remarkable to see how society as a whole somehow condones or enables such behaviors. A myriad of sad excuses are given for individuals whom harm another either physically or by destruction of or deprivation of hard-earned property. Amazingly, many such a — holes seem to arise to positions of power and prominence in society and even within our own department.

It is thus that officers come to expect most individuals confronted to lie. They expect politicians to make false promises. And they expect department commanders to make decisions based upon personal gain, rather than societal benefits.

With police officers, trust must be earned. Once such is earned, a person or group exists beyond reproach. Above all, cops trust their peers most implicitly. It is those peers with whom they must trust with their lives. It is those peers whom are expected not to attack with the ignorant acrimony of endless criticisms so often received from the public and the media.

Police officers are often treated by the public as if they are lepers. Much of such treatment is unintended. Yet, the result is the same. Officers become isolated and only trustful of those with whom they can co-relate. Even family members may become offensive in their fascination toward such a unique vocation.

The most common greeting a uniformed officer receives at any circumstance is, "Uh oh, I didn't do it." Often otherwise reasoned individuals will throw themselves against a wall inviting a search. Similarly, when seated at a restaurant for lunch, the beleaguered officers will inevitably receive numerous rancorous approaches by members of the public. Usual greetings include, "I got a ticket ten years ago, and it was bull--t." "Have you shot anybody?" And the ever popular, "Junior, you better eat your spinach or these here cops are gonna take you to jail!" The stunts are annoying on the first occasion, and highly offensive after the thousandth. The same scenarios even eventuate at family parties. Often in-laws may scream out, "Hi Officer!" upon entrance to a party. Or recent police controversies in the media are immediately broached for heated debate. Above all, a simple "hello" would be greatly appreciated.

It is thus predictable that cops tend to wish to associate with their own. Yet, such choices can lead to myopia and an unhealthy lack of well-roundedness to lifestyles. Officers must struggle to retain confidence, esteem, and patience with those whom do not understand.

***

Chapter 3: A contract hit and another notable case

On April 14, 1992 at 12:28 in the afternoon, your author was working patrol unit 2-Union-1. I was, however, directed to focus attention upon nearby patrol district Union 4 as well. The district was a scenic area, mostly surrounded by the Lake Washington Ship Canal, an historic and scenic waterway between saltwater Puget Sound and freshwater Lake Washington. Kayakers, university crew teams, and pleasure boats filled the canal on any given day in a serene, but steady aquatic traffic. Many small businesses dotted the area, and historic bridges connected the small-town neighborhood district with the trappings of downtown Seattle. It was a mixture of blue-collar groups of people—most notably commercial fishermen and related business partners—and liberal university types whom seemed to view a nearby Stalin statue as a prideful icon. All seemed to mix amicably in numerous local cafes, serving fresh seafood and delicious Greek cuisines.

It was a very quiet Tuesday to begin the daytime shift. I sat parked in my patrol vehicle, engine idling, watching passing vehicles through a controlled intersection, watchful of red-light violators.

Three high-pitched tones suddenly vibrated from the police radio. Known as "alert tones," the sounds were indicative of very serious in-progress incidents. The sounds guarantee an instantaneous doubling of a pulse-rate. A male dispatcher voice spoke calmly, yet emotionally, "All units, be advised we are receiving multiple calls of a shooting…The Fremont Dock

Restaurant… 1102 N. 34th Street… unknown where the suspect is at this time." The restaurant was very familiar to me, as it was a popular spot for wonderful seafood brunches, friendly waitresses, and great prices. The business was a mere six blocks from my location, and I arrived within seconds. Multiple units advised via radio they were mere minutes away. I was greeted by two panting men on the sidewalk one half- block north of the business. They indicated that the shooter had fled the scene, and that they were unable to successfully pursue him.

I was summoned frantically by numerous restaurant patrons and employees to enter the restaurant. The setting within the small and quaint café was eerie. Numerous patrons stood in horror and shock against a five foot wall partition, staring downward at a lifeless bloody body on the floor. Others huddled at nearby tables, screaming, crying, and seeking to console one another. More than thirty people were present at the time of the incident. It seemed that the room was both deadly silent and deafeningly raucous at the same time. The victim, a Mr. David Tippett—well-known local commercial fisherman—lay on his side, blood splattered upon his face, with a vast amount of blood pouring from the back of his head.

A sixty year-old stocky restaurant patron by the name of Don was beginning chest compressions upon the victim, as he rolled the victim onto his back. He immediately screamed "Please! Help!" toward me. The heroic gentleman was retired military, it would later be learned. He had been the shooter's earlier accompaniment at the bar, Don would later advise.

It was readily apparent that the victim had been shot in the head. There were no discernible signs of life, yet some attempt to resuscitate had to be made. I clamped my mouth upon his blood-spattered mouth and began to blow. The blood tasted sweet and sickening. I found it strange to watch his chest rise, just as did practice mannequins a few months ago in training. But I did not have blood smeared across my face in training, as did I at that moment. The heroic patron and I continued for several repetitions, with no apparent success. We both thought we might have found a pulse at one point, but our racing heart rates may have deceived us.

I ultimately heard the radio at my side squawk, "Union One…your status?" While only a few seconds had passed, I had forgotten to communicate to my peers. I had, after all, been somewhat preoccupied. I alerted radio to advise waiting paramedics that it was a "good shooting" (meaning verified), and that the scene was secure. I further obtained a basic suspect description for broadcast. Don continued to provide oxygen to the victim as I addressed the radio. Paramedics, waiting a block away were thus assured of their safety, and free to render aid. For what seemed like hours, yet was in reality a couple minutes, blood-smeared Don and I continued CPR and waiting. Ultimately, white-shirted paramedics scurried to kneel at my side, obtain our CPR information, and continue the largely symbolic efforts. Blue uniformed officers began pouring into the business, seemingly numbering in the dozens, like frenzied ants toward their foe.

Finally released from the victim, I was free to try to make sense of the incident, with the assistance of my many peers. Juan Palacol, the respected and trusted Hawaiian officer previously mentioned stood nearby. He brought a reassuring demeanor to any scene, and calmly asked, "Where do you wanna start, Steve?" We began to identify witnesses — some 33 it would be in total, and seek to piece together the story that had unfolded. Juan's priestly calm demeanor and James Earl Jones-like bass voice evoked a corresponding calm in witnesses, as his pen scratched rapidly across his note pad. He spoke in a quiet and comforting voice to the witnesses. His head nodded often in acknowledgement of vital information. No information is considered more poignant and accurate than such immediate witness recollections. It is then that obtained recollections and observations are more accurate of an event, before conversations amongst witnesses and personal doubts begin to bias their beliefs and recollections.

Sergeant Glenn "Blinky" Miller, a 30-year beloved veteran soon arrived. The Sergeant was a large man, standing some six feet two inches and 220 pounds. His graying black hair drooped down over his puppy dog brown eyes, and an ample belly hung above his worn gun belt. His nervous blink was evident, decrying the cause of his unkind nickname. He had long ago been marked with the nickname by unappreciative former squads whom confused his profound interest in their police-work for meddling. Nicknames were never shaken. Sergeant Miller had nonetheless earned deep admiration from his new squad of young officers whom marveled at his willingness to join his troops in physical confrontations and toss a suspect to a patrol car hood. He quietly ensured that homicide detectives had been summoned and the entire scene contained and protected. He sagely did not interfere in any way during the investigation, but lent insight and assistance as needed. He acted like a veteran movie director, quietly assuring that all logistics were to be handled.

A supremely calm bartender by the name of Donna Rask was first to be interviewed. She immediately volunteered that she had preserved a beer glass from which the shooter had drunk. She had the presence of mind to immediately secure the glass by locking it inside the bar accounting office. I was thus able to submit the glass into evidence in a paper evidence bag. It was hoped that fingerprints would be present. Ms. Rasks' attention to detail was remarkable as she related her keen observations. I sought to lighten the mood by asking her if we could sign her up for SPD. She laughed politely and declined the offer, noting that she was a "20 year veteran bartender and darned good at it."

Ms. Rask explained that she had observed the shooter calmly enter the small restaurant. She eventually observed the shooter approach her at the tiny bar in the rear of the business. He was described as an Hispanic male in his 40's, five feet seven inches tall, 150 pounds, with shoulder length black hair that was thinning on the top. He had worn sunglasses, but eventually removed them to engage Ms. Rask and other bar patrons in limited but cordial conversation. He was said to have been wearing a denim jacket with white fleece lining about the collar. He kept the coat partially zipped, although the bar area was stuffy. Ms. Rask remembered that he had a mustache. She even remembered that the shooter had mentioned that his name was "Don," to a fellow bar patron, who was also named Don. Ms. Rask recalled that the shooter had ordered Michelob beer. Eventually, she said, shooter "Don" arose to approach nearby Mr. Tippett, who was sitting across the table from an acquaintance at a center table, some 25 feet away. She paid no further attention to the man. She soon heard two pops, described as the sounds of popping balloons, and then "all hell broke loose."

Elena Droutzukas * was a 25 year-old waitress at the restaurant. She worked part-time to support herself while attending the nearby University of Washington. She often helped prepare the Greek foods in the kitchen, for which the restaurant had a favorable reputation. Ms. Droutzukas was the second witness to be interviewed. Ms. Droutzukas smoked intensely from a Marlboro cigarette, as she tried to control the profound shaking of her hands. Having been the closest to the victim at the time of the shooting, she was clearly disturbed by the shocking events of the day. Her fragmented recollection and highly agitated state lay in deep contrast to the demeanor of Donna Rask.

One by one the many witnesses in the crowded restaurant related amazingly similar versions of the event in question. The tablemate of the victim appeared to be in total shock, unable for the most part to relate events or converse. Experienced homicide detectives had arrived and were taking over most interviews, although they remained ever respectful of the patrol officers. They encouraged your author to continue interviews of witnesses whom almost seemed like instant friends.

David Tippett, it was stated, was a successful commercial fisherman. He was the owner of at least two Alaska fishing boats of considerable size and value. He had been having plentiful harvests of salmon on his spring and summer runs of late, and his cash flow was thriving. For some reason unknown to his peers, Mr. Tippett was known to always travel with a large briefcase, in which, it was known, he carried a large .357 caliber revolver. Mr. Tippett was described as cordial, yet somewhat distant, almost paranoid in demeanor. He was known to all, and truly known by none.

On that April 14th day, David had seated himself at a center little metal table with a simple checkerboard plastic tablecloth. He had joined an acquaintance, unknown to the regular clientele, and seated himself across the little table. He bid the waitress a cordial greeting and maintained his dark metallic briefcase beside him on the floor. The briefcase was leaned against his right leg, as if he had to feel the presence of such at all times. He faced south, ever watchful of the comings and goings at the only entrance and exit to the restaurant. He drank his coffee black, and toyed with the daily Seattle Times. He occasionally engaged his male acquaintance in conversation, while awaiting the arrival of his seafood omelet and biscuits.

Upon walking into the restaurant, the shooter was seen to approach Mr. Tippett calmly. He engaged Mr. Tippett briefly in conversation, and the two appeared to be cordial. He was heard to have addressed the victim by his full name—Dave Tippett. He had further been heard to ask Mr. Tippett if he was hiring any fishermen for his business. The man was told no hiring was occurring, but that he could apply for future opportunities. With a shrug, the shooter then ambled back to the bar to drink.

Approximately twenty minutes later, the shooter was then seen to approach Mr. Tippett from the bar area. He then walked past his prey as if seeking to exit the restaurant. Yet, he immediately turned around, and without further word pulled what appeared to be a .38 caliber "snub-nose" (short barreled) revolver from his waistband. From nearly point-blank range, the shooter fired one shot directly into the rear base of the skull of David Tippett. As the victim fell forward from the blast, vast quantities of blood geysered out of the small wound. The victim's head rattled the table and dishes, as his forehead collided with the surface. Two seconds later the shooter calmly pressed the firearm to the back of the victim's skull and fired another round.

The bar patron was named Don Goldman and he was retired military. Mr. Goldman was first to react and sprinted toward the table, as the waitress dropped her tray of dishes crashing upon the floor. The waitress stood in shock and then screamed. The shooter quickly pointed the gun at Mr. Goldman and David's acquaintance, both of whom sat frozen in shock at the death table. Mr. Goldman quickly froze. The shooter turned the weapon toward the shocked crowd as if on a turret.

Seconds later, he rapidly walked out of the entrance to the restaurant, gun still in hand, and the door slammed loudly against its frame. The shooter was seen to run northbound uphill on a sidewalk and past the eastern windows of the restaurant. Numerous male patrons of the restaurant ran out of the restaurant in attempts to monitor his escape.

But the shooter was nowhere to be seen.

An hour later, Sergeant Don Cameron of the Homicide Unit stood in the corner of the restaurant, away from other gatherings of humanity. His arms were crossed against his chest. Sergeant Cameron was a huge bear of a man at 6 feet 2 and some 280 pounds of "mostly" muscle, and reminded many of a huge Winston Churchill. "Big Don" commanded respect both for his physical presence and his 30 years of intense and decorated police experience. He summoned Sergeant Miller and me over to him very discreetly. He looked at Sergeant Miller smiling, and stated with hand over mouth, "Glenn, you know what we have here."

"A contract hit, I would presume," Sergeant Miller quickly answered.

Sergeant Cameron then opined, "Been a while since one of these, hasn't it buddy?" The two renowned Sergeants with a combined experience surpassing 60 years simply frowned and nodded.

Sergeant Cameron then motioned to your author, "Good job, kid. Go back to the barn and clean yourself up. I'll see you down in the Homicide office after- while."

It was only then did I realize that my face remained smeared with blood, and my uniform shirt soaked in the life source of what was once a human being.

Reported Seattle Police Incident number 162, 838 for 1992

would notate the taking of one human life by another. A case file was thus begun, with a lengthy investigation to follow.

The Homicide Unit, or "H & R" (standing for homicide and robbery) as it was coined, was then located on the sixth floor of a 50 year-old abomination of a Public Safety Building. The 12-story building had been constructed during World War II as a "temporary" housing for the police department and municipal courts. Fifty years of growth and unaddressed wear in both endeavors had left the building an overcrowded and dilapidated mess. The blue and grey building was replete with mold, asbestos, and rusted mildewed walls and ceilings. Rodents made homes in the ceilings and electrical workers cringed at the thought of repairs from within. Nonetheless, it was home for over 2,000 city employees and a vital downtown hub of activity.

H & R dominated the space on the sixth floor of the cavernous building. One needed a badge, police ID card, and an ability to reassure the detectives on the intercom phones beyond a substantial steel door and bulletproof windows, that an entry buzz was merited. The ultimate test of character was acceptance by legendary beloved secretary Ila Birkland. Ila literally knew all and had seen all. She truly ran the unit. Numerous dusty and foul-smelling holding cells filled the center of the floor. Spacious dimly lit "lineup rooms" reminiscent of 1930's cop movies adjoined the area of activity. Twenty homicide detectives filled small cubicles wrapped around the south portion of the floor. Reams of case files were stacked on each cubicle, orderly, yet seemingly overwhelming in quantities. The two nearby Sergeants showed the status of rank, as their cubicles stood at nearly twice the phone-booth square footage of their subordinate detectives. Only the unit Lieutenant and Captain possessed respectable looking offices.

Against one concrete wall stood a replica of bloody scrawlings , with the words, "I am the destroyer of worlds" upon such. The wall was a copy of that found in a victim's home during the infamous Manson killings. One knew immediately upon being buzzed into H and R that the business that lay therein was serious and surreal. A replica skull stood atop the cubicle partition of partnering Detectives Tom Pike and Al Gebo — two of SPD's brightest employees. All who were familiar with Homicide Unit traditions recognized the skull to be indicative of "next up" status for a pair of detectives to receive a case assignment. The hit would be their case.

Ironically, and strangely, all of the detectives actually looked forward to a murder case assignment. Muffled celebration thereof was known to be seen. They meant no disrespect to the egregiousness of the crime thus committed, but they knew they would be relieved of investigating overwhelming quantities of armed robberies and muggings, and would move on to "serious business." They were also supremely confident in their abilities, and enthusiastic to send an "a---hole" to the joint. The thrill of the hunt served as motivation, and copious amounts of overtime pay didn't hurt the cause.

Legendary unit commander Larry Farrar oversaw the elite unit. A decorated Vietnam army veteran, the Captain had served in virtually every capacity within the department in his 30 years of experience. The huge and imposing man was said to resemble his beloved and ever-present boxer "Bismark" in general appearance. Many officers would say they were identical in demeanor. Yet, when Captain Farrar smiled, even that was on a large-scale, and all whom encountered him would be put instantly at ease. He had recently been assigned to the Homicide and Robbery unit as a promotion, of sort, both in prestige and opportunities. He had come from the North Patrol

Precinct and was thus very familiar with your author. There had been no one in the precinct in which the Captain was not familiar. He was beloved by all within the precinct, who looked upon him as a father figure.

Captain Farrar extended his huge hand in greeting and his smile was endless. He encouraged me to converse with the two investigating detectives and complete the mandatory statements and follow-up for beginning the investigation.

Detectives Gebo and Pike were pouring through reams of statements, sorting photographs, and ensuring that every piece of evidence had been properly noted and submitted. They paid particular attention to the beer glass now stored in the SPD evidence room on the 7th floor. It was their hope that condensation upon the glass would not ruin any subsequent possibilities of drawing a fingerprint of the brazen shooter. Al Gebo was a 14-year veteran of "H & R" and nearing the final 18 months of his illustrious career. He remained fit and youthful looking. He was a muscular five foot ten and 200 lbs, despite his 53 years, and his reddish mustache showed mere glimmers of grey within. It was readily apparent that he was a former Marine. Tom Pike served as the direct physical contrast to his partner. An exceptionally bright officer, he had quickly risen to robbery detective and then homicide detective as a relatively young age. He was a slim and slight man of approximately six feet tall. He bore the demeanor of a minister, well dressed, with his hair parted perfectly to the side. He was tremendously humble, mannered, and charismatic.

Captain Farrar ultimately ushered the three of us into a nearby conference room, and the room began to fill with all the detectives. He leaned over to me and stated, "I have a surprise for you." He unfurled paper coverings of massive grease bulletin boards to display a very detailed accounting of the murder in question some four hours earlier. Resembling General Patton with his long wooden pointer, the Captain expertly described all aspects of the case—the brazenness of the shooter, the crowded restaurant, the evidence located (to include the firearm in the victim's briefcase), and the known background on the victim. The Captain did so with the precision of any former military commander. A large group of detectives would be involved in the investigation, as he labeled the case an obvious "contract hit." He even explained to questioning detectives that in times past such hits had commonly occurred in the city. Mobsters, he explained, had often found that crowded rooms provided perfect cover for assassinations. He said that the pandemonium hid their escape and later led to confused and unreliable witnesses.

Captain Farrar indicated that the case would take a very high priority, and that additional resources would be needed. He indicated that your author would join the investigative team, assisting with menial sorting of paperwork and taking all tip calls from the public. Ultimately, Juan Palacol would be selected to assist as well. For two patrol officers who usually patrolled the most peaceful neighborhoods in the city, it was like going to Disneyland.

The investigation would span two and a half months. Hundreds of tips came into the homicide office hotline. Amazing arrays of wild conspiracy theorists pontificated regarding the case. Some blamed the Russians, some blamed the devil. Others had brief glimpses of what may have been the suspect, and a getaway vehicle description was ultimately obtained.

Others had possibly seen the suspect lingering around the nearby boat docks, seemingly very familiar with the environs. Through it all, Detectives Pike and Gebo kept meticulous and voluminous documentation of the progress of the case. The case file would ultimately number over one thousand pages in length. The detectives kept the entire unit apprised of poignant information on a bi-weekly basis. Hundreds of interviews were conducted. It was most difficult to interview the widow of the victim. Rumors of clandestine activities persisted from many sources. But they remained always rumors. Financial records for the victim indicated unusually high cash flows, but nothing that could be described as extraordinary. Some detectives suspected drug trade, but nothing could be proven. Few motives for the killing could be gleaned, other than business rivalries and revengeful dismissed employees. The victim was not renowned for his tact and diplomacy in the business world.

As weeks passed credible anonymous tip-line calls came in, advising that two brothers-- Gernard and Joe Casbon, had been overheard in Everett Washington boasting of "teaching Tippett a lesson." These tips would lead to extensive surveillance of the two brothers in their restaurant and marina workplaces. Background checks indicated that both were familiar with the victim. Joe Casbon was a recent parolee from Louisiana. Information would indicate that they had alternately worked as welders for Mr. Tippett. They were said to have been greatly disgruntled at their termination from his employ. Phone records of the two brothers indicated that they had extensive phone contact with a Michael W. Lindquist just prior to the murder. Lindquist was a bitter estranged former partner of Tippett. He had been fired for drug use, an alleged habit that Tippett had walked away from.

Ultimately, solid witnesses to the brothers' boasting came forward. This led to their arrests. The partial fingerprint taken from the beer glass came back as a probable match to Joe Casbon. He was soon identified in a lineup as the shooter.

Witnesses then identified Gernard Casbon as the driver of the getaway vehicle. Eventually, convinced of pending convictions, the brothers discussed confession to their parts in the murder. Gernard Casbon was more willing to implicate Lindquist for the contract hit. Joe Casbon only gave ambiguous information regarding the incident, maintaining the innocence of Linquist.

The murder trial of Michael W. Lindquist and Joe Casbon would last just under two weeks, or roughly a year less than that of O.J. Simpson. Predictably, the key witness would prove to be the bartender, Ms. Rask. The astute woman had unequivocally selected the shooter (Joe Casbon) from a lineup without hesitation. She even pointed out how he had sought to change his hairstyle. Impassioned defense attorneys seemed to lose enthusiasm after they could not shake her on the stand.

One by one the dozens of witnesses were paraded upon the witness stand. While stories varied slightly, the ultimate basis of their accounts remained amazingly consistent. Many wept openly upon the witness stand. All expressed that the incident was the most devastating event in their respective lives.

Gernard Casbon escaped prosecution for his part in the murder in exchange for testimony against his brother and Lindquist. He was sentenced to Snohomish County Jail after pleading guilty to rendering criminal assistance and witness intimidation.

Joe Caspon was convicted of aggravated murder and sentenced to prison for life.

Michael Lindquist was also convicted of aggravated murder and sentenced to prison without the possibility of parole. The price for taking the life of another human being was all of $9,600 dollars. The exact motive for the acts of

Lindquist were never fully discovered. He steadfastly denied his involvement. The myth or innuendos of the victim's alleged secret life were never fully put to bed.

The restaurant in question had remained closed for many weeks following the murder. It was said that the blood stains could be removed, but that the patrons would still see the sight. Attempts to re-open soon failed when the regulars stayed away. It was as if the business were cursed. Arrests and convictions of the killers only brought more negative attention.

Several witnesses were to experience extreme bouts of depression and anxiety for many months following the incident. Indeed, one such witness would ultimately commit suicide, often remarking that the murder had been the final straw in her challenging life. Lifelong happy marriages suddenly ended among witnesses, and the restaurant eventually ceased to operate. The single brutal act of three callous men had implacably affected the lives of countless people. It was as if a stone had been thrown into a placid pond, sending endless ripples, and dredging unpleasant sediments from below.

Nearly eighteen years later, the old restaurant finally re-opened. New owners unfurled dust- coated table tops and removed seafood brunch specials inked upon a grease-board wall from that fateful date. They hoped that a new history could be generated in the lovely waterfront neighborhood.

***

A brutal rapist and the legal "system."

During the summer of 1986, several brutal knife-wielding rapes would occur in the Columbia City portion of Seattle Washington. Columbia City was a primarily poor multi-ethnic residential area southeast of downtown Seattle, dotted with public housing, inexpensive rental homes, and aging houses owned by senior citizens. The area would be gripped by fear for most of that summer, as patrol and detectives struggled to arrest and identify a commonly described suspect. The suspect, described only as a very large black male in his 40's, seemed indiscriminate in his choices of victims. A teen young lady was raped in her back yard, and a 78 year-old woman raped in her bedroom. The warm weather provided the suspect with innumerable easy targets, as bedroom windows were left open and women sought relief from the heat on rear decks and in back yards.

An exhaustive investigation ultimately led to the arrest of a Gary Minnix. Minnix, it would be learned, lived in a nearby neighborhood and could easily gain access to victims on foot. The SPD held a collective sigh of relief as the case was solved. Yet, the relief would be very short-lived.

Numerous King County Superior Court judges alternately ruled that Mr. Minnix could not stand trial for his crimes. Mental evaluators for the defense had argued that Minnix was mentally retarded, and thus not responsible for his actions. He was described as having the reasoning of a five year-old child. The judges claimed that no state law, at the time, addressed such mental incompetence. Prosecutors would argue to no avail that Minnix could hold down a job, take a bus to work, pay his own bills, and otherwise display competence in daily life. Minnix would not even be relegated to mental facilities for his horrific crimes. Instead, he would be returned to his neighborhood, free in every respect to roam.

In the late summer of 1987, 28 year-old Marcia Fredericks* was gardening in the back yard of her spectacular Magnolia home. The spacious pillared and red brick home abutted scenic Smith Cove Park, and held incomparable access to a rocky beach and Elliott Bay views. The skyline of downtown Seattle shimmered across the bay. Marcia was working in her dahlia garden while her five year-old son Jason* played Tonka trucks in the nearby sand. Her husband was out of town on business, as he was often known to do. It was a beautiful sunny day, and the breeze provided perfect relief from the 84 degree "heat," as Seattleites labeled such conditions.

A large and perspiring black man appeared out of nowhere beside Marcia. She had not heard her wooden gate open, and was startled at the appearance of the individual. The man asked, "You got any jobs?" to which the puzzled Marcia answered no. He then asked, "Can I use your bathroom?" and again, the answer was no. Marcia offered that a public restroom existed nearby in the city park that would be open all summer.

Suddenly the man closed the eight-foot distance with profound quickness. Marcia felt her head jerk backward from a fierce pull upon her hair. She felt a brutal blow to the side of her face and heard the ringing of her ears. She saw shards of light and tasted her blood, and the ringing intensified. She could feel that she was being dragged by her hair, as her consciousness became fleeting. She could strangely relate to victims of bear mauling at that moment. She knew she had to fight the bear.

Marcia kicked and flailed and screamed at her captor, but she was no match for the huge man. The captor punched her again repeatedly and darkness soon encroached. Minutes, seeming like days, passed, and Marcia regained her consciousness. She had been dragged to water's edge of the beach, and the huge man was atop her, breathing hard from his frenzied movements. His eyes did not blink as he stared into her eyes and smiled. She sought to scratch the man's face, but her hands were pinned down beside her. Her assailant punched her again, and the ringing in the ears grew louder.

The last words she could recall from the rapist would haunt her for the rest of her life, "There, bitch, now you be all full of come." He left the victim for dead. She was bleeding, thrice raped, and nearly drowning in the oncoming tide. Her five-year old son stood ten feet away, screaming, "Mommeeeeeee!" as the suspect turned and ran.

The call rang out to all patrol units of the brutal events endured by the victim and her son. Rapidly approaching units, including your author, descended upon the area. The district officers attended to the welfare of the victims, and broadcast the suspect description. The victim would insist upon providing a suspect description before agreeing to a fire department transport to Harborview Medical Center. Her son would not stop crying.

Magnolia is essentially an island, adjoining with the rest of Seattle by only two old concrete bridges. It was thus believed that the suspect had no means of escaping the 16 square mile area. All bridges were blocked and search teams began to envelope the park. A daytime canine team was summoned. The legendary police dog "Tally" and highly capable handler Jon Emerick arrived post-haste. Patrol units, including your author, slowly scoured the area, ever careful of the dog on track.

Tally appeared on a long leash coming up the hill of a residential street, some three quarters of a mile from the scene of the assault. Jon was panting much harder than the 9 year-old German shepherd and the dog began to almost skip, as he was known to do when he detected a nearby suspect. I was directed to follow the team toward a nearby bungalow on the east. A side door was open, and showed signs of force. Guns drawn, the dog and two officers entered the home. No lights were on within, and only filtered sunlight escaped the trees of the yard to provide any illumination. Flashlights were used to search the upper floor of the home. Nothing appeared to have been disturbed. Tally crawled and slid down a steep set of wooden steps to the basement, and Jon and I quickly followed. The dog paced in circles upon the linoleum of the basement, and his toenails made a "click click click" upon the surface.

No signs of a suspect were apparent. Yet the dog finally stood still, almost as if to work out a mental puzzle. Tally burst past the two officers to a narrow hallway and laundry room. He growled and clawed at a huge industrial drier. The experienced canine handler, once-again took amazement in the greatest dog to- date in department history. Jon merely smiled at me. He moved forward and pointed his .357 magnum at the door of the drier and called out, "Do you wanna come out, or do you want my dog to drag you out by your a---hole?" The six foot 2 and 240 pound man unfolded himself from within the drier and emerged. It was amazing that he could fit himself within the drier in such a way. He was extremely compliant in allowing his handcuffing, as he was clearly terrified of the snarling dog at his feet.

The suspect was transported to the West Precinct by a nearby tandem of officers. Tally received his usual reward for great work by receiving 15 minutes of chasing the "kong" (large rubber chew toy) thrown for him to retrieve repeatedly.

Your author returned to the precinct holding cell area in time for Sex Crimes Detective Kevin O'Keefe to approach the suspect. Without hesitation, Detective O'Keefe greeted the suspect, "Hi Gary." West Precinct officers had only been familiar with Minnix by general history, as his previous offenses had all occurred in other precincts. Detective O'Keefe would provide invaluable assistance in the investigation of the crime. He, and other talented detectives would provide very detailed documentation of the lengths to which the rapist had planned his crime. They were able to elaborate upon how the rapist had surveyed the victim's home to confirm the absence of her husband, located the most remote residence in the area, and even drawn an escape plan upon a bus route map. It was hoped that no one could argue that this was the equivalent actions of a five-year-old child.

Experienced prosecutors knew that additional pressures would lie this time upon the presiding judges. While it would never be overtly stated, the brutal rape of a wealthy white woman gained much greater attention and scrutiny. Judges who were elected to their positions would take note of the public outcry.

Once ordered competent to stand trial, the ensuing proceedings were a mere formality. A serial rapist was finally no longer free to roam.

Over the following several years, numerous on-duty patrol officers, including your author visited the victim to check on her well-being. She recovered from her broken jaw, ruptured eardrum, and many lacerations. But the other pain would never subside. Her son would need intense counseling for the rest of his life, and complete healing seemed impossible. The victim would ultimately suffer divorce from her husband. She would not venture from her locked home without a police escort to and from any nearby venue. She was a prisoner of her circumstances, and one day moved away to whereabouts unknown.

Her attacker would one day gain his freedom, but she would not be so fortunate. The "system," it would seem, had failed her miserably.

***

Chapter side note: Officer Fred Kilmer—World's meanest and sweetest cop.

Few whom have worked for SPD during the past third of a century will argue that Fred would be the most noteworthy officer known during this era. Fred's reputation always preceded him. He was said to have saved many an officers' lives during past times of riots, and Black Panther attacks in the 60's and early 70's. Several months before Fred was forced back to work from years of disability retirement, all West Precinct talk focused upon him. Veteran officers alternately spoke reverently about the legendary beat cop, or roared uproariously about his innumerable antics. All they would tell your author, then a 31 year-old, ten-year "veteran" was, "Kid, you're in for a treat."

Fred arrived at the West Precinct one morning for his first shift in years. He was greeted as would have been a rock star at a high school. The Chief of Police, Assistant Chiefs, and the precinct Captain scrambled from their upstairs offices to witness the arrival of the enigmatic grizzled cop. Senior officers lined the walls of the hallway in a quasi-receiving line as Fred entered from the "G-Deck" parking lot, inside the cavernous Public Safety Building.

The greasy steel entrance doors slammed open as Fred made his grand entrance. A large black boot appeared from where the door had received a kick. The attached legend soon emerged. Fred Kilmer stood some six feet two inches tall and weighed nearly 240 pounds. He was a combination of obvious strength and obvious excess in eating. Fred stood tall in a brand new rookie uniform with a very worn gun-belt hanging low on his right hip. He blew a massive cloud of cigar smoke into the building and began his gravelly laugh. He had black and grey hair, neatly combed to one side, and he was enormously tanned and weathered in appearance. Half Yakama Indian, Fred looked as if he had just returned from commercial fishing — which was exactly where he had been.

Fred was known by all of the dozens of senior officers in his receiving line. He pounded his huge hand into the equally huge extended hands of the older cops. He was back amongst friends. Fred showed no obvious bitterness for the abrupt cessation of his retirement.

Fred was greeted at the end of the line by the Chief of Police. The chief held out his smallish hand toward the living legend and received no response. Fred looked disdainfully downward at the five foot eight Chief momentarily, and merely growled, "Hey, shorty." His return was thus complete.

Newly transferred to walk the downtown foot-beats, your author would have many occasions to walk the beat with Fred. This would occur on days when his partner had a day off, or simply by walking the adjoining beat. It would prove to be an adventure and an honor. Yet, Fred would not allow me to walk the beat with him, on the first outing, until I had a sip of coffee at a local restaurant. It was while seated with the other veteran beat cops at a back table. I thanked Fred for the offer, but indicated that I did not drink coffee. He was not impressed and indicated that I was not a "real cop" at that point. "Have a drink, kid, I insist!" I thus took a slurp of the massive mug. There might have been a drop of coffee somewhere in the vast regions of the mug, but the contents nearly took my breath away. I managed to swallow the contents without retching. Fred and the other cops then laughed, patted me on the back, and said I was alright. I could then be trusted.

Fred would be assigned to the toughest beat in the city — David 90. The beat encapsulated historic and beautiful Pike Place Market on the west side of 1st Avenue and the filthy and crime-laden east side of 1st Avenue and Pike Street. The area was a fascinating dichotomy of environs. A spectacular massive open-air fish market was surrounded by hundreds of small booths of fresh fruits, vegetables, and worldly foods. Artisans displayed beautiful works, while streets musicians entertained with incomparable talent. Yet, junkies, drug dealers, thugs and hoodlums pervaded within the fabric of such. Just across the street stood "Live Girls" shops every 100 feet. It would thus seem an assignment of strategic wisdom by the Sergeant to place Fred in the roughest beat in town. It was like a fish to water. His partners were equals in immense physical stature and toughness toward the "sh-t-birds," as they preferred to call the bad guys. Drug dealers, prostitutes, pickpockets, and newly emerging gangs were trying to establish themselves in the area. But they had never encountered a cop like Fred.

All of the downtown beat cops seemed huge. The veteran officers had very broad shoulders and enormous hands that could land like thunder upon the backs of criminals' necks. They wore very heavy leather gloves inlayed with lead, called "sap gloves" that added to the inertia of any hand strikes to suspects. Your six foot six author was lucky to finally be filling out his frame, so as to not look like the little guy amongst his peers. But no one stood larger than Fred. Twirling heavy nightsticks became an established art form amongst all beat cops. Fred was the finest artist.

Fred quickly established himself as the new sheriff in town. He made it clear, in his less than gentle ways, that the criminals were not to be seen on his beat during his shift. Many was a time that Fred would twirl his ironwood nightstick deftly as he approached a local thug on a street corner. He would encourage me to go purchase him coffee within a café, and await him. He made it clear that the kid need not witness his manner of communicating with the bad guys. Several days later, the target of his communications could sometimes be seen on the city streets. They would often be in a cast of some sort, for broken bones suffered during an earlier "fall." Fred would thus remind the drug dealers, pimps, pickpockets, muggers, et al, that he might need to communicate again with them, were they to return to his turf. The bad guys would put forth tremendous efforts to leave the area.

Fred had interesting old school interpretations of local laws, ordinances, and procedures. Were Fred to tell a bad guy to leave downtown, a law had just been written. Upon the return of a criminal to Fred's beat, they would go to jail for "trespassing." That was if they were fortunate. Others received "attitude adjustments." Fred really seemed to have a way of connecting with the street thugs.

Fred and others somehow came into possession of a large city-owned cargo van for use by the Police Department. Young officers like me were amazed at how quickly he could navigate governmental bureaucracy, and requisition equipment that had been badly needed for months. The West Precinct had needed a spare prisoner van for months, and no such equipment had arrived. Suddenly, Fred and veteran peers were seen out on "G-Deck" painting what was once a yellow van, a perfect shade of SPD blue. Large magnetic badge logos capably covered other insignias previously on the van, reading "Seattle City Light." Fred and the boys knew how to get things done.

The van would be a multi-use facility. The front of such would be a mobile precinct—replete with department paperwork, food, and beverages of all sorts imaginable. A vast library ranged from local papers, to Sports Illustrated, to various curled girly magazines jammed between the seats. The rear spacious suite of the van was the true coup de grace. Various sundry criminal guests could make themselves comfortable upon one solid steel bench in the front of the cargo, and nothing but oily, rusty metal for further seating throughout. The restroom facilities consisted of…the rusty metal surface. The ventilation system was a work in progress. In fact, no progress had been made.

Fred immediately christened the tastefully renovated van, "The penalty box." On a daily basis Fred would park the van at 1st Ave and Pike Street for use by all patrol officers. The multiple purposes for the city equipment were spelled out clearly by Fred, and prioritized wisely. The van would serve as an interim holding facility for all downtown corridor arrestees. There was no point in taking one bad guy to jail, it was opined, when the cops could fill the large van with many suspects over the day. *This* was efficiency. The van could provide *eventual* ample transportation of multiple suspects to booking facilities. And, above all, it was determined that the van would serve as a visual crime deterrent. The street thugs would see the van and realize several things: One — That Fred Kilmer was on the beat; Two — That Fred Kilmer was coming after them for being on his beat; Three — That they would have to sit in that van for hours with other disgustingly smelly bad guys; and Four — That there was no restroom.

Hot summer days seemed to be the most stressful for street thugs. Fred assured them of a lovely sauna setting in the penalty box, guaranteed to ensure rapid weight loss. He was so incredibly strong that he could spare the suspects the need to climb into the van, and could kindly toss them the entire length of the suite.

Fred hoped that all suspects would appreciate his magnanimous efforts toward rehabilitation. However, occasional ingrates would present themselves. In those cases when they insisted upon rapid transportation to the station or jail, and thus freedom from the penalty box, Fred was sure to comply. Fred would light one of his huge cigars and take the street thugs on their rides. However, Fred was not a polished driver, it would seem. After all, Fred was a foot beat cop. It would seem that Fred's route planning was sadly lacking. Often, he would drive the van in the incorrect direction and become inescapably mired in vast construction zones. Embarrassed, and concerned for his impatient passengers, Fred would rapidly accelerate the vehicle through the area. Yet, unfortunately, this caused the vehicle to speed awkwardly over massive bumps and potholes, causing the captive passengers to resemble popcorn in a popper. Fred could hear the street thugs screaming profanities and insisting that he stop. Ever the compassionate one, Fred would thus slam on his brakes. But, sadly, this would simply propel his cargo against the steel inner wall of the vehicle, like racquetballs. Sometimes the van was seen to be airborne!

While some may have considered Fred Kilmer's methodology to be unconventional, amazing results could be measured. The streets, it would seem, would soon be "clean" in the David Sector environs. Even on Fred's days off, his presence could be felt. Often, your author and his other young partner would encounter some of Fred's clientele on the sidewalks and in the alleys. We would happily greet the street thugs and point out that Fred was nearby. We would reach for our portable radios while asking the street thug if they were willing to remain in their place, while we'd call Fred to come visit them. It was amazing how fast a human being could run.

On very rare occasions, street thugs would think there was merit in filing Internal Affairs complaints against Fred. Fred would immediately point out to his younger officers, that such complaints were indeed prima-facie evidence of his failure. He had clearly not caused enough pain with the first encounter to discourage any such considerations. Follow-up visits with Fred's clientele always guaranteed no further such occurrences.

There were only two such exceptions to the rule known to your author. On one occasion, a street thug child molester, rapist, and mugger of little old ladies filed complaint number two about Officer Kilmer. The thug went by the name of Randy Eisel*. Fred affectionately referred to the lad as, "Eis- Hole!" It would seem the lad had repeated a complaint to Internal Affairs, alleging that Fred had repeatedly inflicted "attitude adjustments" upon him. Randy apparently further voiced displeasure with the accommodations in the penalty box.

Fred was thus grossly inconvenienced to have to write mandatory, detailed Internal Affairs statements, addressing serious allegations of police brutality. Fred devoted nearly an entire day to the serious written correspondence to Internal Affairs and department command. Ultimately the statement read as follows: "No." Thus exhausted by his efforts toward legal justification for his efforts, Fred made it known on the streets that he was looking for "Eis-Hole."

Randy Eisel was able to dodge Fred for many weeks on the downtown Seattle streets. In fact, he had not been seen in a few months by any daytime officer. It was believed that he had escaped the fate of facing Fred one more time. Yet, destiny, as it would seem was a fickle thing. One evening, all the daytime beat cops were held past shift due to high call loads in the area. Fred, and your author, were assigned to a patrol car for four additional hours on overtime. We were thus dispatched to a disturbance upon a Metro Bus in the Pioneer Square environs of downtown Seattle. It would seem that a drugged-out thug was mugging elderly riders, and intimidating others with a small knife.

The bus was stopped and nearly emptied upon our arrival. We were told by the driver, outside the bus, that the assaultive and intimidating thug remained in the back seat of the coach. The thug was said to be smugly celebrating his control of the situation. Fred donned his trademark leather gloves and boarded the stairs of the coach first, as I followed. Before I could even look up from the stairs of the bus I heard Fred call out in glee. His booming, gravelly voice, bellowed, "ICE-HOLE!" Fred lit a cigar and began to laugh.

I thought for a moment that the wily Mr. Eisel would evade Fred once again, as he extended a middle finger in our direction and began to lower a back window of the bus. Eisel smiled delightedly as the window began to slide downward on a track at 4-inch increments. But, alas, it was not to be. The window was only designed to slide a mere eight inches downward. Randy made a gallant attempt to fit his moppy head and five foot eleven frame through the small window opening. The thug's efforts were fruitless as his head became inexorably wedged in the window. The young man even tried to push his body through the glass and metal, but fine window engineering prevailed.

Fred implored his young partner to go to a nearby restaurant and order him some coffee. Unwilling to leave my partner alone, Fred reminded me, "Kid, you have a long career ahead of you. You can't be here. I'll be just fine."

I abided by Fred's wishes. Upon his return to the restaurant Fred seemed to truly relish his cup of coffee. And Mr. Eisel was never again seen on the downtown Seattle streets. It must be assumed that he chose to no longer rape, rob, and pillage. Fred had a way of changing lives.

On another occasion, there was an individual by the name of Rob Velmont* whom had gained ownership of a downtown fleabag hotel. The man had come from the boroughs of New York City, and was a reputed crime lord. The man quickly established a kingdom in his twelve-story building and began to purchase other properties in the area. Mr. Velmont brought in very seamy clientele to live for free within his properties. But his clientele paid in other ways. Velmont ran child prostitution within his confines, and saved the most desirable little boys for himself. He quickly trained and mentored the boys and young men to run drugs for him. They were further directed to burglarize neighborhoods, steal cars, and mug little old ladies.

Velmont, a tall and extremely thin man, was actually very effeminate. However, he countered for such outward demeanor with his knowledge of how to run a crime syndicate. He intimidated the innocent and the guilty in the area by waving a huge .44 magnum revolver in their faces. He was crazy, smart, and dangerous, and people feared him greatly. But he did not intimidate Fred Kilmer.

A few months after Velmont had established himself as the unquestioned crime leader of downtown Seattle, the man bumped into Fred. It would seem that Velmont was in the process of intimidating an elderly woman, when Fred and partner walked across his path. It must be assumed that Mr. Velmont did not find a subsequent discussion with Fred to be pleasant. Velmont, it would seem, must have fallen in that dark alley. He was seen with both arms in slings shortly thereafter. It was hoped that the area was thus freed of the crime lord.

Velmont, it would seem, was not so easily dissuaded. He summoned an expensive attorney from New York City, and serious allegations of misconduct were lodged with the city. It was worried that Fred may have gone too far. He was told to lay low by supervision, and some worried that his career was to end. Velmont openly bragged upon the streets that his influence was unquestionable. His criminal operation in the hotel thrived as never before.

One summer night a few days hence, a call came out to the Seattle Fire Department. It would seem, a multi-story old downtown hotel was fully engulfed in flames. Apparently, a Good Samaritan was able to pull the alarms at a very early juncture. All occupants were able to escape the inferno. But, sadly, the entire hotel was lost in a ball of fire.

As media crews gathered around the crestfallen hotel owner, Velmont stood tearfully in front of the cameras. One of his arms was still in a sling, and Velmont stated, "I know it's Officer Kilmer who did this. He's the devil!"

Velmont would eventually die a lonely death at a small downtown apartment from the drugs that he promoted. His criminal enterprise had already ceased to exist abruptly, and he had never been heard from again. He had also never cooperated in any further Internal Affairs efforts.

People can hold differing opinions on Fred and company's mode of law enforcement, yet one thing cannot be disputed—wherever Fred patrolled a beat, crime went down to nearly nothing, and normal people felt safe again. To the young officers, Fred was held in awe.

A few years later, your author had transferred to the North Precinct of the department, and somewhat lost touch with Fred and the rapidly retiring cadre of beloved and revered beat-cops. One day an old veteran Sergeant announced that we would have a new squad member—none other than Fred Kilmer. Most of the young officers of the North Precinct had only heard of Fred in legend. Yet, I began to laugh. The Sarge asked if anyone would be willing to take Fred along as a partner for a few days, while he adjusted to the very different area. I was delighted to volunteer. I knew Fred would find it strange to move from the sometimes filthy, crime-ridden downtown melting pot of humanity, to the primarily white upper middle class residential demographics of out north.

Fred soon had his own patrol car district and sought to fit in. I enjoyed coffee (well, hot chocolate for me) with Fred almost daily. I enjoyed his company greatly. I learned from Fred that he had been moved by the new and despised West Precinct Captain in an effort to remove all of the "dead wood." I would learn that the legendary desk officer Nick Carnovale had been similarly forced to retire. Fred, easily at retirement age by then, would not give the Captain that satisfaction. Within the first week of Fred's assignment, he displayed to the more laid-back north-end officers, how to "commit police-work" West Precinct (downtown) style.

On a particular sunny summer's day, circa 1991 a young street thug sought to intimidate a young Asian woman within her tiny floral boutique. The thug had stolen flowers and gifts, and proceeded to trash many displays within the shop. Numerous officers were dispatched in response to the victim's 9-1-1 calls. The drug-infested thug was cornered on the sidewalk outside the business. Officer Kilmer, being the senior officer, had authority over our response.

Fred attempted earnestly to talk the thug into passively accepting handcuffing and transport to the North Precinct for booking. However, the thug, unfamiliar with Officer Kilmer, proceeded to spit upon the front of the officer. The thug expected a gentle and reasoned response attributed to the demure north end officers. However, Fred merely started to laugh at him. Your author honestly tried to convince the thug that it was in his best interest to come with me. Yet he refused.

Fred gave me a nod, and I advised the other patrol officer to leave the scene. The other officer protested, yet I advised that

I would explain later.

Approximately ten minutes later, Officer Kilmer arrived at the rear parking lot to the North Precinct, where I and the other patrol officer had stationed ourselves. Just as I predicted to the other officers, Fred seemed to have the thug under control. Fred retrieved the bedraggled suspect from the rear of the patrol car. He then proceeded to drag the suspect by his hair across the parking lot, all the while counseling the lad, "You don't know who you were talkin' to, F--kbag." Virtually simultaneously, the legendary North Precinct Captain Farrar drove into the parking lot. The Captain's head seemed to spin a full 360 degrees as he caught a glimpse of his new officer at work. The Captain quickly placed his hands to the sides of his eyes, as if blinders, and hurried into the station. He was heard to mutter under his breath, "God help us all," as he disappeared toward his office.

I absolutely and thoroughly enjoyed working with Fred. He was a very intelligent, highly well-read individual. Fred knew something about everything without coming across as arrogant. As it turned out, Fred had been an all-state catcher in baseball, back in his days in Central Washington. A baseball player myself, from the same area, we could talk sports for hours. Fred loved great literature, and the outdoors. He was an accomplished commercial fisherman, and could repair anything mechanically. He held a deep love *and* fear for his wife, Crystal, whom I knew of as the only person on earth tougher than Fred. Fred and Crystal were and are great couple. They seemed a perfect match for each other. A former bar owner in the toughest part of town, Crystal had become a highly educated teacher. When Fred got too carried away in all night "choir-practices," it was Crystal who would make him put his guns away and behave. She was said to be a far more accurate marksman.

Fred and Crystal ultimately poured their hearts into two young granddaughters, for reasons I care not to expound upon. And it was Grandpa who volunteered to coach their Little League and umpire many games. It was obvious to most, that the grandpa was protective of the girls, as evidenced at a particular little league game. According to legend, a parent became too vocally abusive toward Fred's granddaughter. Fred was described as patient, yet firm in admonishing the parent. But, alas, the parent was said to persist. Legend continues that the man found himself cart-wheeling uncontrollably down a steep nearby embankment. Your author has little doubt as to the veracity of the story.

Fred was obviously hell on two feet toward criminals. But he was profoundly compassionate toward any victims, or those who were down and out. He often gave money or groceries to the homeless. He repaired cars for those whom could not afford repairs. And he would give his fellow officer the shirt off his back if needed.

Fred Kilmer has now long since retired. Yet he can be seen occasionally in a different uniform, providing security at certain venues. He does so for two reasons — one, in order to fund any needs his beloved granddaughters; and two, so that he may still see his friends upon occasion.

I think the world of Fred. I will forever appreciate that he and the other "old crusties" accepted the kid into their esoteric world. I've been forever grateful he chose to be on the side of the good guys. Lord help us, if he hadn't.

***

Chapter 4: Harborzoo

Harborview Medical Center rises above the downtown skyscrapers of Seattle on a shining hilltop. Aptly named, the hospital stands like a huge gothic castle, boasting a spectacular view of Elliott Bay, several blocks to the west beneath a daunting hill. That is not the only view possessed by this historic and vital institution in the city. Built in 1931 as the King County hospital, Harborview serves as one of the country's first emergency-response programs. While it may be said that police officers view thousands of lives in a career, employees of Harborview Medical Center, or "HMC" as coined, view hundreds of lives in a single grueling 24-hour shift.

The old and formerly very dingy building has turned away no visitors. From the acutely injured arriving by helicopter in several pieces, to the mentally ill, to the truly down and out, every segment of society walks through those doors as equals. Harborview was a key player in developing Medic One, as one of the country's premier paramedic programs. Indeed, an entire television series was once filmed to display the life-saving deeds of the hospital and the Seattle Fire Department paramedics whom the doctors and nurses trained. Dr. Michael Copass, a grizzled and highly decorated Vietnam War Medic led and guided the hospital for over a quarter century. While feared by many employees for his undiplomatic attention to detail, few may deny learning more and faster from the legendary genius than anywhere on the globe. A neurosurgeon by trade, Dr. Copass developed innovative programs that have saved countless lives. He never ceased to learn nor innovate, and he could not refrain from performing miracles. Retirement only served to bore him. Michael holds a profound sense of affection and guardianship toward any man or woman in uniform, and he is still considered the patron saint of SPD officers. Most officers refer to Dr. Copass, simply, as "God."

The doctors and nurses, many of whom hail from the nearby University of Washington, are second to none. What they see and experience on a daily basis, while doggedly seeking to save and improve lives, leaves this author in absolute awe. They treat the mentally ill, the gunshot victims, the burn victims, the accident victims, and victims of rare diseases, all with dignity and enormous skill. The doctors and nurses of H.M.C. are, quite simply, the salt of the earth. But, my, are they stories unto themselves.

A Friday or Saturday night at" the zoo" is the ultimate adventure into the surreal. Full moons may even further the spectacle, as no one may un-convince the hospital personnel or police and fire employees of the reality to the phenomenon. The massively overcrowded emergency room shall soon be packed with mental committees, overdoses, shooting victims, rape victims, accident victims, angry gang families, and the regular clientele just seeking attention. Teams of police officers and hospital security guards may struggle to pin down a mental patient, brought in by ambulance in restraints, while paramedics quickly shuttle critically injured patients from the hospital helipad.

Mental patients may rise from a restraint bed as if starring in an exorcism movie, while feeble little old ladies amble in with false maladies so as to simply seek solace with compassionate, albeit harried hospital personnel.

Dr. Copass and staff are so advanced in their medical skill that they have been known to assemble makeshift operating rooms around victims at an accident site. At least on two occasions, a sterile tented O.R. was constructed around individuals whom were pinned between loading docks and huge trucks that backed into them. Heroic efforts were made to stabilize the victims before the trucks were instructed to slowly pull away. Sadly, neither victim survived. But the efforts were testament to the heroic and brilliant efforts to which the Harborview staff will attempt in order to save a human life.

Through it all, the HMC staff maintains an incredibly organized response entity to all situations. They prioritize quickly, and seek to provide care and compassion to all whom enter. Well, *almost* all. See below.

***

Circa summer of 1991 — The sorry bad guy

Once a "seasoned" veteran of ten years of gainful employment, I was fortunate enough to work one of the dream patrol districts of the fair city — 2-Union-1. The daytime district assignment basically entailed circling the most beautiful lake in the city, surrounded by running paths, beaches, wading, pools, and sports facilities. The grueling assignment involved unlocking doors of cars with keys left within, resolving "out or safe" issues at the little league parks, advising thong-clad young ladies if their skimpy swimsuits were indecent or not, and other demanding big-city tasks.

Yet, on a sunny August day the radio reported a burglary in progress in a neighborhood a few blocks from the Green Lake. I, backed by adjoining units, motored toward the residence. A radio update indicated that shots had just been fired. Suddenly, my size 12 shoe was pushing the pedal in a rapid downward motion and the patrol car came to life beneath the wailing siren.

Multiple units came skidding to a halt in front of a stylish bungalow, and exiting officers found one individual on the front porch of the home in a bloody pulpy mess, screaming for "help" and complaining of "murrrrrderrrr." A male stood at the entrance with a shotgun in hand and a glazed look on his face. Two officers drew weapons and pointed them at the shotgun-toting individual, as they propelled him to the front lawn of the home. However I noted that the "suspect" appeared to be clean-cut, wearing expensive sandals, and a tastefully matched designer tank top and Bermuda shorts. He was cooperating fully, whereas the "victim" was screaming incessant profanities, had tattoos and piercings, body odor, and apparent drug usage sores.

The wise and sage officers on the scene ultimately concluded that the man whose face had been driven into the turf was an innocent victim, and that he had shot a knife-wielding burglary suspect with bird shot. An estimated 55 darling little pellets had penetrated the suspect's every extremity. His level of pain was inestimable.

The lucky contestant was transported to Harborview Medical Center by aid car for conscientious and compassionate care. I followed the air car to the hospital E/R.

Attending physician number one made a grand entrance around a drawn triage-room curtain like Jay Leno onto a stage. Having just begun his shift, the young intern was enthused for a night at the zoo and the opportunity to save humankind. He looked at the tortured young man, who looked like he had lost a fight with an ant-hill, and wisely inquired, "Now what seems to be the problem?" Apparently not impressed with the intern's powers of observation, the less than patient patient promptly summoned phlegm that must have begun somewhere near his large intestine region and gathered reinforcements on the way upward. With expert marksmanship, the young man was able to successfully launch an impressive quantity of personal fluids toward the face of the attending physician. An erudite oration followed, consisting of the combination of the words "F--k" and…."You."

Attending physician number one was apparently less than impressed with the patient's non-verbal and verbal forms of communication, as he quickly exited the room to sanitize himself. He returned shortly thereafter with a blissful smile upon his face. Apparently there were no hard feelings, as he sought to clean each and every pellet wound thoroughly and completely. As a supplemental bonus to his patient, he added copious amounts of saline (yes, salt) to his massive syringe of cleaning fluid, just to be thorough. While this author has rarely felt a wisp of pity for a piece of garbage burglar, the screams of appreciation for the doctor's great work did eventually evoke profound pity.

It was apparent that the young lad had learned commandment number eleven: "Thou shalt not ever, ever, ever piss off the attending emergency room doctor." The suspect was thus prepared when the second attending physician entered to relieve his predecessor of the time consumptive task. He gently attended to each and every wound with the patience of Job, while the contrite patient purred that he was a saintly man indeed.

The good doctor eventually asked your author how the poor lad had come to become so egregiously injured. Yours truly, ever happy to share a story even then, was quick to relate the circumstances. Fate, it would seem, had again taken an untoward turn regarding the young scofflaw. The doctor immediately turned a lovely shade of red and exclaimed, "I *live* in that neighborhood…I was robbed just last week…cleaned out the whole damned house…it was probably *you!*" It was at that point that the poor patient seemed to truly miss doctor number one's bedside manner, as the new physician pulled out the wire brushes for even more thorough cleaning. Your author is quite sure that, had the suspect indeed possessed international secrets, he would have surrendered such info to the proper authorities.

One would think that the poor patient would have learned every life lesson imaginable after his thorough bathing. But, alas, the pain may have yet again dulled his senses as an attending nurse sought to roll his gurney to another room. While it may have been thought that the lad had emptied himself of all possible expectorants at that point, his actions would indicate otherwise. The sweetest, most compassionate little nurse was the recipient of a perfect bulls-eye shot to the face. But before attending officers could come to her aid, she waved them off with a "fear not." Showing profound concern for the patient's eventual need to urinate, the experienced nurse produced a catheter for the patient's comfort. However, untrained observers opined that it may have been excessive to insert said catheter so deeply into the privileged areas of the patient. It would have been their sworn testimony that the catheter was seen to exit the patient's nasal passages at some given time during insertion.

The officers left the hospital knowing that the troubled lad was indeed in good hands, and had seen the error of his ways. Harborview has a way of changing lives for the better.

***

The great chase, sponsored by VISA

In late summer of 1985 an individual was arrested after attempting to rob a local convenience store. During the arrest the individual had attempted to further his armed intimidation tactics toward the responding patrol officers. The result was a bullet hole in his shoulder. As is procedure, the individual was treated for his wound at Harborview Medical Center. He was hospitalized in a seventh floor private bay view room, courtesy of the taxpayers of King County. As was protocol between the Seattle Police Department and King County Jail, the robbery suspect would be subject to police guards for several days prior to the filing of formal robbery charges by the Prosecutor's Office.

Young Officer Chris Wrede was assigned the daytime shift of prisoner watch. An affable and carefree officer, Chris took the assignment with feigned appreciation and humor. At that time in his career, Chris was not renowned for taking the job inordinately seriously. Such a detail was generally dreaded by officers due to the extreme boredom of standing in the doorway of a hospital room. Many officers were further offended by the pampering the dirt-bag would receive, complete with pity for the wounds, and pillow fluffing. It would seem that half of the hospital's nurses were extremely liberal, and often resentful of police hardline attitudes. Yet, the more experienced nurses whom had seen it all usually presented more realistic attitudes--at least in the opinions of the police.

The robbery suspect was fortunate enough to be receiving care from a cadre of younger, more liberal nurses. It was the belief of that nursing team that locking leg restraints for the suspect were barbaric and unnecessary. After all, the "victim" of police violence had promised them that he would be a good boy.

Hour after hour dragged by, as the suspect commenced to snoring loudly. Cartoons played on his television set. Not to be outdone, Officer Wrede positioned himself in a comfortable chair near the doorway and was heard to produce his own snoring sound effects.

Officer Wrede awakened, almost instinctively. He found that the suspect was not in his bed and rose nervously. A nurse walked by the doorway. He asked the nurse if the suspect had been removed for some sort of treatment. The nurse responded that the suspect had just walked down the hall for reasons unknown. She had assumed that he was exercising. Officer Wrede sprinted down the hallway. He was just in time to see the suspect in his hospital gown entering a stairwell and disappearing. Wisely, the excited officer communicated on his radio that a dangerous felon was attempting an escape.

Dozens of officers responded to the hospital, inclusive of myself. We sought to surround the enormous campus. The young officer's gasping narration of the foot pursuit sounded like a Notre Dame football broadcast for drama and suspense. The suspect ran down two flights of stairs. He ran across the entire wing of a floor. He tipped tables while running through the cafeteria. At one point, the suspect even sprinted through the morgue. Despite the efforts of dozens of SPD officers, Harborview Security Officers, and nearby State Troopers and County Sheriff's officers, the suspect eluded the dragnet. Thus, a dangerous felon was loosed upon society.

Many days passed and extensive detective-work and interagency collaborations were conducted while seeking to locate the robbery suspect. Ultimately, he was located by alert Alaska State troopers, somewhere outside of Anchorage. The suspect was thus arrested and incarcerated. Extensive extradition proceedings were processed between the two states.

Ultimately, the suspect was flown back to Seattle for booking and formal charges.

Young officer Wrede was summoned to the Chief of Police's office. He was immediately highly anxious. The Chief was known for his intimidating demeanor and dominating command of the department. He was often referred to as "The Ayatullah" and "Little Hitler." The Chief graciously seated the young officer at a conference table. He even offered the young man a glass of water.

Then the screaming began. The Chief could be heard far down the hallway of his tenth floor office. Other command staff and secretaries felt profound pity for the young officer. Yet, Officer Wrede maintained his composure throughout the lengthy high volume diatribe. The Chief proceeded to expound upon the costs to the department for paying for Alaska State Patrol overtime, Jail Costs, Air Fare for two robbery detectives to fly to Alaska and return the suspect, and additional county costs for re-filing of charges. The Chief was even able to cite to the young and terrified officer the exact monetary loss from losing a prisoner. He bore down into the face of the seated officer, while he held a commanding standing position. His demeanor resembled that of a baseball manager versus an umpire.

Ultimately, the Chief of Police asked the young officer how he was to pay for all the expenses of his foible. He jabbed his finger into the shoulder of the officer and asked if he had thousands of dollars in cash.

Young Officer Wrede gave a legendary response to the Chief of all Police.

The young man, from a local affluent family, reached into his wallet. He retrieved a shiny platinum credit card, reached such forward to the Chief and asked, "Do you take Visa?"

To this day, some thirty years later, the now highly respected retired Detective Wrede remains embarrassed by the story. He somehow suspected that he might someday receive honorable mention in my book.

***

Cop Culture
Chapter side note: "Gallows humor."

In trying to understand the unique sub-culture of the men and women in blue, one must take into account some of the macabre occurrences too often observed by all cops. Laughter—albeit seemingly inappropriate and forced, provides a brief modicum of levity, and the vital "medicine" derived thereof. The humor often emerges at moments when the cops can seemingly take no more of the surreal, twisted, or grisly.

From the very onset of this career, your author viewed this condition eventuate. Our academy class was forced to observe an autopsy, first-hand. This training was ostensibly designed to teach forensics to the young recruits. However, the intent appeared most clearly to involve separating the weak-stomached from the tenacious. The autopsy "field trip" occurred during the second month of the five month academy session.

In the room of the autopsy gathered 22 wide-eyed recruits of class #144. The coroners and present training officer seemed to delight in their pursuit of causing young recruits to "lose their lunches." The stench was horrible, as "ripe" bodies had been selected for a particular reason. Ever mindful of the monitoring training ("Tac") officer, and their huddled peers, all recruits sought to present a stoic persona. The opening of a gaseous body cavity increased the stench exponentially, and one recruit left the room retching.

A smirking coroner then took a saw to the skull of the cadaver. A horrible grinding sound made dentist drills seem tame by comparison. Smoke actually rose from the skull of the body.

As the slicing of a human skull had nearly ended, and the brain matter began to appear, recruit stomachs reached the apex of tolerance levels. It was at that point that Marysville Police recruit Steve Winters spoke clearly above the noise, "OK, do you give?" With that, the entire group laughed uproariously. But the horrible moment had magically abated, with only one recruit resigning.

It is thus that officers on the street will apply such humor to come to grips with the horrific and tragic. Terms such as "road pizza" and "crispy critters" will sometimes be voiced, not as an attempt at irreverence, but as an attempt to label the reality unreal.

It is amazing how the human mind shall process the macabre. At least in the case of your author (but often confirmed by peers), the mind shall convince itself that the horrific is, indeed, unreal--that surely something of such proportions could not have truly transpired. Strangely, many peers agree, that true-life scenarios often do not immediately severely affect us. However, photographs and television shows of simulated such scenarios bother us greatly. It is because our defenses have been lowered, and we have been conditioned from youth to believe that photos or videos are reality. We cannot convince ourselves otherwise. Your author cannot stand the grisly scenes portrayed on the television CSI shows as they are, indeed, realistic. I am forever appalled that young children may be watching the show, shortly after their dinnertimes. My, how the world has changed.

As police officers, we must remain forever vigilant, however, so as not to become too hardened. We reaffirm to one another a sage oath of sort-- that on the day that the horrible has no effect whatsoever, it is the day to leave that chosen profession.

In terms of "gallows humor," no group surpasses this phenomenon more so than fire fighters or emergency room nurses. And this would ultimately seem to make sense. Perhaps no one views more human suffering than they do. But the folks in blue are not far behind.

Most police officers develop extremely thick outer skins for their own mental preservation dealing with blood, gore, and twisted circumstances. Officers must fight not to become so callous as to lose their humanity in the process. Most officers can handle tragedies and grisly scenes involving adult victims. But none that I know of can shake off the horror of children suffering a violent death. They will gladly handle one hundred adult dead bodies in exchange for avoiding one dead child or baby. Delivering a message of the death of child to the respective parents is nearly as devastating. This is true of officers whom have their own children. Yet those without children still possess affection for children and the pain is just as intense.

***

Chapter 5: Death from above and other astounding accidents

On a cold January evening in 1989, your author and partner Tony Jensen were walking a foot-beat in the downtown corridor. Assigned to the ever-fascinating Pike Place market area, we were walking northbound on a Second Avenue sidewalk, two blocks south of our area of assignment. We had completed an arrest of cocaine dealers in the market, and were set to return to our beat to complete the final hour of our shift, until 2000 hours (8 P.M.). We were content to twirl our nightsticks and raise our coat collars against the chill. We could see our respective breaths as we paced.

From a half block behind us came a tremendous metallic crashing sound, but we did not turn around. The sound was often heard from nearby construction sites and did not strike us as unusual. Seconds later, upon our portable radios, we heard the exasperated voice of a fellow patrol officer, Sekfai "Paul" Leung. Never prone to excited utterances, he hurriedly broadcast impassioned exclamations. But we could not understand what he was announcing. It soon became apparent that he was calling out in his native language of Vietnamese. He quickly managed to calm himself and pleaded for more units to assist at his location. His location was a half block to our South, and clearly was the source of the earlier sounds.

Thinking that our fellow officer was imperiled, we ran rapidly toward the nearby street corner at 2nd Avenue and University Street. We arrived within seconds to find Sekfai crawling into a crumpled pile of three automobiles. The damage to the vehicles was tremendous and we wondered how a fender–bender could have generated such consequences. While joining Sekfai in the crumpled pile and searching for victims, we realized that one car was totally atop the other two. We quickly realized that we could not penetrate the twisted metal and withdrew from the pile. Fire engines with jaws of life apparatus arrived momentarily.

As the fire department crews set to cutting away the metal, we asked Sekfai how an accident could bring one vehicle atop two others. "Where did that car come from, Paul?," we asked. He shook his head in bewilderment and pointed his powerful flashlight straight upward. We craned our necks and then could see his intended site. Seven floors above in the darkness we could see the source of tragedy. In a brand-new parking garage there was a broken cable fence and pieces of metal flapping in the wind. Debris continued to fall downward from the site, pelting the nearby sidewalk.

Tow trucks arrived very quickly to assist in pulling the vehicle from atop the others. The car had imploded in an inward fold and had totally entombed two bodies within. The metal groaned as two different tow truck cables "gently" slid the car from the two others. Fire crews immediately placed tarps over the two bodies within the removed vehicle. It was clear that no aid could change their fate. Within the remaining two vehicles another twisted pile of carnage remained. Green anti-freeze dripped from the vehicles, as if the machines themselves were bleeding.

Large and muscular fire fighters pulled two bodies from what remained of a small import car and dumped them unceremoniously upon the gutter of the street. They appeared to simply be sleeping, and actually looked peaceful. Paramedics knelt to check for life signs, but the largest member of the ladder company called out, "Don't bother. Code black. Look at the back." Vast quantities of "cottage cheese" (brain matter) was escaping from the ears and skulls of the man and woman. The firefighters started to hose the brain matter and blood down a nearby drain.

Progress was made with cutting through the second vehicle, and a sole driver of the Cadillac had been broken and folded by the force. Another tarp would be placed across him until the rest of the cutting could be completed. Huge crowds of onlookers had arrived, and media trucks began to set up. From the sidewalk a father took his young son by the hand and walked toward the site. "Look son, look." He sought to take photographs of the bodies for a memento. We chased him away with total disgust. Others in the crowd would strain to get a look at the gore.

As our attention turned back to the first "victim" vehicle our hearts stopped. As metal was further pulled away, a small baby seat lay within the rear of the car! Cops and firefighters searched frantically through the debris, but no child could be seen. We checked repeatedly, with the same results. Five persons, in total, would die in an instant on that street corner. Three of them, literally, never knew what hit them.

Responding Accident Investigation detectives soon arrived, with laser measurement tools, and high priced camera equipment. Like precise tacticians, a team of investigators would meticulously piece together the entire incident. A macabre vision appeared in my mind. They appeared, for all intents and purposes, to resemble crabs, scurrying over a beached decaying animal. I felt sick at my own twisted thoughts.

The profoundly thorough detectives and officers would

determine that a sixty year-old male had been driving a sports car on the 7th floor of the parking garage in question. He was accompanied by a 39-year-old female on a social outing. He was driving from the top of the parking garage, when he apparently suffered a massive heart attack and lost control of the vehicle. The vehicle somehow accelerated as his foot pinned down the pedal. The vehicle would crash through a five-foot under-enforced cable barrier "wall" and immediately become airborne.

Below, a young couple in their early twenties sat stopped in their small compact at a red traffic light. They were in the easternmost lane on the southbound one-way street, nearest to the parking garage in question. Beside them was stopped a young businessman in his Cadillac, headed home from a long day of work. Only 30 feet to the north was officer Leung in his patrol car, also stopped for the traffic light.

In a cruel twist of events, we later learned the reason for the empty child seat in the rear of the couple's vehicle. Just one week prior, the child had died of SIDS. The couple had just buried the child the day prior. The couple's family would soon have yet another crushing funeral to attend. Five lives ended instantly upon the horrible impact of the car from the sky, perfectly perpendicular upon the two vehicles below. God's aim, for inexplicable reasons, was deadly accurate that night.

Many months later, lawsuits against the parking garage company would come to fruition. Several officers, including your author, and detectives, provided testimony. The trial lasted several days. We never heard the verdict. It was our understanding that the defendant ultimately paid a substantial settlement to victim families in an out of court settlement. But the money would never bring back the tragic victims. Numerous officers later offered to one another how vividly the incident had displayed that "when your number is called, your number is called." The difference between being a vital human and mere pulp, it would be said, was very slight indeed.

***

Half a woman

It was a very warm early August morning, at around 0215 hours (2:15 A.M.) in 1991. Your author was working a "third-watch" patrol shift 3-Boy-1. It was yet another highly coveted beat to work, as the district entailed tremendous hillside views above Elliott Bay, and the northward Puget Sound, spanning all the way to Canada. The lights of the city could be seen to the south during darkness hours. Fifty miles of the snow-capped Olympic Mountains brushed the sky to the west, across the Puget Sound during daylight hours and full moons. Spectacular parks, such as Sunset View Park on the steep eastern hillside, and Golden Gardens Park, two miles below adorned the area. A long strip of sea-side restaurants and upscale singles nightclubs completed the ambience along Seaview Avenue. Expensive tudor-style homes dotting the neighborhoods and touristy businesses seemed to coincide neatly in the area.

It was a typical Friday night, turned Saturday morning in the sector. Numerous bar fights had been interrupted in the area. Family arguments had followed at the predictable hours of high alcohol consumption. And bonfire-lit "keggers" were monitored in the nearby park, so as to not get out of control. For the most part, young people were mannered and compliant, and few had to be told twice to tone it down, or face expensive tickets.

A quarter moon shone off of the gentle beach waves, as the tide was coming inward. A rare plenitude of stars was present, giving cause for celebration to the young revelers on the beaches. Guitars were being played, and young couples took advantage of blankets to draw closer to one another. It was a perfect summer night.

A nonchalant radio dispatch came out to your author. "Three-Boy-One." I gave my response. "Boy One, we have a possible accident near the 5800 block of Seaview Avenue. A caller advises that he was awakened by the sound of screeching tires, and he believes he heard a sound of a collision...unknown how many vehicles may have been involved." It was not uncommon for fender-benders to occur at that location, as young drivers often became inattentive coming down the scenic hillside curve. They would often become distracted at the sights of the bay and glitzy nightclubs, and rear-end other vehicles that had slowed for the thick traffic below.

I arrived uphill to the scene within 4 minutes. Traffic seemed to be flowing normally for the time of night, as bars had just closed and patrons were driving uphill and homeward. I could see no signs of any accident, as I drove uphill for several blocks, along the curving two lane roadway. I thought the accident, if such had occurred, must have been resolved amongst the participants. As I reached the hill's apex, I chose to come around and make a downhill pass.

Two blocks down the hill I could see what appeared to be fresh skid marks. Yet, new skid marks were a daily occurrence in the area. I noticed, however, that the skid marks took an abrupt jaunt to the right, and away from the roadway. I slowed the patrol car and shone the spotlight to my right. I could see that eight feet of guardrail had been blasted away by an obvious impact. The edges had been peeled outward, and hung jaggedly above a cliff. I engaged my red and blue "overheads" and exited the patrol car. I pulled my 30,000 candle-power flashlight from the belt-holder and peered over the cliff. All that could be seen far below were acres of blackberry thickets, and distant railroad tracks. A great deal of garbage had been thrown over the embankment, and reflections of metal refracted from many locations. Each would appear to be hub-caps, aluminum foil, and even entire garbage cans.

I again scanned the entire area with the powerful flashlight, wondering if I was looking for nothing. I re-focused again upon what looked like an errant hubcap and realized that I was actually viewing an entire wheel of a vehicle. Looking downward some 60 feet, I could finally determine that an entire automobile lay partially on its side. It was tilted forward somewhat, and leaned toward the driver's side. The vehicle had crashed upon a combination of blackberry bushes, dirt, and boulders. The front bumper was bent around an old telephone pole. It was apparent that speed had been involved, as the vehicle had sailed a considerable distance outward from the roadside above.

I radioed for additional units and for the fire department to respond. Radio quickly replied that fire dispatch sought clarification for the need of their response. Fire crews wanted to know how I knew there would be injuries. My response was a sarcastic, "Radio, tell 'em to just get moving."

I donned black leather gloves, and carefully guided my long legs over the guardrails, careful to choose solid ground beyond. The twisted metal was like razor blades, and I was grateful for the protective leather on my hands. I held the guardrail with one gloved hand, while lighting below with my flashlight. There would be no easy pathway toward the crash site below. My polished size twelve shoes sunk deeply into the rocky, sandy hillside. I struggled to maintain my balance while alternately walking in choppy steps and sliding in the dirt and rocks. Numerous tentacles of blackberry plants attacked my shins and immediately bloodied my legs upon my descent. My tailbone scraped rocks, as I leaned backward during the sliding motion. My pants and skin were torn.

I finally reached the bottom of the ravine, almost out of control. I braked my sliding and running motion with a dusty thump against the victim's car. My mouth was caked with dust that I sought to spit outward, while my shins stung, and tailbone throbbed. I thought myself a wimp to even notice my minor condition, under the circumstances.

"Mommy?" "Is that you, Mommy." A voice came from an unknown location. I shone my flashlight toward the back seat of the vehicle. Clothing items and paperwork littered the seat, but no one could be seen. I moved the strong beam toward the front seat and had the same results. The dashboard had imploded inward upon the impact, and the glove-box contents had been strewn violently within the car. The driver's side windows had all been shattered. The vehicle smelled of oil, anti-freeze, and the ever-present dust.

I panned the flashlight to the windshield, from right to left, and top to bottom. There was very little left of the windshield, and only jagged edges remained. Still, no signs of humanity were readily evident. As my beam glided downward, I noticed a small amount of blood and something shiny draped across the driver's side windshield shards. I re-directed the beam upon that area.

At first it did not register what I was seeing. It looked, for all intents and purposes, to be a snake. Almost yellowish in color, and glistening, it reminded me of corn snakes, often seen at the local zoo. For mili-seconds my mind sought comprehension. I trained my beam to follow the "snake" forward from the glass. The site spanned the entire length of the hood of the large luxury vehicle, as I inched forward through the blackberries. The snake held the strange smell of uncooked poultry, and my stomach began to churn.

"Mommy?" came the voice again, more strongly. My flashlight's beam first shone across a woman's face. She was staring at me intently, almost smiling. I could then recognize her entire upper torso, strangely posed across the front hood of the vehicle and against the cliff-side. Her arms were reaching toward me immobile. Her fingers were alternately clenching and releasing very slowly.

"Mommy, are you mad at me?" she again spoke in a strangely childish voice. She appeared to be a woman in her mid- thirties. She was clearly a highly attractive affluent woman, with perfectly groomed brunette hair and clear blue eyes. Expensive diamond earrings hung from her ear lobes, and a small amount of blood was brushed upon the left side of her face. Her glistening intestines spanned immeasurably into the distance, and I could not determine the location of her lower torso, somewhere in the darkness. Her arms fell to her side. Her mouth then seemed to gesture inaudible words. Slowly the lower jaw bobbed and quivered. The motion resembled that of a fish out of water, gaining final desperate gasps of precious oxygen.

A voice suddenly came from above my right shoulder "F--k, meeeeee...", and my flashlight beam grew exponentially brighter. Startled out of a near trance, I turned to find a young pair of dusty, suspender- clad firefighters panting behind me. Their industrial flashlights cast a wide beam, and the luminescent macabre scene appeared like a Hollywood set. I could then see the flashing lights far above from other patrol cars. A paramedic van had just arrived. Multiple flashlights shone downward. I heard the firefighters' radio crackle a request from the paramedics up above. "Ladder 14, your status." The senior of the two twenty-something year-old firefighters quickly answered, "You gotta see this to believe it."

The woman uttered no further words, as my attention immediately returned to her. Her lower jaw quivered more slowly, and she took one final deep "breath." Her beautiful blue eyes stared at us eternally. They do so even now.

The recovery of twisted metal and what was once a human body began.

A week later, no one would be able to notice that a life had ended on that twisting, scenic curve, on a warm summer night 1991. A guardrail was replaced and life went on as if nothing had occurred.

I was reminded of the tragedy many years later, during a bizarre scene in the movie, "Signs." M. Knight Shymalayan had captured such a sight perfectly. The movie scene drove your author from the theater.

***

Chapter side note: Officer John Patrick Sullivan — A Policeman's policeman.

If one were to draw up on a board the epitome of what a police officer is to represent, Officer John Patrick Sullivan would grace such a board en- toto. To borrow a phrase my Irish grandfather often uttered, John was, "As Irish as Patty's Pig."

John, as were most beat cops of the 60's through 80's was a big man, who seemed even bigger. He stood some six feet two and a half, and he carried 220 pounds of muscle and strength. He had the trademark enormous hands that most beat cops possessed. His grip could nearly crush a person, and his handshake made your author wince. Officer Sullivan had flaming red hair and a flaming red beard. Only the beat cops were allowed to wear a beard. His beard matched the 1940's style wool beat uniform often allowed for beat cops as showmanship for tourists and business people.

John was without doubt your author's idol as a policeman. He used his slight brogue to apply incomparable charm and wit toward nearly any situation. He stood perfectly erect, with his wide shoulders thrown back proudly. His walk was patient and purposeful. John was harsh and iron-fisted with street thugs. He was intolerant of dishonesty, scams, or taking advantage of the vulnerable. His wrath was swift and unmerciful toward those whom victimized in any way. Many a street thug knew John's fists or his ironwood nightstick.

Yet, toward the peaceful thousands of occupants of John's Pioneer Square beat, he was the most kind and compassionate person imaginable. Officer Sullivan knew every street person on his beat, and knew them well. The stories behind the street people were often shrouded, yet John took the time to learn every detail over the years. While he never admitted such, John Sullivan was widely known for his generosity on the streets. He provided innumerable down- and- out persons with food, clothing, and money — even if such money did lead to a bottle of wine. He sought social services for those whom truly needed such, and quickly ran out those scamming the system in greed.

John Sullivan was the gentlest officer I have ever seen. I will never forget watching the officer offer his arm to a tiny and elderly woman whom sought to cross busy 2nd Avenue at Yesler Street during rush hour. The woman was very feeble and struggled to shuffle across the street. John patiently bent far downward to grasp the woman's arm like a gentleman taking a lady to a grand ball. One fiery glance from Officer Sullivan toward the angry traffic sufficed to ensure all drivers' patience. The light changed to green for the traffic, then back to red, and back to green again. John gently guided the woman across the street through two cycles of the traffic light—and the drivers understood his act. The tiny old woman kissed Officer Sullivan on his cheek. He tipped his hat and walked away, his iron-wood night stick again twirling like a blur in his hand. John Patrick Sullivan was straight out of the movies. But I was honored to work with the real thing.

***

Chapter 6: Traffic stops—Human-kind at their finest moments

Traffic enforcement is a vital cog in law enforcement in any kind of town. In the scope of human events it is insignificant. Yet, few aspects of law enforcement bring about more public interest. Neighborhood groups will demand heavy enforcement in their area to slow down the speeders that endanger their children. Yet, they will be the first to complain when it is *their* exceptional speed that registers upon our radars. Traffic enforcement is like being a little-league umpire. Nobody wants the job, but somebody must do it. And everybody shall complain about the calls.

Many people in the real world shall never have contact with a police officer for any event other than a traffic stop. It is thus the ultimate measure of public to officer interaction. And, oh, my, what interactions do occur.

In response to innumerable inquiries as to the existence of traffic quotas, the answer is Yes. And... No. It all depends upon the agency, and the assignment within that agency. To be sure, if one is assigned to a traffic enforcement task, whether on our State Highways or in municipalities, the expectation is to write tickets. Otherwise, job performances would be viewed similarly to cannery workers viewing the passing cans for the beauty of the logos, and sending empty cans ahead.

All municipalities of any size look upon the revenue generated from citations as vital income for the government coffers. Seattle may rake in over fourteen million dollars in a particularly profitable year. But the income is never a factor in staffing, budgeting, and directing traffic enforcement. Uh, huhhhh…

Some officers absolutely love the traffic enforcement side of the profession. To be sure, officers from tiny entities may view such task as the most exciting occurrence in a given day. Others may enjoy the power yielded thereof, or maybe truly believe that tickets save lives. (Studies may show that they do). Officers' opinions on the level of enforcement differ as much as those of the citizenry. There is no bottom line to the business.

Many citizens seek a magic formula to escaping the scribing of a ticket by the detaining officer. Sadly, no such formula does exist. At best, a few considerations are recommended as follows:

DO--

- Respond to the flashing lights behind you by pulling over as soon as possible, to a safe right side of the roadway.
- Stay behind the wheel of your car.
- Have your window rolled down, especially if the window is darkly tinted.
- Have your license, registration, and proof of insurance available.
- Keep your hands on the wheel, in clear view of the approaching officer.
- Be mannered and briefly informative. Politely point out perspectives, without arguing the merits of the stop. You will lose an argument every time, guaranteed.
- Be honest. If you made a mistake, you made a mistake. It is amazing how sincere contriteness can benefit a human being in life. And traffic stops are part of life. This is not to imply that you volunteer that you've recently beaten your wife, cheated on your taxes, and

are concealing two kilos of cocaine beneath your seat. But, consider that it is amazing how rarely a driver will offer a sincere admission. Thus, many, but by no means all officers will consider releasing the driver with a warning.

DO NOT--

- Jump out of your vehicle. (You would instantly pose a threat).
- Allow your passengers to jump out of your vehicle. (Same reasoning).
- Seek to impress the officer with how important you are, or how important your friends are.
- Ask the officer if they have "something better to do." (Obviously they don't.)
- Lie about never having had a ticket before. Those darned things called in-dash computers are highly informative.

All officers have personal pet peeves for which tickets are nearly automatic. For your author, tiny children being bounced on mommy's lap while rolling 60 MPH was number one. Number two was the throwing of lighted cigarettes or other debris from a vehicle. Stale red light violators were assured to receive a ticket from me. To each their own in that realm. Realistically, you probably cannot talk your way out of a ticket. But you most assuredly can talk your way *into* one.

Those things said, there most certainly have been violators whom managed their way out of the wrath of my trusty ballpoint pen. Yet others talked themselves into a full quill's worth of the trusted sword of justice. Cases in point are, as follow...

The wrong-way comedian

One sunny Friday afternoon your author was driving southbound on Roosevelt Way in the 5000 block thereof. It was a mostly commercial area, abutting a beautiful residential zone to the east. The roadway was a three lane southbound one-way street, clearly signed every other block. A black sedan drove slowly *northbound* in the center lane, and ultimately "split the uprights" by driving right between and past two Southbound vehicles in the outside opposite lanes. The driver of the offending vehicle immediately seemed to have an Exorcist type of epiphany. It would seem that his head spun a full 360 degrees while passing at a slow rate between the two on-coming vehicles.

Ever the trained patrol observer, your author recognized the error of the violator's ways. Emergency lights were immediately engaged, and the pursuit of the hardened criminal followed. Sadly, the offender pulled over immediately, and rolled his window down. The chase, it would seem, was over before it began.

The hardened criminal was a white male, in his late forties. He had a tremendous head of black curly hair spilling over his large head and curling over his puppy-dog brown eyes. He held the appearance of comedian — almost like a Groucho Marx.

He hung his hands over the window ledge closely bunched together, wrist to wrist, and lowered his head in defeat.

"Take me. Take me. I did it. I'm so baaaaaaad."

Your author wondered from what planet the man had emerged. He produced ID and licensing info immediately upon request, and your author commented upon how quickly he did so. He responded, "Oh, believe me, officer, the way I drive, I've had lots of practice. For that reason I keep it all Vel-Crowed to my steering wheel."

As I examined his paperwork for validity, he peered upward with his puppy dog eyes and asked, "If I may be so bold as to ask, what's the speed limit on this street?"

I answered, "It's 35 miles per hour."

The criminal put his hand to his chin and wrinkled his face. "Hmmmm, I see. How fast do you think I was driving?"

I answered, "Only about 20."

The criminal immediately responded, "Do you have a calculator, officer?"

Incredulous, I asked the meaning of such a strange question.

The criminal then replied, again striking a thoughtful pose, "Hmmmmm, well I don't mean to be obstinate officer... and I'm no math wizard, and have no calculator on me, as you can plainly see... but the way I'm figuring this thing... it's 35 that way, and I went 20 this way... I think *you* owe *me* money."

At that I could no longer maintain my stoic posture. The driver had cracked me up. That is when the detaining officer knows that all control has been lost, and no ticket can thus be drafted. How, of course, could one ruin the day of someone who has just made yours!

A brief conversation would follow with the driver, as I returned his cherished paperwork. He actually taped it to his steering wheel as we spoke. As it turned out, the man was from Los Angeles and had never been to the confusing streets of Seattle prior to the date in question.

The driver had flown up for one weekend of employment — As a stand-up comedian at the nearby "Giggles" nightclub. He even offered me free tickets to his show that night, but immediately saw the error of his ways. He again dropped his head and placed his hands out of the window for handcuffing. "Oh God, I tried to bribe you… Oh wait, you haven't seen my show, it's more like a life sentence for *you!*"

I had no doubt the crowd would be in stitches that night, as I declined his kind offer. I told the violator so, and wiped the tears from my eyes.

The city would gain no revenue from me on that fateful date.

***

The "hikers."

Many an attractive female seeks to gain forgiveness from their myriad of tragic offenses by adjusting their skirts or dresses upon the approach of officers. Affectionately referred to as "hikers", some of these talented women can reach record heights for hiking such apparel. It is claimed that some skirts have been sighted at or around the earlobes of the lovely offenders. Officers take such acts as highly offensive, and many a ticket have been produced. Equal amusement in such circumstances arises when the approaching officer happens to be *female*. The skirts quickly are adjusted to cover even their shins. Sometimes female drivers may actually offer sexual favors in lieu of citations. (Males offer to argue egotistically, ultimately with the same results.)

One February Wednesday afternoon, circa 1993, your author was ever vigilant on patrol, positioned to view a controlled intersection at Elliott Avenue West and West Mercer Place. Elliott Avenue is a very busy multi-lane northbound- to-southbound arterial in Seattle. And West Mercer place is a busy feeder street from the nearby bustling Seattle Center, home to the famous Space Needle, et al.

A speeding red sports car passed northbound on Elliott Avenue, still a considerable distance away, when the traffic light turned red. The sports car accelerated the approach to the intersection and passed through a very "stale" red light. Oncoming traffic had to stop to avoid a collision with the offending vehicle.

Your author, confident of the kill, engaged the patrol vehicle, and commenced upon the traffic stop. The violator pulled over and rolled down her window immediately. She was a highly attractive blonde woman of about twenty-six years of age. She wore a red, low cut dress that was clearly very short in length. She was clearly very proud of her long shapely legs. The violator was tremendously friendly. She offered that it was a lovely day, and even complimented your author on his appearance. She seemed to take the confrontation in good spirits and giggled constantly.

As I examined her driver's license and paperwork for validity, I addressed my attention back to the driver. Apparently, some sort of malfunction with her clothing had occurred. The poor woman had lost control of the wild-spirited dress, and the garment had ridden its way to well above her waist. And to further add to the woman's misfortune, she had apparently forgotten to don underwear on that fateful date.

The poor woman seemed to handle the embarrassing situation competently, however, as she continued to giggle and compliment my appearance. But the dress just kept moving upward.

Your author couldn't resist commenting, "That's nice, but I've seen one of those before...I'll be right back." The violator's upbeat demeanor seemed to wane slightly, as I walked back to my patrol vehicle with the paperwork. As I commenced to write the red light citation, I thought to myself that I believed she would somehow regain control over her maverick dress. I proceeded to write the word "hiker" on the lower portion of the citation narrative, in case of future court appearances.

Confident that I would suddenly see the violator wearing a parka upon my return with the ticket-book, I was quite surprised to the contrary. While the dress in question had remained above the driver's navel, she had added more weaponry to her efforts. In full and plain view, the woman had retrieved a bright pink vibrator, from whereabouts unknown, and was animatedly seeking to pleasure herself in front of the citing officer. I took this to be a strange coping mechanism for the stress of the situation. However, she seemed to immediately cease such attempts to cope, upon the presentation of my steel ticket book. The violator's friendly mood changed dramatically, and she made comments about my probable unnatural affection toward my mother.

Your author attempted to remain his composure from the onslaught of insults and profanity, and profoundly asked that the driver sign the citation--- "Er, ma'am, using the other hand please?" I even let her keep the pen.

***

Sometimes, traffic violators win the battle of emotions merely by the sad state of affairs surrounding them. Contrary to popular belief, we *do* have hearts. But hearts don't help us make our quotas.

It was a cold rainy day in late winter, circa 1993. An unfortunate 60 year-old man drove slightly late through a red light in the scenic Ballard area of Seattle. The traffic stop would immediately follow. Immediately after the man rolled down his window, a horrible sound poured forth from within the vehicle. The sound reminded me of a combination of fingernails across a chalkboard and a dying elephant seal. As it turned out, it was the driver's wife. The woman harangued the poor man loudly and incessantly, with a voice that could crack the finest crystal in town.

The driver readily admitted that he had run the red light. He thought he may have been somewhat "distracted" at the time, and offered no real excuse. He then silently mouthed at me, "Help me... Shoot me." Unfortunately, I could not put the man out of his misery, and released him with a warning. The wife's constant berating never ceased, even then. It was my belief that the man had already been relegated to a miserable life sentence.

***

On yet another cold rainy day, an elderly man was seen to drive the wrong way on a busy University District street. Traffic swerved, and horns honked, as other drivers alertly avoided an imminent collision.

A spry looking 75-year-old man peered upward from his vehicle upon my approach. He wore a checkered French-styled hat, and a perfectly tied bow tie. I asked the driver what he was doing driving the wrong way. His response was memorable for years to come, "Well, officer, I guess I got a little confused... but you know, now I know how Custer felt."

I responded, "Sir?"

His answer, "Well, sir, everywhere I tried to go, there seemed to be arrows pointed at me!"

Once again, your author failed to walk away with a ticket on his stats.

***

To be sure, the opposite gamut of emotions can stem from

traffic enforcement. Many is the time that guilt encroaches when realizing that you ruined a person's week. But sometimes, such emotions can be overwhelming.

Violators, both male and female often seek to escape the wrathful ink pen by telling enormously sad stories, making grand excuses, or, in the case of women, crying uncontrollably at the scene. The crying might have been a successful ploy for your author, were it not for an old girlfriend from college days whom often bragged of crying her way out of innumerable citations with "dumb cops." She sealed the fate for many a woman to thus follow her. The problem lies in non-stop phoniness of tears, excuses, and totally contrived sad stories. Officers become hardened to the phenomenon.

One late night in the early 80's in the Southpark industrial region of Seattle, I made a stop of a driver weaving badly upon the roadway. The driver appeared to be a blue-collar construction type of man, and he was clearly highly intoxicated. I ran the drunk driver through the litmus of field sobriety tests, to which he failed miserably. An arrest was clearly mandated, and I sought to perform my legal obligation. The intoxicated man threw his arms over me, slobbered, and began to cry. I righted the man away from me and he stated, "Oh, please, oofthicer (sic), you don't understand... the doctor told me today that he is gonna cut my legs off next week... you gotta let me go."

Taking the slobbering drunk's act to be yet another artificial ploy to escape their rightful punishment, I processed the man for DUI and later released him from the precinct to a cab driver. Total fines at the time would surpass two months' pay, I estimated.

Approximately one month later, I would see the same man driving down the same stretch of roadway at which I had once arrested him. Yet, he was not driving the same vehicle as previously seen. The man was driving a motorized wheelchair — sans both of his legs. I don't think I have ever felt so low.

***

Guilt can be quite a motivator toward traffic decisions, on certain occasions. Case in point, my beloved 7-year patrol partner Kent Carpenter (please refer to subsequent full future chapter on my partner and I) were working downtown patrol unit 2-David-4. Circa 1987, on a blustery May afternoon, I was driving toward the scenic Alaskan Way corridor. Partner Kent was providing enthusiastic back-seat driver input, as always. The district included bordering rows of businesses upon sparkling Elliott Bay and historic Pike Place Market rising above on a nearby western hillside. Numerous ferry terminals and outstanding seafood restaurants lined the waterfront environs. As we approached a green westbound traffic light, we were forced to slow as a white station wagon drove through the red light northbound. The vehicle had not slowed in the slightest. We sought to catch up with the vehicle down the very short waterfront blocks, only to witness the vehicle again pass through another red light.

A traffic stop was thus initiated. I approached the driver's side and was greeted by a black man in his early thirties, sitting perfectly straight behind the wheel. His window was rolled down and all appropriate paperwork was held for my convenience. Kent stood at the passenger window of the vehicle, conversing with an adult female passenger, and simultaneously seeking to hear my conversation with the driver. We both expected to hear the traditional cry of "racism" by the black man for daring to enforce the laws he had broken.

However, the driver remained extraordinarily polite and respectful. He made no excuses for his actions, other than to apologize for his mistakes and invite the lawful penalty. We could see that he had three young children in the rear of the station wagon, and that they were typically active little boys. The driver again apologized for his errors and blamed himself for becoming distracted. He again invited the inevitable two citations. He did seek, however, to obtain directions to a nearby neighborhood. He offered that he and family had just arrived in Seattle after driving across the country to begin his new job.

I sought to flush out the driver's true hostility by advising that we would soon return with citations in-hand. Yet the driver held his ground and merely smiled and acknowledged the appropriateness of our actions.

Partner and I returned to our patrol vehicle to strategize our next moves. I bit into my lower lip and began to write one red-light ticket. Kent did not say a word, but released a tense breath from his position. Completed ticket in hand, we soon sprung from the car in unison for the return approach to the violator vehicle.

I was confident that the driver's demeanor would turn instantly abusive as I handed him the citation book. I knew that in a moment he would decry Kent and myself as being reminiscent of klans-men, and crucifying the victim black man. Yet, the driver simply signed the ticket and smiled, and my heart began to sink. I was encouraged, however, when he asked if he could ask but one question. I allowed the man to inquire, certain that a venom-laced tirade would follow. The man then asked, "Well, I ran two red lights... shouldn't you write me *two* tickets? I deserve it."

At that point I heard in the back of my mind, the classic song, "You're a mean one...Mr. Grinch." The guilt became overwhelming. As I handed the man his citation, the conversation continued momentarily. The driver thanked us for our time, and apologized for the inconvenience. He offered that he was a United States soldier, just reassigned from Maryland to Seattle. He and family had just driven nearly non-stop across the country, and he was clearly very tired. His shiny green uniform lay neatly pressed in the rear of the station wagon. He thanked us for our service to the community, and Kent I returned to our patrol car.

I looked at Kent, and my partner looked at me. "I can't do this, Kent," I volunteered. Kent smiled and immediately answered, "I sure can't either." Always on the same ethical wavelength with my beloved partner, we both instantly sprang from the patrol car and approached the driver's car.

"Sir, may I please have that citation back?" I asked. The driver politely returned the green document and acknowledged that I should write the second ticket.

I responded, "Please, no more!" I took the citation and tore such into a dozen pieces. The driver and his attractive wife seemed incredulous at our actions. We visited for a few minutes with that true gentleman and his true lady wife, and greeted his darling young sons.

We wished the man nothing but success in his assignment to Seattle and commented that we were lucky to have such a mannered, responsible family in our town.

To this day, Kent and I are thankful for that decision. We could have never lived with ourselves otherwise.

***

Other violators may win the game, simply by superior reasoning. Case in point a Mercedes taking an illegal left turn. It was not far from Seattle Center and the Space Needle environs where the black Mercedes made such a turn, where the multiple signs had stated, "Left turns for transit only." (This is intended to convey metro bus transit only).

The gentleman visiting from Germany could not fathom my explanation for the stop. He stated with a heavy accent, "Yah, I saw da signs. But, sir I VAS en transit." In the translation, the man had a point. Away he went on his merry journey, without a charitable donation to his host city.

***

Some drivers simply talk themselves into greater legal turmoil. Case in point, a seriously inebriated motorcyclist stopped for weaving badly in and out of traffic. He was clad in all black leather, with his customary red bandana, tattoos and ponytail. It was clear the man had just come from a weekly meeting at a local biker bar. Errantly, I asked the man if his motorcycle were a Kawasaki or Honda.

The biker responded heavily slurred, "It's a damned Harley, man....I wouldn't drive no f---ing Jap bike for nothin' in the world....in fact, I hate everything that is Jap...Jap bikes, Jap TV's, Jap Cars....I especially hate Jap people...we shoulda nuked another million of em...fact, I'd drive right over any of those squinty-eyed bastards if I saw em tomorrow." Ever the dutiful scribe of a story, I took copious notes of the suspect's drunken diatribe for future reference in court.

Court did indeed follow, some 3 months later. The defendant appeared replete in a stylish three-piece suit, and his ponytail had been replaced by a short-cropped look. He sat next to a very expensive DUI attorney, angelic and confident. His attorney bragged of the prospects of a courtroom victory.

However, the confidence and joviality of the tandem of defendant and attorney seemed to change almost instantly. A new judge entered to replace the other presiding authority at the bar. None other than Judge Ron Mamiya, a highly regarded

Japanese judge, sat down to review the reports. The tandem set a world-record for changing a plea to guilty. Sometimes, it just isn't your day.

***

The attitudes of some drivers remain a permanent source of bewilderment. Clearly, we do not always encounter human beings at their very finest moments on those roadways.

Kent and I were patrolling the historic Pioneer Square district of downtown Seattle on a cloudy summer day in the mid 1980's. Kent was driving, as we were rolling on a northbound street at the posted speed limit of 30 MPH. A bright red sports car suddenly approached from out of nowhere, at a profoundly high rate of speed. The speeding vehicle passed our rolling vehicle as if we were standing still. The vehicle continued at a high rate of speed as we began to pursue. The vehicle passed through a stale red light as we engaged our emergency equipment for the stop.

The young white male driver, a clearly pleasant individual, rolled down his window. The driver greeted approaching Kent with a smoking cigarette tossed at his feet. He offered the customary greeting of, "What the f−k do you want?" The ever non-plused Kent responded with the customary acknowledgment, "I want to write you some tickets."

Before the driver could even complete the customary sentence, "You can't...." Kent had begun to display to him that, oh, yes, he can. Copious amounts of ink were injected upon the traffic documents. The driver was rewarded with a Reckless driving ticket in the amount that would total two weeks' pay for the average citizen.

The driver managed to sign the citation without incident and bid farewell to ourselves with the traditional verbiage of

"F—k," and "You." We were hopeful that he had seen the error of his ways. But, alas, that was not to be.

The driver proceeded to push his gas pedal to the floor, causing his rear wheels to spin and billow smoke. The vehicle slalomed sideways in rapid acceleration before moving down the street. We thus were given the opportunity to again greet the young man, and again write him another reckless driving ticket. The process was quite convenient, indeed, as we did not need to even ask for his paperwork. We could copy off of the previous citation.

Utterly convinced that no one would be fool enough to seek another ticket, we were proven to be wrong in our assumptions. The young lad was able to yet again spin the vehicle out, and sent gravel and oil flying upon our patrol car hood.

Kent was thus happy to hand the third reckless driving citation to the driver and invite him to occupy a jail cell for any further attempts at bravado. Either the driver was a very wealthy lad, or he saw the error of his ways in eventually forwarding six weeks' pay to the city's treasury. We never saw him in court.

***

Your author will never forget the most vile of all offenders ever personally witnessed. The date in question was quite significant. One day prior, Officer Dale Eggers was murdered, while working a uniformed off-duty assignment within a local bank. A bank robber would complete the robbery and then, for reasons unknown, return within the bank and empty a shotgun into the head of the unaware officer. It was thus with heavy heart that all officers took to the streets to patrol the city the following day. Yet, the job needed to be done. A forty year-old female was stopped for an expired license plate on that date. The intent of the stop was to simply remind the driver to obtain her current license tabs at her earliest convenience. The driver, however, made such a benevolent act impossible. The woman offered that she was enormously pleased about the brutal murder of my fellow officer. She further advised that it was her earnest hope that your author would suffer a very similar fate in the near future.

I was somewhat pleased to return to the woman with her requested citation and watched her scream in primal rage while signing the citation.

My return to the station to relate the occurrence to other officers only reinforced a very low view of humankind by myself on those two days of my life.

***

I would be remiss not to mention my personal best at a paced speeder. I was working a Detective Sergeant assignment in the late 1990's in the Gang Unit. I was responding to a call-out of a serious, but non-emergent nature at three o'clock A.M. on a Sunday morning. I was in an unmarked Gang Unit pursuit vehicle. I was passed by another vehicle while on Interstate 5 Southbound, approximately a mile north of what is known as the "Ship Canal Bridge," nearing downtown Seattle. The BMW product passed me at such a speed as to shake my vehicle. I attempted to gain on the vehicle and obtain a solid pace. I was able to pace the BMW at 133 miles per hour plus. I was not sure that my amped- up Chevy Caprice could keep pace. It took a couple more miles to near the vehicle and seek to make a traffic stop. I was surprised to find that the driver immediately responded to my flashing grill lights and spotlight and pulled to the side of the road. As I approached the vehicle in my Gang

Unit jacket, he rolled down his window. A twenty-something year-old well- dressed male tossed a burning cigarette at my feet. I could see that an attractive young woman was his passenger. The young man said, "What the f---k do you want?"

My immediate response was, "To take you to jail."

The young man maintained his recalcitrant attitude and offered, "You can't do that." (I would offer to my readers that such a comment is very nearly the *last* thing to ever utter to a cop.)

The driver seemed to realize the error of his ways as he was abruptly dragged from his car and cuffed. He nearly left his feet while being escorted back to my car. Once away from the young lady whom he obviously had sought to impress, the young man literally cried for his mommy. I offered that his mommy could bail him out of jail. He was booked for reckless driving. I knew that, had he struck another car, only a charcoal etching of the vehicles would have been located upon the roadway.

***

Traffic stops as a highly dangerous venture

Drivers should be aware of all the dynamics of a traffic stop. While it is obvious that the violators experience a profound level of anxiety on the stop, that is only half of the equation. Most members of the public are unaware of the fact that the approaching officer(s) are undoubtedly experiencing exponentially greater anxiety. The drivers are considering the ramifications of the encounter in terms of fines and increased insurance costs. The approaching officer(s) are concerned for their lives. We are trained from day one of the academy of the following safety concerns:

That individuals have, in fact, emerged from vehicle

trunks to shoot officers; that motorcycle gangs have built shotguns into the handlebars of the motorcycles and used such to shoot officers; that passengers have leapt from vehicles to surround and murder troopers; that drivers often shoot officers through their rolled down windows; and finally, that drivers have shot officers and troopers through the driver's door of the vehicle.

It is thus that all law enforcement officers are instructed to approach violator vehicles with some basic safety precautions. These precautions often don't entail initial pleasantries. Officers must first place the patrol vehicle at a diagonal angle to the offender vehicle. This is so as to provide an engine block as a barrier to gunfire. The vehicle also serves as a barrier to passing cars that have so often bring death to law enforcement. Officers are further expected to instinctively test any trunk lid upon their approach. Above all, they are instructed to stand well short of the driver's window upon engaging the driver. This is intended to keep the officer's face, eyes, and hair out of reach of the driver. This is also intended to limit the ability of the driver to pull a weapon and shoot directly out of the window or through the door. A former SPD motorcycle officer is forever paralyzed after neglecting that final proviso.

Thus equipped with such training, your author once approached a red light violator in the Central District of Seattle. Immediately upon approaching the vehicle, I stood well short of the driver's window. I heard a muffled pop like that of a small firecracker. I did not immediately recognize the source of the noise. I quickly recognized the driver as a member of a notorious crime family in the area. He slumped over in his seat, and I could see blood pouring from his stomach. I drew my .357 revolver as I noted the handgun in his right hand. Yet, the driver tossed the weapon to the passenger side floor of his vehicle.

The driver looked upward to me and pleaded, "Help me man, I'm bleedin' to death." My fury arose instantly. The driver had tried to shoot me! Yet, because of my proper positioning behind his window, he had been forced to turn too far around. He had shot himself in the left side of his abdomen during the rapid draw and shoot motion. I had not even seen his very quick motion. He was bleeding profusely.

For a few seconds, I looked at the driver and smiled. It seemed longer than seconds as I actually pondered letting the man bleed to death. As he continued to beg, I called for backup units, and summoned an aid car.

Unfortunately, the man recovered nicely under the care of Dr. Copass' amazing staff at Harborview Medical Center E. R. He was later charged only with being a felon in possession of a firearm, and served a paltry ten-day sentence. Prosecutors opined that I could not prove his intent to shoot me. My furious response was, "Do you think his intent was to shoot himself in the gut to get out of a red light ticket?!"

The criminal would find himself in prison for a very long time a few months afterward. It would seem he had pistol-whipped a McDonald's employee nearly to death during a robbery. I couldn't help but think of other earlier legal options that might have averted the terrible events for the McDonald's manager.

***

Cop Culture: Conservatism run rampant

A prolific public stereotype of law enforcement officers often seems to be that all cops think alike. This perception most assuredly begins with the "uniform" appearance of the officers. Indeed, they *look* alike at first glance. But I would invite the public to take a closer look down the line of blue, black, green, or khaki uniforms. No two human beings truly look alike. The opinions and beliefs of police officers may be as diverse as their physical appearances. That said, there are certain core values that have profound commonality with most police officers.

In the political sense, I would opine that nearly 88% of all police officers would label themselves conservative in views. That is to say, that the overwhelming majority believe in a legal justice system of strict interpretations of laws. They believe in swift and sure punishment and holding criminals accountable. They know that many criminals are only stopped from heinous acts upon innocent victims by two factors: Death or imprisonment. And they see, on a daily basis, that tax dollars are wasted in tremendous amounts. Thus, they feel that the average American citizen is grossly *over*-taxed.

As far as political party preference, I would estimate that 85% of all cops are Republicans. I know that a change occurred within myself very quickly when I entered law enforcement. I had never believed in the death penalty. That changed very quickly when I saw my first homicide scene. It was extraordinary to behold what one alleged human being had done to another. Interviewing murderous convicts within prison walls, and hearing them brag and giggle about their offenses, also affected perspectives.

I recall exactly the moment when I became a Republican by preference. A huge gathering formed outside the Pike Place Market in order to listen to presidential candidate Walter Mondale speak. Innumerable members of the crowd cursed at and spat at officers who were providing security and traffic control at the event. Massive groups ignored orders to wait to cross a street. Instead, they uttered, "F--k you, pig," and crossed the streets in the middle of traffic.

A warm-up speaker at the rally uttered profanities from

the stage and berated Mr. Mondale's opponent, Ronald Reagan. Her final remark was, "All I can say is Damn Reagan." The crowd erupted in support. Candidate Mondale's presentation was quite similar. He spent 35 minutes criticizing his opponent and giving no ideas about himself.

At the conclusion of the event we counted three totally trashed patrol vehicles. The crowds had stood atop the patrol car roofs in vast numbers, and thus collapsed the bodies of the cars. The crowd was so huge, police were rendered helpless. As the crowd separated to leave the event, great celebration of the trashed police cars resulted. There were mass amounts of garbage strewn everywhere.

The following day, candidate Reagan and supporters arrived at the same venue. The crowds were extremely respectful of the officers. They minded every instruction to the letter. They thanked the officers for providing security and traffic control. They apologized for the trashing of patrol cars the previous day and offered to raise funds to reimburse the police department for the losses. Numerous leaders within the gathering were appalled at the garbage strewn by the previous throngs. They quickly obtained large trash bags at a local store and cleaned up the mess.

Your author, and many of my peers quickly acknowledged that we felt a huge kinship with the folks from the right.

Such a scenario would repeat many many times over the years. While this may be a simplification of ideologies, it remains our reality to a vast extent.

***

Chapter 7: Ya can't make some of this stuff up, folks

The crazy lady by the zoo

One dark and lonely summer's morning, at half past midnight a radio call was routed my way, disturbing any chance for meaningful sleep. I was working a third watch 7 PM to 3 AM shift in the north end of the city. My district ranged from the eternally busy and dirty state highway to the east, to the fringes of beautiful Greenlake to the North. A very established middle class Ballard neighborhood abutted the district to the west and south. It was a warm summer evening turned morning and a half-moon aptly illuminated the parking lot, which I inhabited. "Three Boy Three," came the female dispatch voice. I responded bored.

"Boy Three, I have a woman calling to advise that her backyard cherry tree is full of orangutans and that their screaming is keeping her awake."

Radio would further advise that dispatch had checked the woman's name in the notorious "220 file" (lists of well-known insane callers) and that we had never heard of her. Radio asked if I desired a backup unit in response to her calls. Your author could not resist responding, "Only if Marlon Perkins (TV animal adventure icon of the era) is available."

With that information, your author drove nonchalantly to the nearby residence. Your author expected the caller to come to the door in nothing but a hospital robe. I looked for a straightjacket on the coat rack, but nothing seemed out of order. Her hair was neatly quaffed and was not standing on end in errant patterns, as preconceived notions would lead one to believe. She even spoke in complete and clear sentences. Strange screaming and screeching sounds caused a near deafening din within the lovely split level home. I was sure the woman's teenagers were watching movies at a ridiculous volume.

Perplexed at the woman not readily displaying her obvious lunacy, I accepted her invitation to vacate my front doorway position. I followed her, entering the deep reaches of her home. The screeches increased in volume, as I was guided toward the rear kitchen. A sliding door led to a large cedar upstairs deck. The porch light was turned off, and I sought to turn the light on.

"Oh no!" loudly chided the complainant..."You'll make them mad when you turn on the light... they'll beat against the windows and throw things around."

(Uh-huhhhh, I thought, now we're making progress... I will soon locate this woman's Prozac and will be on my merry way.) As I sought to slide open the door, the woman whispered, "Careful, they will throw things at you... you won't shoot them will you?... I love animals."

I assured the woman that I would be plenty safe, and there would be no need to shoot the poor little monkeys. "I think they're orangutans, if I'm not mistaken," she again whispered. I whispered in return, "Ohhhh, OK, orangutans." I resisted the urge to wink at her.

Unable to handle any more of the farce, I opened the sliding door and flippantly cast my flashlight above to the huge overhanging cherry tree.

I believe my jaw hit the floor of the decking. Not more than six feet above in the tree were several *orangutans*! And they were throwing leaves and branches downward at me, and spitting! They made quite a wail, as well.

I instantly turned off my flashlight and re-entered the woman's kitchen. "Ma'am, there are a bunch of monkeys in your tree!" I almost gasped. The woman immediately countered, "No, I believe those are orangutans."

Your exasperated author communicated with dispatch to contact curators of the nearby Woodland Park Zoo, using dispatch's vast list of emergency phone numbers. Radio advised that they were successful in reaching a zoo official who lived nearby. They would check the primate exhibit for missing animals. I thought to myself, "Well who else could be missing these baboons, or whatever they are!"

Radio soon advised that the zoo had determined that inmates had escaped their facility. They would soon be arriving, equipped to capture the hardened prisoners. True to their word, an entire team of zoo employees and volunteers soon arrived. They were highly apologetic for inconveniencing the police department and immediately commenced upon counting the inmates. All of the creatures were referred to by humorous names such as "Mutumbo," and were found to be present in the tree. The escapees almost looked resigned to their fates as they looked downward at the keepers.

Soon the keepers had stretched vast netting beneath the tree and the heavy artillery was brought forward. Quiet little dart rifles emitted slight hissing sounds as the keepers tranquilized each of the cherry tree pillagers. The orangutans fell softly, one by one, into the nets. They were gently carried to nearby cages. I was privileged to assist in carrying one such primate toward a waiting truck. He or she was heavy!

The zoo officials again expressed their apologies for the inconvenience. Apparently seeking to compensate me in some way, they offered that I follow them into the darkened zoo to release the primates. I was thus honored to join them within the dark and huge zoo grounds to experience a nocturnal exhibit few could experience. The acres of animals were much more active and vocal by night, and it was eerie to guess what animals lay behind the gleaming eyes in the darkness.

The groggy primates soon recovered their wits, and were disappointed to find that they were back in their asylum. They seemed highly disappointed to find that no further feasts of cherry tree leaves would occur. I thought to myself, as I returned to my patrol car, "Someday I've gotta write a book about this job."

***

Life choices, according to the Bible.

The Lord said, "If your hand causes you to offend, cut it off. It is better for you to enter into life maimed, than having two hands to go into hell, into the fire that never shall be quenched." And, He said, "If your eye causes you to offend, pluck it out. It is better for you to enter into the kingdom of God with one eye, than having two eyes to be cast into hell fire." (Mark 9).

The above is a Bible passage with which I had little familiarity at one time. That would change on a summer afternoon in 1984. Numerous officers were dispatched to the area of the 300 block of West Ewing Street. The dispatch information indicated that an employee of an investment firm was acting in a bizarre manner. He was said to be incessantly reciting bible passages and speaking of his imminent death. He had walked out of the building, warning concerned peers to not follow him or he would kill himself. He therefore was allowed to walk out of the building.

Numerous patrol units began to arrive in the area. The business was part of a vast complex of glass-encased ten-story buildings looking over the scenic Lake Washington Ship Canal. Numerous small boats, fishing vessels, kayakers, et al were traversing the canal. The watercraft looked like water skippers upon a pond. It was a perfect summer day. Radio updates from the first arriving officer indicated that employees believed the individual had walked across a grassy field westbound. They felt he was headed toward the concrete bulkheads that abutted a ten-foot drop to the canal water. Officers exited vehicles and began to walk the embankment, looking for a possible man in the water.

Several officers ultimately came together from different approach directions. We converged upon a grassy hillside at the shore, obscured by a huge weeping willow tree.

All officers heard an individual loudly reciting the above bible passage. We saw the individual in question standing beneath the tree. His back was turned toward us, and he was facing the canal. A nearby squad-mate called out, "What the f−k?" He pointed downward toward the water. A bloody hand was bobbing in the water and slowly sinking.

All of the officers rapidly approached the individual with guns drawn. The squeaking sounds of gun belts and jingling of key sets on hips attracted the man's attention. He quickly spun around and faced the approaching officers. The officers froze immediately. The man stood staring at the silent group of police officers. He held a hacksaw in his left hand. His right hand was gone at the wrist, and blood was coursing from the amputation. He screamed the bible passage more loudly, almost angrily. The man was missing his right eye. A large and jagged hole remained, bleeding only slightly. The eye was seen lying on the ground, next to his right foot. A bloody string of optical connections remained with the eye. A bloody screwdriver lay next to the carnage.

The individual then dropped the saw and began to move robotically toward the canal wall. He was quickly tackled and pinned upon his stomach. All officers were showered in blood as they held the amazingly strong individual upon the ground while an ambulance with restraints and a paramedic unit was summoned. There was no way to handcuff him. He continued to call out bible passages, and referred to the officers repeatedly as "Satan." A medic unit arrived nearly immediately. Paramedics, usually known to avoid physical confrontation at all costs, eagerly dove into the pile of humanity. Officers held the individual's severed wrist while a tourniquet was applied.

Ultimately, the 28 year-old business partner was transported to Harborview Medical Center for medical and psychological treatment. Peers within the business were interviewed. They related that the individual was an up and coming investment broker who was widely respected within the firm. He was expected to make partner within the year. Yet, they added, his behavior had altered greatly following a recent bitter divorce. But they had no idea as to the extent of his mental illness.

***

The noisy bachelorettes

One particular summer Friday night, your author was dispatched to a nearby North-end residence in response to a loud party complaint. It was one of dozens of calls in the sector for the same circumstances, and typical for summertime.

Upon arrival, I could hear the music thumping rhythmically from inside the house. I could hear loud and jovial voices emanating from within the tasteful classic home. I rang the doorbell repeatedly, but no response was to occur. Clearly, the music was too loud for the doorbell to be heard. As every cop would then opt to do, I withdrew my three-foot heavy flashlight from my belt and banged upon the door.

Eventually, a highly intoxicated and attractive blond woman of approximately 28 years of age answered the door. The noise instantly wafted outward oppressively. The woman held a martini glass in one hand, and her drink sloshed errantly upon the hardwood floor. "Is there a problem ofthicer (sic)?" she slurred and giggled. I could see that the living room and kitchen area of the house seemed to contain nothing but many women of varying ages. Most of the women continued to gulp their beverages, and even increased the volume of the music. I eventually determined that the intoxicated greeter at the door was the owner of the home.

At an ample volume to be heard, I advised the woman that she needed to turn the music way down immediately. She responded by extending her hands outward to me, dancing with the music, and yelling, "Yeah, officer, I'm a baaaad girl, arrest me!"

Becoming mildly annoyed at the apparent lack of responsiveness, I sternly increased my volume, then yelling, "Turn the music down NOW!" At that, the woman was joined by several other women, dancing and spilling more drinks. They began to dance in front of me, hips gyrating suggestively, and tugging at my gun-belt. I slapped a hand away from the tugs at my gun (nobody touches the firearm). One woman tugged the flashlight from my belt and illuminated her fellow party-ers. My anger grew immensely, and I thought I would grab the stereo and unplug the nuisance.

At that point, a woman grabbed my police radio from the belt holder and feigned speaking into such, "I'm the chief. Arrest 'em all." The women began to grab at me in highly inappropriate ways, at which time the police radio suddenly squawked. I grabbed the hand of the female holding the radio to return my equipment. The women suddenly grew silent, and the music suddenly stopped. They stared at the radio as a dispatcher's voice boomed from the device.

The homeowner then spoke, "Is that thing *real*?"

"Of course it is," I responded, irritated. As if in unison, over a dozen women gasped a loud, "Oh my Gawd!" The homeowner seemed to set a world record for instant sobriety, as her face turned a profoundly crimson color. She covered her face with her hands.

Clueless, I asked the woman why she and friends were behaving so obnoxiously. She responded, "OK, I just wanna make sure. You're not the stripper, right?"

I responded, "Stripper?"

"Yeah, he was supposed to come her dressed as a policeman... Oh my gawwwwwd... hey, he never showed up."

The humor of the entire situation finally reached my dense reaches of brain matter. It took a couple of minutes to convince the homeowner that she was not losing her house, her freedom, or her spotless reputation.

Your author then could not resist asking, "How much were you to pay him?"

The women jointly answered, "Two hundred bucks." I was astonished at the going rate for a male stripper in the mid 1980's.

The homeowner then quickly quipped, "Hey, when do you get off-duty?" I then conveyed to the woman that, while my mother thinks she gave birth to a beauty, Robert Redford had not recently called me to work as his stand-in. I was even more convinced as to the woman's level of insobriety.

At the end of the shift, while back in the station, I relayed the story to my veteran Sergeant Bill Greene. The gravelly-voiced beloved Sarge immediately offered, "Kid, ya shoulda taken a halfer. A new career coulda been launched tonight."

***

The proud papa breaks the sound barrier.

Circa the summer of 1984, your author was a seasoned "veteran" of two whole years of police-work with SPD. I was on regular patrol in the southeastern corridor of the city, known as Holly Park. My district was 2-Sam-33. The district entailed an interesting mix of government housing, areas of prostitution, and drug dealing. Yet, the people in the "projects" would become my favorite demographic group I would ever work around. For the vast majority of the residents in the area, they were simply the salt of the earth. They appreciated tough, but fair officers in the area, and wanted the thugs to gain no ground therein.

I was patrolling along the very southern border of the city of Seattle, in the very heart of rush hour. At the five o'clock hour, tens of thousands of Boeing workers were escaping their daily duties and flooding the insufficient surface streets toward residential areas. Traffic was literally at an angry standstill. Suddenly a white male in a Jeep Cherokee approached my patrol car from the rear. The Jeep was up and over a curb, straddling a sidewalk and planting strips. The driver appeared to be startled as he passed my clearly marked blue and white car on my right. His much deserved traffic stop would quickly follow.

Your author diplomatically asked the man at the window of his car if he suffered from some sort of insanity. The man perspired heavily, panted, and shook his head.

He offered, "No officer. I may *seem* crazy… hell, maybe I am… you see, I'm trying to get to the hospital. My wife is in life threatening labor for both she and the baby. They're at Northwest Hospital."

Your author immediately thought to oneself, "Uh huh. Surrrrre." One becomes rather cynical after hearing every lie and excuse imaginable. Yet, I quickly noticed all the baby apparel in the rear of the man's vehicle. He had a baby seat, balloons, diapers, and formula. He was clearly ready to take care of business.

However, Northwest Hospital was nearly 15 miles to the

exact *North* of our location. And traffic was absolutely snarled. Your author immediately recognized the earnest need to assist one of the fine citizens of our fair city, *and* have an excuse to drive like a bat out of hell. I quickly called to the man to abandon his vehicle on the sidewalk. I radioed my peers to ensure that his car would remain secure and untouched. I then gently called to the totally exasperated gentleman to fear not, get in, shut up, and hold on. I tossed my briefcase and paperwork, known as a "kit" toward the back seat and strapped the man in.

The gentleman was fascinated with the elaborate electronics in the vehicle, then resembling a cockpit of a 747, and the low-tech but effective shotgun beside his left knee.

Lights and siren set at full warp-speed, I began to navigate in a wild slalom through the surface street traffic. The passenger was screaming that he was surprised how loud a siren is within a patrol car. He was grinning from ear to ear.

Your author ultimately escaped the backups of traffic and gained freedom upon the on-ramp to the freeway, some 4 miles away. My high quality Goodyear Eagle tires screamed in either glee or pain as the vehicle alternately leaned left and then right while rounding the curving ramp at an unreasonable rate. The passenger was then pounding on the dashboard and calling out, "Whoo hoo, rock and roll!" Traffic was more manageable upon the freeway, and the real fun was to begin. I accelerated the patrol car to warp 9 as the force propelled the passenger back in his seat.

During the next ten miles the passenger commented that he had never traveled so rapidly in a vehicle. I looked at the odometer and commented, we were only going 100. The odometer indicated a need to speed up. I forgot to look after that point.

I escaped the freeway and again had to fight through dreadful traffic in the north end of the city. Ultimately, the vehicle spun aggressively into the parking lot of Northwest Hospital and came to a rest at the Emergency Room entrance. Smoke billowed from the brakes and the engine idled wildly. The passenger released his seatbelt and extended his hand toward me, gearing up to thank me. I simply told him, "Go, go, go!" Off to the races he sprinted, into the hospital and out of sight. Medical staff had been contacted by radio and advised to be standing by. The man was in very good hands.

Your author sought to take in a couple deep breaths, calm down, and return to the far end of the city. Later in the shift I returned back up to the northern hospital. I wanted to hear how the family had fared.

A beaming father came downstairs in the elevator to greet me. I received a large hug and a hundred thank-yous. He had treasured the moment of the arrival of his new son. Both the child and the mother were in good health. The gentleman announced to family and friends circled around he and I, "That was the biggest thrill of my life!" I agreed that nothing could surpass the experience of the birth of one's child. But the papa countered, "Oh that was fabulous too, but man, that ride... Awesome!" Laughter erupted in the small gathering enjoying the glee of the young father. He again shook my hand demonstratively and thanked me another dozen times. He even offered that he and his bride wished to name their first born after me. But all he had referred to me by was "officer." He forgot to ask the first name.

It is my profound hope today that there is not a young 30-year-old man walking around with the first name of "Officer."

***

Larry's Leprechaun Luck

It was a blustery March 17th daytime in 1991 when your author was patrolling the Lake City Corridor area of Seattle, designated as "Nora-6." The district was dominated by a state highway, slowed by innumerable traffic lights and congestion. State Route 522, better known as Lake City Way ran north-south above tremendously scenic Lake Washington, obscured by trees and buildings a few miles eastward. The area was dotted with car sales lots, ranging from huge and corporate, to tiny lots offering bargain sales to Latino customers. Errant streetwalkers, whom had been banned from higher volume areas of prostitution by the courts, would dot the corridor. Two strip clubs on the south and north borders of the district made the ambience complete.

A radio broadcast emanated at around 1300 hours (1 P.M.) of a massive explosion in the area. Your author was located only about twelve blocks to the north of the purported blast sight, and immediately reversed travel from northbound to southbound. Immediate recognition occurred, as one could see in the distance mass clouds of smoke and apparent heat rising. The smoke and heat looked to be battling forces, tumbling in and out of the other cyclonically, rising rapidly. It appeared that the radio description of the occurrence was accurate.

Multiple police and fire department units arrived in the area within 3 minutes. The location of the occurrence was a tiny car sales lot on the west side of Lake City Way. All the police officers were very familiar with the owner-victim at the blast site.

The owner was a well-known colorful used car salesman. He was nicknamed "Scary Larry." Larry was a large-framed man with a grayish crew cut. He was about sixty years of age and claimed he had lived his life previously as a merchant marine. Larry worked from sun-up to sun-down at the lot, purchasing repossessed vehicles, and rental cars taken out of fleet service. He was known to have a shrewd eye for a bargain. He had a knack for finding quality vehicles for little or no cost and making ample profit in the re-sale thereof. He was a very hard-working man, and literally lived at work. His "home" was a 35-foot single wide mobile home that he had placed unobtrusively in the northwest corner of his tiny car lot. Scary Larry was also known to imbibe freely in adult beverages before, during, and after his working day. His favorite beverage was known to be McNaughton's Irish whiskey, which he was willing to share with any friend or acquaintance.

On the date in question, business was very slow. Larry had received nary a visitor since seven o'clock A.M. He thus thought it prudent to place a closed sign on his office window and retreat to his residence. He also sought to ponder life's meaning and relax with copious amounts of his beloved McNaughton's whiskey. He turned the stove's gas to the on setting and looked for matches to light his burner in order to cook dinner. But a prospective customer drove into the lot and ignored the closed sign nearby. An interested party was walking about the lot, admiring Larry's newest treasures within.

Always happy to make a sale, Larry emerged immediately from his home, clad only in his long dirty robe and sought to charm the buyer. Apparently unimpressed with Larry's presentation, the buyer soon drove away with cash still in his pockets, much to Larry's disappointment. Larry sought to diminish his disappointment by imbibing from yet another bottle of McNaughton's whiskey he had secreted strategically in his office desk drawer. His mood immediately improved, and he eventually staggered back to his mobile home.

Larry happily entered his home and sat upon an old metal chair in front of his television and set upon lighting the Marlboro cigarette dangling from the corner of his mouth. The lighter flame immediately joined inhospitably with the mass of inert gases. An enormous fireball instantly annihilated the mobile home, and a maelstrom of gases and smoke arose.

As emergency units converged upon the site, nothing whatsoever remained of the mobile home — with the exception of Scary Larry. Larry still sat upright in his old metal chair. Half a cigarette still hung from his mouth. He was totally naked. His crew cut appeared to be singed, and his ample potbelly hung unsupported. He was conscious and alert, blinking repeatedly, and staring at his on-coming attention.

"Larry, you alive?" your author brilliantly asked.

Larry smirked and giggled slightly. "I guess I *am!*" Larry shrugged.

Fire crews immediately descended upon Larry, as he sat still naked in the chair. They began to check his eyes, take his blood pressure, and measure his pulse. As another officer brought a blanket to cover Larry, I listened as he answered questions for the medics. I watched the incredulous reactions by the medics, as all of Larry's vitals checked out perfectly. Blood pressure was perfect, respiration as well. No constriction of pupils. No scratches on his less- than sculpted body could be found. Larry's pulse rate was a bit high, but quite understandable under the circumstances.

Incredibly, as fire fighters hypothesized, it would appear that the blast removed Larry's robe in a colossal upward and outward motion. The tremendous force of the blast had driven the walls of the home outward and all contents within upward. The roof had been propelled upward and northbound in two large pieces and crashed into a vacant lot some fifty yards away.

The only injury that Larry could be found to have suffered may have been a ruptured left eardrum. He said his ears were ringing loudly.

The date being March 17th, I could not resist but to ask Larry, "Larry, are you an Irishman by chance?"

Larry responded, "Well, hell yeah, three quarters... why?"

Your author followed, "Well you've had a helluva Saint Patty's Day."

Larry could not contain his laughter. "Well, ya know, I do believe the good saint bestowed all his luck upon me on this Saint Patty's Day. And I may have out-bargained the devil yet again. I think I'll drink to that!"

All the emergency responders who were gathered around Larry answered in unsolicited unison, "You've had *enough* to drink Larry!"

***

The most revolting shooting (It's not what you think!)

A boring and gloomy February day in 1982 was suddenly disturbed by three shrill "alert tones" coming across the police radio. Moments later, the Chief Dispatcher reported a shooting. The shots were said to have been fired within a notorious Central Seattle criminal hangout. The hangout was known as the Fox and Hounds Tavern, located in the 2000 block of Madison, in the denizen of drug dealing and prostitution. Fire department trucks and aid cars, as usual, arrived before racing police vehicles. Your author, then a 21 year-old rookie, very fresh off of the field training program, arrived second at the scene. I was relieved to note that Officer David Peppard had already arrived, and was waiting for his backup units. Dave was a seasoned veteran of the East Precinct, known as the roughest precinct in the city, for the quasi-ghetto environs and resultant crimes. Ironically, Officer Peppard had been the second of two training officers for me, and I was very familiar with his tremendous patrol skills and toughness.

Several other officers were arriving as Peppard and I drew firearms and crept into the bar. The interior resembled a movie set from 1930's gangland settings. The smallish dive of a bar was filled with cigarette and cigar smoke. A jukebox played rhythm and blues music at a piercing volume. Prostitutes sat at the bar, cigarettes burning, accompanied by the cigar- smoking pimps. They all sat on stools, sipping at drinks, as if nothing had happened. One enormously obese retired prostitute was propped atop two stools at the bar and ignored us. A mustachioed middle aged black male bartender, clad in white apron, was running a wet rag across a slimy bar counter. Middle-aged ex- cons blended into the corners of the room, leaning back on chairs and watching basketball on small televisions.

Officer Peppard un-plugged the juke box and held his .357 magnum revolver toward the ceiling. The noisy room suddenly went silent. Several more officers poured into the bar, followed by nervous paramedics. The police and paramedics scanned the room for a body, or for pools of blood. But nothing seemed amiss. Peppard told all patrons of the bar to "Shut up!" He then motioned to the bartender to approach. He asked the bartender where the shooting had occurred. The bartender responded, "I dunno."

Peppard immediately spoke into his portable radio and inquired as to the previously frantic source of the 9-1-1 call. The dispatcher indicated that the bartender had placed the call.

Peppard, sided by my six –foot six self, then leaned angrily toward the bartender and said, "I won't ask you again, what happened?"

The bartender then stated that an argument had occurred within the bar between several patrons. He advised that a known felon had pulled a .38 caliber revolver from his waist band and fired one shot toward the patrons at the bar. Peppard and I thus sought to find the location of a bullet hole to confirm the story. We parted the intoxicated and drugged patrons of the bar while checking the floor, ceiling, and walls of the bar counter. Nothing could be found. The bartender shrugged his shoulders and said, "I swear to God, man, dude leveled that gun and shot right at em... I dunno where the bullet went."

At just that moment, the enormously obese woman began to scream profanities at a tremendous volume. She jumped from her over-stressed stools and began to jump around, as if in a frenetic dance. We were initially baffled as to the source of her anxiety. She then began to scream, "Hep me, hep me, I'm dyin'!" We still could not identify the source of her anxiety. Peppard asked her, "What the hell is wrong?"

The woman screamed her reply, "Looka here, looka here." She pointed toward her enormous back-side. Reluctantly, the standing officers and paramedics dropped their glances to the region in question. Still, nothing could be seen, other than a short, red sequined dress stretched beyond normal endurance. The woman then pulled up her dress and pulled down her enormous girdle. The girdle fell complete with a highly utilized maxi-Maxi pad! Aghast, the stunned emergency personnel witnessed enormous rolls upon rolls of cellulite. Yet, barely able to penetrate the tremendous rolls of fat, was seen the end of a bullet.

Ever cordial police officers immediately made magnanimous gestures toward fire fighters and paramedics to approach the wounded woman. A pecking order within the firefighters was quickly established, and the youngest of the paramedics was selected for treatment of the injury. He retrieved a pair of tweezers and easily removed the .38 caliber slug from the woman's enormous assets. The paramedic placed the bullet in a plastic bag and handed such to Officer Peppard. The paramedic calmly remained knelt at the backside of the woman, while she kept her girdle down at her ankles and her dress pulled up above her waist. The woman shrieked, "Damn, damn, damn, that nigga done shot me in da ass!" She regained her poise and immediately directed her wrath toward the kneeling paramedic. She said, "Boy, you best stop staring at my ass and put a bandaid on....damn, can't you see I'm bleedin'!?" The paramedic sought to calm his shaking hands and placed a three inch, four cornered gauze bandage upon the woman's very slight wound.

Upon completion of the entire shooting investigation, the departing officers and paramedics marveled at the situation. It was opined that fat cells might well surpass the Kevlar in bullet proof vests in stopping bullets. A rather rotund policeman offered that he suddenly felt safer.

As the paramedics began to stroll away from the parking lot of the bar, older firefighters cautioned the young attending paramedic, "Yeah, boy, you stop lookin' at her ass." The paramedic shuddered demonstrably and mimicked vomiting motions.

**

Captain Laurence Farrar

Captain Larry Farrar was a legend in the department, and revered by officers of the North Precinct, whom he commanded for six years. He could be aptly described as Douglas MacArthur meets Santa Claus. Larry Farrar was a huge bear of a man. He maintained a very short-cropped hair cut that looked like that of soldier in boot camp. Indeed, Larry was a decorated soldier during the Vietnam war.

Captain Farrar brought an instant presence of leadership to any setting. His physical stature quickly drew attention to him as a powerful man, both physically and figuratively. He had piercing brown eyes and a chiseled jaw. This only added to the effect when he would scowl at young officers. Those young officers whom first met the Captain would find him to be a fearsome and imposing presence. He could easily resemble a bulldog on guard. In fact, Captain Farrar looked like a distant human relative to his beloved dog "Bismark," who was ever present at the precinct.

However, first impressions would rapidly change, when time was spent around Larry Farrar. All would quickly learn that the Captain's bark was much worse than his bite. His smile would soon emerge, much like the Grinch who stole Christmas, and the secret would escape. Larry Farrar was a warm and kind soul, who cared greatly for the safety and welfare of his officers.

Captain Farrar was a master tactician during any critical incident. He almost seemed to enjoy hostage and barricaded suspect scenarios. He knew what to do. The Captain would quickly establish a command post and set up logistics. A mini compound of mobile precincts, patrol cars, supply vans, et al would be assembled. The good Captain would puff on a pipe and review his situation report board with profound scrutiny. Every minute detail of an incident response would be crafted. Thoughtfully conceived plans would be carried out to perfection. Larry Farrar ensured that each and every one of his officers, SWAT officers, or detectives would be accounted for. The professionalism of incident command would nearly always convince suspects to surrender. And, on one known occasion when a bank robber sought to take the lives of cops, the suspect died alone in a trailer in a hail of gunfire.

Captain Farrar was responsible for most logistical planning for the 1989 Seattle Goodwill Games. The games were a privately sponsored version of the Olympic Games, produced by billionaire Ted Turner. The bulk of such events occurred at the campus of the University of Washington. Iconic Husky Stadium was to be used for Opening Ceremonies, involving fly-by's of Russian Mig 23 fighters in formation with U.S. F-16 Eagles. Rock groups were to perform as well. Track and field, volleyball, and basketball events, among others would be fielded on the campus.

Thus, Captain Farrar was responsible for coordinating security requiring hundreds of officers on extended shifts. Somehow, the Captain found a way to schedule copious amounts of extra overtime for a certain 29 year-old officer. My scheduling seemed to entail interesting assignments to famous athletes and interesting celebrities. This was during a time when your author was experiencing a sudden financial and emotional devastation of divorce.

(The same Captain had previously taken me off of a waiting list to work a day patrol shift. I was moved to the front of the list. Apparently, the Captain felt it was important for me to see my young daughters. It would seem, the Captain did not miss anything when it came to his troops. I heard many stories from peers about great considerations made for their professional and private benefit.)

The Goodwill Games event was a very tiring and difficult challenge for the patrol officers whom staffed such. Yet, the Captain made a point of caring for each and every one of them. Scores of officers staffed posts around and within Husky Stadium during an unusually hot August. Temperatures neared 100 degrees. Bulletproof vests increased that temperature by approximately another twenty degrees. Officers did not complain, but seemed to fear melting in their shoes. Yet, it was Captain Farrar whom circled the venues in a golf cart, the pipe in his clenched teeth. Behind the cart he pulled a rolling container of iced refreshments to be dispersed to all of his officers. He could be seen patting his officers on the back and loudly commenting, "Now remember, if you're not peeing, you're not drinking enough liquids."

The food for the event was provided by the department itself. The city had sought to save money in doing so. Thus, the patrol officers at the University venue were generously provided several year-old re-frozen airlines food, far beyond expiration dates. Most was barely edible. Officers did not complain, as they tore mold off of breads and tried to stomach frozen and micro-waved eggs.

The moment Captain Farrar noted the horrible quality of department-provided food, he ordered all such food to be re-gathered. We were perplexed as we observed the Captain and his assistants throwing the foods into nearby dumpsters. We thought we would go very hungry.

Yet, within a couple hours, a convoy of food catering service personnel began to arrive. Barbecues were set up, spectacular salad bars assembled, and chicken, burgers, and pork chops were sizzling on the grills. A grateful cadre of officers tipped their hats again to Larry Farrar. We were all exponentially more impressed when we later learned that Captain Farrar had used his personal credit card to pay the vendors. I have never heard whether or not he was ever reimbursed by the department. Regardless, his legend grew.

***

During the initial Persian Gulf War of Desert Storm vast protests were held in left-leaning Seattle. As with both Iraq conflicts, the war was highly controversial. The mayor's office ultimately directed the Chief's office to demand strict neutrality of Seattle police officers regarding the debate. We were to provide professional security at demonstrations and show no personal beliefs. To a vast extent, the professionalism was maintained by the SPD officers. Mass platoons of officers stood in the middle of 35,000 marchers. We stood calmly while a Catholic archbishop directed his followers to spit upon us. We saw vandalizing marauders stand in freeway traffic with middle fingers extended, until traffic slammed to a halt.

Captain Farrar was soon to learn that a young Seattle man was one of the first casualties of the war. A twenty year-old Army private had paid the ultimate sacrifice. Despite orders to the contrary, Captain Farrar quietly informed his staff that he would attend the funeral of the young soldier. Captain Farrar would wear his full Seattle Police dress blue uniform at the nearby event. Further, he would drive his police car in the procession. Captain Farrar would thus risk severe discipline from the department for disobeying orders.

Captain Farrar hinted to a couple of his patrol officers that he hoped someone could pay their respects along the funeral procession route. He made no demands, nor orders. He knew that he could not jeopardize our careers. He simply hoped for a couple of officers to be seen somewhere along the procession route.

I am quite sure that Captain Farrar was astonished by what he viewed, while driving in the soldier's procession route. Along the entire way, some three miles from 145th Street and Aurora Avenue North to Lake City Way, police cars could be seen at each major intersection. Each and every member of the North Precinct, both on and off duty, were on posts at the intersections. As the lengthy procession drove past, sets of officers stood in their finest uniforms and saluted the entire procession. I will never forget the sight of the fallen soldier's parents driving by, folded flags in their hands, looking gratefully at the flashing patrol car lights and saluting police officers. I shall further never forget the friends and family passing by in subsequent vehicles. Several members of the procession smiled, cried, and displayed grateful thumbs-up for our gestures. Yet, we will all most greatly treasure the sight of beloved Captain Farrar beaming with pride at the sight of his troops. We were there for the soldier and his family. But we were ultimately there for Captain Farrar. He was family to us.

***

Larry Farrar would act as a father, of sort, to the 150 or so officers of his command at the North Precinct. He chewed us out when we did something stupid. He patted us on our backs when we did something smart. Yet, he was always there for us for work, or personal issues. Were an officer's car to be in the shop, he would offer the Captain's car to be borrowed. He always insisted that his people worked *with* him....not *for* him. He was instrumental in recommending me for eventual promotion to Sergeant.

Captain Farrar's distinguished career ended with his final

assignment being a coveted job. He was assigned to command the Homicide Unit. The officers of the North Precinct were saddened to learn that their beloved Captain was moving downtown. But we were delighted to see his career end in style.

It was requested that the Captain address and inspect his troops one final time, on a warm spring mid-day. The officers stood at attention in several military ranks in the parking lot, in our finest uniforms. Captain Farrar paraded past each and every officer, many of whom from night and graveyard shifts. He stopped and shook the hand of each officer. Most embraced him in a hug. The Captain related very personal and gracious comments to each of his officers. He knew all of us. He knew our kids. He knew our loved ones.

We presented the Captain with several highly expensive going away gifts. I was very proud to present the Captain with a limited edition lithograph of a recent national champion Washington Husky football team. Legendary coach Don James autographed the plaque, addressed to Captain Farrar. While the Captain treasured the coach's autograph, the tears welled when he saw the reverse side of the large work of art. Hundreds of personal messages to Larry Farrar were on the back of the plaque—from his adoring officers.

***

Chapter 8: The people of the streets

Patrol assignments, in general, provide an extraordinary view into all aspects of human-kind. Literally thousands of lives are lived out within our purview. Walking a beat serves to provide even a closer insight into the microcosm that is a city's downtown streets. A foot-beat is the ultimate exercise in extroversion. A beat officer will come into close contact with hundreds of people on a given day. The uniform is a magnet to all segments of society. Billionaire business owners may stop to visit, and down and out junkies may surprise with latent insight. In a few days one could guard a president and then coincide with skid row winos. Regardless, in the end, they're all just people.

***

"Stumpy."

In "King Sector" lay historic Pioneer Square. One hundred thirty year-old buildings, with beautiful brick arches and courtyards provide settings for yuppies to eat fine dinners in the roped- off plazas of restaurants. They sip rare wines in a carefree manner and watch humanity pass by to local art shops, bars, and nearby stadiums. Street quartets of remarkable singers serenade passersby, in hopes of hauling in donations. Meanwhile, decrepit relics of humanity lay in alcohol- induced stupors only fifteen feet away from diners. The winos are fair game for criminal alcohol citations, while guzzling their fortified wines. A strange dichotomy lay in the fact that yuppies may sip wine legally within the roped area, while those of the streets were guilty of a crime by doing the same. The yuppies were untouchable inside the rope of opulence. The strange sort of caste system has prevailed for decades in the area.

***

"Stumpy" was just another worthless wino in the district, in the late 80's. He was one of many considered a blight upon the area by the business and political community. Stumpy was a man of about sixty years of age, as best one may guess. He had greasy long grey hair tightly bound in a ponytail. He stood around five feet nine inches tall, on the rare occasion when he could stand upright. He always wore a tattered army jacket, jeans, and conspicuously high quality hiking boots. Predominantly, Stumpy stood hunched over, and staggered to his respective alleys, behind dumpsters.

Stumpy was so nicknamed because he possessed only a stump of a right arm, hanging uselessly six inches below his shoulder. He was usually accompanied by a fifth of Wild Irish Rose wine and little else. Stumpy only rarely commiserated with other winos in the Pioneer Square plaza. He usually preferred to keep to himself and bother no one. He seemed most content to drink his wine and read from the latest paperback novel he had picked up for 25 cents at a nearby bookstore. He loved Louie L'Amour, above all. Stumpy only emerged from the alleys in order to panhandle for cash, when his meager social security stipend had been, literally, drained.

If one took the time to visit with Stumpy, he had a profound charm and wit about him. He was exceptionally knowledgeable about literature, and could recite poetry forever. He never forgot the author of a particular poem. He could extrapolate the deep meaning of each respective poet, and even describe the experience of the author which led to such writings. Stumpy was exceedingly well-versed in world politics, economics, and many world cultures. He always greeted your author and partners with a salute, and a "Good mornin' Cap'n." His greetings would always be followed with a raunchy joke, a hearty laugh, and a cough.

Stumpy had a deep abiding love and admiration for the outdoors. He slept in a greasy sleeping bag in a back alley behind a fetid dumpster. Rats would sometimes scurry across his "bed", and automobiles full of drunken bar patrons would sometimes speed past him. Yet, Stumpy referred to his status as, "Going camping." He advised that he and family had camped at many of the nation's great parks — Yosemite, Yellowstone, Glacier et al. He was nearly expert in wilderness survival skills and had once enjoyed teaching nature to his two daughters. He had climbed to the peak of "El Capitan" on several occasions in his younger days, he would offer. He indicated that the peak of the vertical rock climb at Yosemite stood at exactly 7,569 feet. And, as Stumpy often stated, "Believe me, I felt every foot!"

Harold Walter Cummings* had once been a high-ranking official of a utility company in Sacramento California. He had gained a Master's Degree in mechanical engineering from UCLA many years earlier. Harold had a beautiful wife and two teenaged daughters. The girls loved volleyball and running track, and the entire family enjoyed their home on five acres in the canyons east of Sacramento. The deer would literally eat out of their hands on their acreage, when their black Labrador did not chase them away. Harold's wife sold real-estate part-time, while very involved in the girls' school and activities. Harold had been working too hard and too many hours to enjoy all of the girls' activities. It was the reason why he accepted a less demanding job for lower pay in the state of Oregon. That, and the forests. Harold and family loved the forests.

Harold and family ultimately packed their belongings and began a trip to the north. The father filled his van to maximum capacity with items. The mother and two girls took the passenger car and led the tandem of vehicles northward on Interstate 5. Eventually, while outside of Portland Oregon, increased traffic separated the two vehicles. Harold fell several vehicles behind his wife and daughters and lost sight of the other car.

Somewhere outside of Portland Oregon an exhausted trucker was also driving northbound on Interstate 5. He was hauling groceries, and had been delayed by road construction in northern California. He sought to make up time and complete his delivery. The trucker fell asleep, only for a moment. Yet the moment would find his truck colliding abruptly with a passenger car that had slowed for traffic.

Harold Walter Cummings saw the smoke and fire before he could hear the collision. He knew immediately what car he would find afire as he parked and ran ahead. Harold Walter Cummings tried desperately to pull his family from the fireball that was once his family car. He would later tell me that he felt delayed for hours, but in reality only mili-seconds, by deciding which family member to try to first save. The screams of his family would be heard for the rest of his life, he stated. He could remember fire fighters and troopers dousing his own flaming clothing and ultimately pulling him away from the car.

There was no hope for Harold's family, and no hope for his badly burned right arm. In subsequent months, Harold would recover from the loss of his arm. Yet, there would be no recovery from the loss of his family. Harold told me that he never felt the burning of his arm, but he felt his family burn. Research in newspapers confirmed every word of the man's story.

Harold took to the bottle for solace, and lost everything he had once owned. He sought to camp in local Sacramento city parks, but he would be soon moved onward by local authorities at each. He needed more trees for comfort and stowed himself aboard a Burlington Northern cargo car.

"Stumpy" ended up in Seattle Washington, because he slept through Oregon and Seattle "had more trees." His adventures brought him to the concrete forests of downtown Seattle, out of a need to panhandle money and pick up a tiny check at a local government office. He would be spat upon by passing bar patrons, mugged by street thugs, and stabbed in the shoulder by gang members. But nobody ever took away Stumpy's dignity.

Your author ultimate gave Stumpy my finest subzero sleeping bag, and all hiking gear possessed. He looked at the meager amount of equipment as if a treasure. The little man snapped off his regular salute and commented, "You're alright, Cap'n." Visits with Stumpy would span two years, until one day his hiding spot was vacated. Yet, a lump in the throat disappeared when word on the street passed that he had caught a train to California. He was hopefully going home.

Stumpy had been just another worthless wino on skid row, Seattle. But the man was a somebody.

**

Little Alice

During any daily walk through Pioneer Square a frail and tiny four foot eight woman in her sixties could be seen endlessly sweeping the cobblestone streets. She wore a very tattered full-length fur coat that must have been stylish decades earlier. Weather conditions never merited a change of such attire. Her head was always covered by a dark blue scarf, and her eyes could barely be seen above the drooping cloth. She rarely looked upward, and muttered to herself while shuffling up and down the streets. Automobiles would honk at her in the street and drivers would dodge her angrily. She would never acknowledge the existence of the passing cars. Her name was Alice.

Alice was yet another worthless, wildly insane individual plaguing Seattle's downtown streets. Most business people and tourists considered her a frightening and revolting presence. Some businesses would employ Alice to sweep their entrances, for a meager two dollars. Many people complained of her poor hygiene and odor. Still others felt that she should be institutionalized, and blamed the seemingly heart-less police for their indifference. Yet, it was by state law that Alice could not be removed from the city's streets. ACLU lawsuits and state legislation sought "freedom" for nearly all mentally ill persons whom did not present an "imminent danger" to the public. Thus, Alice was seemingly remanded to fending for herself.

Alice Rosencrantz* was very well known to all the veteran beat cops. They held a special sense of fondness and protectiveness toward her. They encouraged your author, then a ten-year officer, and my partner, to get to know the tiny woman. Invariably, upon greeting Alice, she would bow demurely to the uniformed officers and hand a very stale cookie over as a gift. It was known that great appreciation for the gift should be expressed, and Alice would giggle demonstratively. She spoke only limited words of heavily accented English, and would pat our hands and say, "Goot!" Alice otherwise spoke only a staccato form of German, and usually directed her speech toward herself.

Your author and partners felt that the veteran beat cops were testing the younger officers to see if we grasped the entire situation of Alice. We offered that she appeared to be healthy and well-fed. To be sure, her hygiene was sadly lacking. We did notice small, but conspicuous tattoos along her right thumb and forefinger. Symbols of some sort. We offered to the veteran officers that Alice appeared to be a woman of about seventy years of age. She had a very bad back and experienced pain when standing upright. She seemed to have profound respect or fear of uniformed persons. We guessed that she was a recent German immigrant, with only nominal comprehension of the English language. She seemed to be a loner. She clearly suffered from mental illness. We were very concerned about her well-being on the streets of Seattle in a notoriously rough area. And we wondered where she slept at night.

The veteran officers expressed their pleasure with our comprehension of the most important aspect of walking a beat—reading people. They completed the puzzle graciously for us. Alice Rosencrantz* was sixty-six years of age. She had actually been a resident of America since 1949. Alice was originally a resident of Munich, Germany. She had parents and two younger brothers. The parents were both engineers, and Alice had studied at a private school, majoring in music.

Alice's entire family became residents of Dachau, Germany, courtesy of the Nazis. Alice was sixteen years of age at the time. She would view the brutal beating of her parents, as they were dragged away to the ovens. They never returned. Alice was beaten and raped by several Nazi officers. They took a profound pleasure in beating her in the back with heavy sticks. Still, she sought to care for her younger brothers, who were starving and ill. Alice charmed some Nazi guards by singing for them. They would reward her with a cookie or two, which she guardedly secured for giving to her brothers. Yet, her brothers would ultimately die of unknown ailments, perhaps by the rampant starvation and cholera.

The tattoos upon Alice's hand were Nazi markings. They indicated that she was to be included in the next wave of slaughters. Yet, the arrival of the American forces ended the macabre plans. Alice was freed. But she had nowhere to go. Her entire family had died in the holocaust. Even her school had been bombed to rubble. During the restoration, young girls could either make food money by prostitution or by sweeping demolished streets for two dollars a day. Alice chose to be a street sweeper.

Fate would bring her to a ship headed for Israel, at one point in time. Yet the terrible conditions of the Exodus negated easy entry into Israel. In an unknown manner, Alice emigrated to the U.S. Seattle Washington accepted limited entries.

Alice would live the remainder of her life in and out of institutions, and sweeping Seattle's streets. The horror of the holocaust never escaped her mind, and recovery became an impossibility. When governmental services for Alice were largely ended, it was the veteran beat cops whom attended to her needs. A tiny downtown apartment had been arranged for Alice. Ample food filled her cupboards, and she was escorted to and from her home on a daily basis. While the officers would never take credit, it was obvious from whom all necessities had come. Those whom criticized the officers openly for callousness were only met with a slight smile. Nothing was ever said. It was made abundantly known on the city's streets to the thugs that no one would dare bother little Alice.

It thus became very clear why Alice feared and respected the uniforms. It was equally evident why she lived to sweep the streets. And it became ever more precious, the gift of the cookies, that she forever presented with a bow and giggle. It became an honor to serve as one of Alice's many guardians.

Alice was just another crazy piece of human refuge. But she was a somebody.

***

Ada Mae the Bag Lady

From Mondays through Saturdays a senior African-American bag lady sits in front of varied entrances to the downtown Seattle Nordstrom store. She has done so for nearly eighteen years, and has become a fixture in the downtown environs. Regardless of the weather or passing seasons, she is always attired the same. She is replete with the finest plastic bag fashions. The color is always green. She neatly wraps the plastic around her legs and tapes the garmentry into place with silver duct tape. Her head is always protected by a plastic bag hood. She rarely speaks to passersby by, but she loves to watch the people come and go. She loves to listen to the conversations swirling about her.

In past years, beat cops all knew the woman as "Ada Mae." Ada Mae was actually found to be a highly articulate woman whom simply preferred to listen, rather than bore others with conversation. She chose each word with painstaking attention to detail and clarity. It was clear that she was a highly educated woman. She was never observed to imbibe in alcoholic beverages and had never been known to abuse her body via drug ingestion. She simply observed the passing crush of humanity with great bemusement. Her smile was radiant and distinctive. One front tooth always glistened with gold. When she chose to laugh at humanity or the vapid jokes of the beat cops, a mouth full of gold fillings could be visible.

Passersby would often hand the woman panhandling money. Yet, she had never requested a dime. She would simply nod and tuck the cash in a plastic bag. Often her bag would be seen to swell impressively by the end of the day. It appeared that Ada Mae simply worked a nine- to- five job at her post, as she would appear promptly at store opening, and depart upon closing hours.

Often citizenry would express disdain for the beat cops, your author included, for the apparent indifference to the woman's plight. Written complaints to the precinct would often arrive, decrying the insensitivity observed. They bemoaned how the cops simply walked away from Ada Mae without seeking social services for the woman so clearly in dire need. Yet, as is often the case on the streets, the beat cops knew the rest of the story.

Ada Mae was well known by the cops to arrive at the sidewalk via a long black stretch limousine. And the same limousine and uniformed driver would pick her up in the evenings. Eventually, the chauffer was asked for whom he worked. He reluctantly volunteered that his employer was none other than a legendary billionaire music producer. The son, a local high school graduate, no longer lived in the area. Yet, he often visited, and purportedly provided his mother with an enormous mansion on Capital Hill in which she resides. Upon occasion, the famous son could be seen stepping out of the limousine to approach his mother. He always expressed appreciation to the officers for keeping a constant watch over Ada Mae, and for providing her companionship and new jokes to relate to him.

While many would consider Ada Mae to be insane, we all found her to be merely highly eccentric. She loved to view humanity as a homeless person. She alternately drew humor and inspiration in observing the snobbishness and compassion of passing individuals. Most, it would seem were too quick to judge. She often commented to the beat cops, "I can buy anything I want… but you can't buy this!"

Few people in Seattle actually know the identity of the sweet bag lady of Nordstrom. And the "callous cops" have kept the secret for many years — until now, as your author spills the beans. Ada Mae was just another misfit on a big city's streets. But she was a somebody.

***

Alvin

In the northern part of downtown Seattle, far away from the hubbub, was a district known as Belltown. In the late 80's and early 90's the area was a run-down haven for violent drug dealers and prostitutes in local parks. Decrepit brick businesses, the welfare office, low income housing, and surplus stores dotted the area. Most winos chose to stay out of the area, for fear of assault or robbery from street thugs. Yet, a huge wino by the name of "Alvin" was found on a daily basis sprawled across a sidewalk outside of "Mama's Mexican Kitchen" — a local dive.

Alvin stood, when he actually did stand, nearly six feet six inches tall, and was a solid 250 pounds. His head was enormous and was covered by a dark and greasy mop of long thick black hair. He often growled at lurking street thugs, and the thugs would drift away, like jackals in search of weaker prey. For all intents and purposes, Alvin was a bear.

Alvin would drink anything he could lay his hands upon. But he preferred whiskey. He could down at least two fifths of McNaughton's whiskey in a day. He was a member of Harborview Hospital's "Sixty-Five Club." This meant that he had, on more than one occasion, been tested to have a blood alcohol level of .65 per cent. To give some perspective, in the state of Washington .08 per cent is considered legally drunk.

And .25 is considered life threatening. Alvin had been drinking consistently and excessively for a very long time.

Alvin was sometimes found to be an easy candidate for the Detox Van to take him to the hospital prior to a local detoxification center. Many times, he was passed out. Yet, most times he was amazingly lucid considering his extraordinary state of intoxication. His endless growling at passing thugs would cease immediately upon the approach of the beat cops. He would immediately right himself to an erect sitting position against a brick wall. After emitting the world's largest belch, he would giggle and beg forgiveness. He would then invariably display an enormous yawn, and the world's longest tongue would fall from his mouth. His tongue immediately reminded one of Gene Simmons. But Alvin surpassed Gene for length thereof. Alvin would smile and pat his hair into place so as to look stylish.

Alvin would thereupon offer the officers a morning serenade. He would clear his throat, hum to find a key, and bellow out a beautiful rendition of, "North, to Alaska." On special occasions he would offer an impressive crooning of "Wasted Days and Wasted Nights." He often chuckled that such might have been his theme song.

Alvin was a man who was sadly rotting away, from the inside out. He had attempted sobriety on many occasions, it would be learned. Yet he could never escape the iron grip of intense alcoholism. He suffered tremendous withdrawals with each trip to the hospital and detoxification center. He would attend a few meetings and swear to counselors that he was a changed man. Yet the bottle would soon find him, and he would soon find the sidewalks or alleys.

One Christmas morning, circa 1989 my partner and I encountered Alvin emerging from a local mission. He stood fully upright in a highly expensive three-piece suit, complete with silk tie. Not a hair was out of place, and Alvin was clean-shaven and completely sober. Alvin, it would seem, was a very handsome and distinguished looking man! We were fascinated to visit with Alvin, and he was delighted to see us. We had to immediately inquire as to his apparent change of circumstances.

Alvin literally told us his life story. At one time he had been an award winning physics professor at the University of Washington. He had been oft- published, traveled the world, and even had an audience with Albert Einstein on two occasions. He had a wife and two grown daughters. In fact, he was preparing himself to be picked up by his family in order to join them for Christmas dinner. But the bottle had been his downfall for many years. He tearfully related how he had received medical treatment, psychological treatment, and spiritual treatment. But he could not conquer his demons. It was thus that Alvin sought to clean himself up once or twice a year, for the benefit of his family. He was still loved by his family. The family was open to him in every way. But he chose the streets to suffer his disease, and did not wish to cause further pain to his loved ones.

Alvin was just another pathetic wino on Seattle's cold sidewalks and alleys. But Alvin was a somebody.

***

Joseph Anthony Gunn – A.K.A. Mr. Christ

On a late October afternoon in 1982 your author was working a daytime patrol district in North Central Seattle, in an area abutted by scenic Greenlake and the Woodland Park Zoo. I was dispatched to a disturbance call at a nearby movie theater. The theater itself was over one hundred years-old. It was a beautiful old brick building tucked into a neighborhood, just north of the zoo. The theater featured old classic movies for two dollars. The establishment stood as a deliberate contrast to mega million- dollar multiplex theaters taking over the entertainment market in the county.

The dispatch indicated that a man was making a scene inside the theater and disrupting the event. Upon the arrival of nearby Officer Juan Palacol and me, we were greeted by an exasperated manager at the curb. The manager immediately said, "Oh, thank God you're here….you gotta see this guy."

We were ushered into the theater itself and found the house lights had been raised. Several dozen angry patrons remained milling around inside the establishment. The actual movie had been abruptly halted, and an individual stood upon the stage, bathed in bright white lights. The gentleman was a white man of about 34 years of age. He was adorned in a stark white flowing robe, tied neatly with a white rope, and brown leather sandals. He was heavily bearded, with perfectly maintained brownish facial hair. His immaculate long brown hair fell below his shoulders.

The individual was calling out to the audience in a booming and melodic voice, "I am the lord your God… bow to me as I have bowed to you." His hands were extended widely outward in a gesture of openness and sincerity. The theater manager explained that the individual had been on the stage for almost twenty minutes. The manager added that the individual had sought to bathe the feet of theater patrons and had orated vast passages of gospel to the unappreciative audience. Yet, some audience members stood and remained, apparently fascinated with the presence of the man upon the stage.

We approached the individual on the stage, with one officer to each side of him. We sought to approach the man with a degree of caution always afforded to "220's" or mental cases. Yet, the individual simply slowly lowered his hands, clasped them together in front of his body, and bowed slightly in our presence. He then said, "Hello Steve...hello Juan...I've been expecting you." Juan Palacol and I looked at one another and then at our nametags. The nametags bore only our last names and first initials! We explained to the man who we were and what our purpose was in approaching him. The man's response was, "Blessed be the peacekeepers... you know that it was a policeman whom arranged the lodging for my mother at the time of my birth... a Roman Centurion in fact."

When asked his name, the individual responded, "I am Christ Jesus, your lord and savior." He stared into each our sets of eyes with tremendously blue eyes, and was never seen to blink. He gave no indication of alcohol or drug abuse. His eyes were crystal clear.

I noted on his wrist a plastic bracelet. The bracelet read, "Harborview Medical Center." The name of Joseph Anthony Gunn was scribed beneath the hospital name. I politely invited Mr. Christ to walk with me to my waiting "chariot." He complied without resistance of any sort. In violation of department policy, I did not handcuff the gentleman nor order an ambulance with restraints for him. While he was technically under arrest for disorderly conduct, he had been as docile and cooperative as anyone ever encountered. Instead, I chose to transport him in my patrol car. He blessed me upon his placement in the rear secured portion of the patrol vehicle. During the short drive to the police station he recited continuous gospel passages. I couldn't help but note his amazingly blue eyes in the rear view mirror and the fact that he was still not seen to have ever blinked.

Once inside the station, Mr. Christ was placed in a pink holding cell while I conferred with my Sergeant. It was determined that the man would receive transportation back to Harborview Medical Center's Mental ward, from which he had apparently come. While Mr. Christ posed no apparent danger to the public, it was feared that the public would pose a danger to him.

As coincidence would have it, the department's legendary Chaplain, John Oas was visiting with the troops of the North Precinct on that particular date. We thus could not resist inviting Chaplain Oas to visit with the remarkable robed man in the pink holding cell. We provided him with the details of our encounter with Mr. Christ.

Chaplain Oas spent several minutes sitting on the cold concrete bench beside Mr. Christ. We almost became concerned for the chaplain's safety as we diligently watched the two individuals through a Plexiglas window. Finally, Chaplain Oas arose and tapped at the window to exit the room. Chaplain Oas displayed his famous grin, which added to the persona of the tiny plump man's elfish appearance.

We asked the Chaplain, "Well?" He continued to smile and shook his head from side to side slowly. Chaplain John related that he had never encountered a man with such vast and complete knowledge of all bible passages and gospels. The chaplain was a renowned theologian in his own right and he continued to marvel at the man's superior knowledge. He further commented that the man never blinked during the nearly twenty minute visit. He finally commented that we should treat the man with all due gentleness and walked away, still shaking his head.

It was thus that I sent Jesus Christ to the mental ward of Harborview Medical Center. As uniformed ambulance drivers arrived to seatbelt the man into a gurney, he asked for one moment to speak with me. He thanked me for my kindness and compassion, and asked that I not judge myself harshly for doing my job. He indicated that his treatment was vastly improved from nearly 2,000 years prior. Lastly, he raised his right hand outward toward me and stared into my eyes again. He said, "You may have that which you seek in life." With that, he was away to Harborview Medical Center, and was never seen again.

To this day I await the arrival of the Dallas Cowboy Cheerleaders at my doorstep. So Mr. Christ remains a mysterious entity to me.

***

Cop Culture: How you can always spot a cop.

It has often been stated by researchers of cultures that cops' attitudes most closely resemble those of convicts. I would agree to a vast extent. There are easily predictable traits in cops that may easily distinguish them from anyone in the public. Even when the uniforms are placed elsewhere while off-duty, the markings are nearly as clear.

To steal a bit of Jeff Foxworthy's wording, please see the following facts about spotting off-duty cops:

If you always sit with your back to the wall in a restaurant, with a wary view of the entrance… you might be a cop.

If you slow upon entering any bank to survey the entire lobby and teller windows… you might be a cop.

If you can be seen backing the family mini-van into a parking space at the grocery store for emergency responses… you might be a cop.

If you interrupt the man at the mall who is begging for money ("to repair his broken down vehicle in order to drive his dying sister back home to Georgia") by saying, "Gee, that's funny, I just saw you drive up here alone in a brand new Chevy Camaro, with Alaska license plate,"… you might be a cop.

If you walk down a city sidewalk riddled with street thugs, look the thugs in the eye, and do not alter your course… you might be a cop.

If you carry a conspicuously large and bulging leather fanny pack, or wear a thin denim vest around your waist, even in the hottest of weather… you might be a cop.

If you are seen driving down the highway, and approach each and every curve with your vehicle positioned high into the curve, low at the apex, and high at the exit of such curve… you might be a cop.

If you hit the brakes abruptly going into a curve, and then accelerate rapidly going into the curve… you might be a cop (or a NASCAR wannabee).

If you drive past an accident, that occurred in the opposite direction of the freeway, and maintain your speed, keeping your focus straight ahead… you might be a cop.

If you would not stand directly in front of a door, even while ringing the doorbell at your mother's house… you might be a cop.

If you drive across the country, on a family trip, and arrive within 3 minutes of your original E.T.A… you might be a cop.

And, finally, if you make serious decisions in thirty seconds, while your spouse takes days to come to the same conclusion… you might be a cop.

***

Chapter 9: Marion, the friendly ghost

On August 8th, 1984 at five o'clock P.M. numerous daytime downtown patrol units responded to a broadcast of a suicide in progress. The location given was that of the historic Arctic Building, which stood directly to the north of the Public Safety Building at 3rd Avenue and Cherry Street. The broadcast indicated that numerous passersby were watching a man standing outside of a 5th floor window ledge on the southwest corner of the building. He was described as a white male in his mid-thirties. He was said to be oddly dressed in a 1930s style thick wool suit, narrow tie, with greased-back brownish hair.

Given the proximity to the combined East and West Patrol precincts across the street, numerous officers simply walked toward the building, while others arrived in patrol vehicles. As officers began arriving, the radio broadcast updated that the individual had jumped from the window ledge. Radio indicated that several calls to 9-1-1 were confirming the update. Paramedic crews were thus summoned as well.

Rapidly arriving officers and paramedics immediately sought to locate the body of the individual upon the sidewalk of 3rd Avenue. Yet, no body could be located. There were no signs of trauma upon the sidewalk, parked cars, or the roadway. Not one drop of blood was evident. No hair strands were planted, and no torn clothing shreds could be seen. Officers looked into traffic for a staggering injured man. Nothing was visible.

Numerous officers set to cordoning off the area and

making a search for the subject. Officers entered the one hundred ten-year-old gargoyle/walrus- adorned building and rode an elevator to the 5th floor. The upstairs officers opened and looked out of the 5th floor window in question toward their peers upon the sidewalk. They spoke on the radio that they saw nothing amiss.

Your author, among other officers, began interviewing the numerous witnesses on the street. We were able to confirm that the upstairs officers were indeed at the window in question and so advised them over the radio. The upstairs officers radioed back that they had had some difficulty in opening the old window, and that all indications were that no one had opened such for many years. They had found dust and a sloppy coat of paint seal that had not previously been broken. The office space in question on the 5th floor was vacant.

Other officers searched the floors directly above and below the window in question. City agencies occupied both floors, and curious employees within reported seeing nothing out of the ordinary. Yet other officers searched up and down 3rd Avenue and adjoining streets, in search of an injured party walking away from the scene. Nothing could be found.

Too many credible witnesses remained at the scene relating identical observations to be discarded as contriving such a story. They ranged from business people to families in the area on vacation. Yet, there was no sign whatsoever of such a suicide. Efforts were even made to maintain contact with local hospitals, in anticipation of the arrival of a badly injured individual. Still, no sign of the individual in question was ever located.

Twenty years following the incident, long ago relegated to faded memory, I was assigned to work a two year stint (sentence) in Internal Affairs. Being that Internal Affairs was a unit regarded about as highly as pit bulls with rabies, actual locations of our offices were not exactly choice. Internal Affairs was ultimately moved from an abandoned city office building that was being renovated. In the department's usual wisdom, the unit was moved from the old Dexter Horton Building only after the unit Captain submitted industrial injury reports on each of his employees for asbestos exposure. We had literally worked in a condemned area wherein construction crews in haz-mat outfits were tearing out the last of asbestos-laden ceilings.

Oblivious of related history, we were delighted to be moved to the historic and beautiful Arctic Building across the street. The Arctic Building was an impressively ornate white brick ten-story edifice constructed in 1917. The atmosphere was complete with a spectacular lower level "Dome Room" conference area with a lofted domed ceiling that was illuminated primarily by dazzling stained glass windows exposed to the outside world. Highly detailed artwork was evident upon the imposing gargoyles and walruses all along the exterior.

Amazingly, the 14-person Internal Affairs Unit, composed of a Captain, Lieutenant, Secretary, and nine investigating Sergeants, was given the entire fifth floor of the building. While other floors were cramped with ever-growing city agencies, the expanses of the fifth floor were wide open. We were delighted with our large office spaces and expressed our pleasure to other city employees on the other floors of the building. However, without fail, the other city employees would shake their heads and make comments to the extent of, "Better you than me," and "They couldn't pay me enough to work on that floor." We had no idea to what they were referring.

Our unit admin specialist (secretary) was the first to gain some insight. One winter night, Leslie Thornburg was working late and alone. It was nearing the midnight hour as she sought to complete voluminous amounts of transcription from interview tapes. She pulled down her ear jacks upon hearing the whistling of our ever-cheerful Captain, standing directly behind her. She turned to greet the Captain and found that no one stood behind her. The whistling continued for a brief instant and then ceased. Leslie arose from her chair and immediately sought to search the entire work area. She called out to whomever was working and present, to end their practical joke. She even searched the male and female restrooms for prankster Sergeants. The floor was completely empty. As a final effort to explain the whistling, Leslie checked the log books indicating entry and exit within the secure 5th floor of the building. She was astonished to discover that the last co-worker had checked out of the building some three hours prior.

During subsequent months, such an incident would occur repeatedly for Leslie. And she was not the only late-night employee to hear the whistling. All members of the unit were fascinated to watch the elevators of the building on a daily basis. At unpredictable times, the elevator light would brighten on the first floor. The elevator would whir upward. The elegant lift would stop on the 5th floor and the doors would open. A very cold wind would briefly emerge from the empty hoist. The door would then close and the elevator would continue upward. Electricians were summoned to check the wiring of the elevator, and no fault could be found.

Other city employees were asked if the elevator stopped on all the other corresponding floors. They simply laughed and indicated that the 5th floor was the only recipient of such service. The city employees then began to relate that we were working on a "haunted" floor of the building. They were surprised to hear that the police department employees were so insulated from other departments that the story had never been heard.

They related many incidents of hearing the whistling. Further, employees had on rare occasion seen the strangely old-styled gentleman standing at or near the 5th floor office window. It was said that other reported suicide events had been witnessed as well.

On one occasion, your author and his Captain were each washing hands in the 5th floor restroom. We each turned the two faucets to the off position. However, the hot water spigots on each respective sink returned to the fully "on" position while we stood transfixed. I finally looked at my Captain in amazement as we both turned off the water again. The faucets then remained in the off position. The ever-comical and lovable Captain Mark Evenson then commented, "Dude, I'd say something about that being the weirdest thing I've ever seen... but I don't want to explain why I was in a bathroom with you." The Captain later had the springs in the faucets checked. They were found to be in perfect order.

Eventually, the trained "investigators" of the unit began to piece together the story of the strange occurrences on the 5th floor of the building. History, it would seem, was very ripe indeed in the Arctic Building. As it would be learned, the 5th floor southwest office of the building was once occupied by a renowned, yet eccentric 1st District Congressman by the name of Marion Zioncheck. While a successful attorney and powerful force for labor in the U.S. Congress, Mr. Zioncheck was known more for his womanizing and the wild parties he and his young wife held.

Congressman Zioncheck was to seek a third term in office when circumstances instantly changed. On *August 8th*, 1936 (see date of above suicide response) he was seen to jump to his death from his 5th floor office window. His body landed directly in front of the vehicle of his waiting wife, down upon the city street. He left at his desk a will and suicide note reading: "My only hope in life was to improve the conditions of an unfair economic system." Congressman Zioncheck was succeeded in his congressional office by long-time friend and District Attorney Warren G. Magnuson. Magnuson would go on to be the longest standing and most powerful member of congress ever to have hailed from the state of Washington.

All occurred as a result of Congressman Zioncheck's suicide.

However, Seattle Police Homicide records that remain indicate that the death was never ruled a suicide. Instead, it was deemed a suspicious death. It was found that the handwriting of the suicide note and brief will did not appear to match that of Marion Zioncheck. Case records also indicated that they found it suspicious that the wife would be present in a waiting automobile directly next to the landing site of the body. There were notations to the possibility that the wife had driven over the body. Powerful political forces ultimately ordered the closure of the death investigation, and no further follow-up would ever occur. Strangely, the usually aggressive D.A.'s office was the least interested in pursuing further investigation.

Yet, the fifth floor of the historic Arctic Building remained a place of mystery and interest....and completely vacated for years. The city ultimately sold the building to private interests seeking to convert such into a hotel. Your author and his wife were some of the first occupants of the very grand hotel. We had a marvelous experience, in spite of Marion's failure to appear.

***

Cop Culture

A common public misconception is that police officers' demeanors of callousness are applied directly toward people of the streets. It is stated by the media, politicians, and passersby that the cops do not care about the homeless. Indeed, many members of the public would attest to perceptions of cops treating the down and out harshly. In some instances this is true. Yet, in most instances, much more of the story is not known by those whom make assumptions.

During the 80's and 90's, when your author was fortunate to walk a downtown foot beat, the vast majority of beat cops were found to be highly compassionate. Indeed, the legendary Officer John Patrick Sullivan epitomized compassion. He, and numerous other beat officers arranged for a myriad of human services for the down and out. John and other officers often dug deep into their pockets to provide for the truly needy. Food, housing, and other miscellaneous needs were often provided by the so-called "callous cops." They simply did not make a big production of such generosity.

Without fail, the police officers detest the fact that many persons posing as homeless or in dire need are scam artists. We have often observed individuals standing by freeway entrances, signs in hand, decrying their pathetic state of life—only to watch them drive away in brand-new Mustangs.

The truly homeless rarely, if ever, stand in the flow of humanity to demand or request funding. If one wishes to help those truly in need, they must travel much further into the city's heart. The truly homeless may be found underneath freeways, in back alleys, or sleeping in the back of abandoned trains or tanker trucks. They won't find you. You must find them.

***

Chapter 10: All the lonely people

Aurora Bridge

A radio broadcast rang out one midnight in late February 1990, of a suicidal man on the rail of the Aurora Bridge. Your author was very close-by on patrol, and arrived in less than a minute. A white man in his mid-thirties stood with one leg over the railing. He was in the very center of the bridge, hovering some 185 feet over the darkness of the Ship Canal far below. Most traffic on the state highway continued to whoosh past the man and my patrol car, now parked in the outside lane with flashing lights. One vehicle stopped north of the site and a concerned couple stood out of their vehicle in concern.

Your author stepped out of the patrol vehicle after confirming a possible jumper to radio dispatch. I put on my heavy winter coat and was immediately soaked by the bitter-cold heavy rains and wind. I was thus obligated to engage the gentleman in conversation. I stood with one foot up onto the sidewalk that abutted the railing four feet above, but held one foot firmly upon the pavement below. As with all officers, I was aware of the possibility of a jumper taking a passenger with them. Physics indicated that no one could counter the pull of a plummeting adult.

Additional patrol vehicles quickly arrived upon the quarter mile bridge and began to close traffic in both northbound and southbound directions. The flashing lights of harbor patrol boats could also be seen far below speeding down the canal from a nearby Harbor Station. I knew that officers were donning dive gear down below in anticipation of a worst-case scenario.

A conversation with the jumper thus began in earnest, wondering what one says to a man seeking to leap to his death. I introduced myself by name and sought that of the jumper. The jumper said, "What the f—k do you care?" I offered that I would not ask if I didn't care, and that the jumper owed his name after I had volunteered mine. The man indicated that his name was "Craig." He was a clearly distinguished man struggling to maintain his dignity. He was very well dressed, while totally soaked by the rains. He had dark hair and a perfectly maintained full beard.

Lacking any professional negotiations training, I asked Craig what could bring him to the abyss of such a choice. He responded that I wouldn't understand, and reiterated that I did not care. I said, "Do you think I'm standing out here in this lousy weather, freezing my ass off to talk to you because I don't care?" Craig emitted a mordant laugh and replied, "I guess you have a point there." I thus inquired again as to Craig's circumstances.

Craig related the story of coming home from a double shift at a utilities company to find his wife engrossed in sex with another man. He added that his two young daughters, ages 4 and 6 were sleeping in their adjoining rooms at the same time. Craig stated that the response of his wife and her lover was stunning to him. They sat in his bed unclothed and simply laughed at him. Craig stated that that evening was the last he would spend in his home, some eleven months prior.

Craig explained that legal proceedings had led to his ex-wife's total ownership of the home; that false accusations of domestic violence had negated any meaningful contact with his daughters; and that exorbitant spousal support and child support orders had bankrupted him. Craig was once a successful supervisor at his company, making a solid living. He was now relegated to living in a downtown flop house with cockroaches. He had recently taken to too much drinking, by his own admission.

Craig again claimed that I had absolutely no comprehension of his current circumstances. I ultimately advised that I had profound familiarity with his state of affairs. I was not lying entirely. During the 20-minute conversation, I actually felt a bond with the gentleman. There was a commonality of recent painful life episodes. He was clearly a decent man, and life had dealt him hardship. It was saddening to see that he could not handle his adversity. Perhaps he had sought help. Perhaps no one cared. Yet I repeatedly reassured Craig that I did care. And I truly did.

Approximately twenty minutes after the conversation began, a white Seattle Police van arrived on the bridge with two trained department Crisis Intervention negotiators. I glanced briefly at the approaching male and female detectives in relief. I felt that I was running out of conversation material with the troubled gentleman. He had not budged from his rail position. As my glance returned to Craig I saw only his wet jacket, lying upon the sidewalk, and flapping in the wind. He was gone.

I re-entered my patrol vehicle and drove the circuitous roadway that travels from the bridge's top to the waterway below. I somehow wished that I was simply experiencing a nightmare. Upon my arrival at the north shore of the canal, Harbor divers were bringing the body to shore. They made symbolic attempts at resuscitation of the jumper and turned "it" over to waiting paramedics.

Craig's body was perfectly intact from an outward glance. He almost looked peaceful. Yet, as medics began to lift him upon a board and cover him with a blanket, his body gave the appearance of total elasticity. His arms flopped below the body like limp pasta. Clearly, everything within the man's body had turned to gel upon the 140-mile-per-hour impact on the waterway turned concrete.

I marveled at what loneliness a human being must have experienced to have chosen such a horrific plunge. I wondered further if anyone cared.

***

The drill

On Christmas Eve, 1988 another nearby officer and I were dispatched to a "check the welfare" call at a Queen Anne home. A concerned landlord had called to report that an adult male had sounded very despondent in an earlier phone conversation regarding overdue rent, and that the door to the home was somehow inoperable. We arrived at the home to find the landlord waiting at the front porch. The landlord advised that he was no "Scrooge," and that he had advised his tenant that the rent could be "worked out." The landlord's motivation for coming to the home of the tenant on Christmas Eve was his concern for the man. He indicated that the man had recently lost his job at a construction company. The landlord added that the man had related that he had no family and few friends, and that the friends had drifted away upon his separation from the common workplace.

The other officer and I thus sought to check on the resident. There was no answer to repeated knocking on the door and ringing of the doorbell. We tried the doorknob. The knob turned readily, yet the door would not budge. We finally kicked at the door and forced it open. We then saw that the door had been braced with a 2 x 4 board. We entered the cluttered bungalow and called out to the resident. No answer came. Yet we could hear a strange humming sound coming from a back bedroom area.

We thus approached the bedroom slowly, and the humming became louder. We heard from behind us the words, "Oh My God," and then noticed that the landlord had followed directly behind us. The landlord had his hands over his face and was transfixed at a sight upon the bed. Upon such lay the resident. A large and powerful commercial drill was imbedded into his right temple. The body lay on its back on the bed in a vast pool of blood, already coagulating in the bedding. Yet the drill was still running, and spinning wildly around, as the large bit had become stuck in the skull and brain of the victim.

I marveled at what loneliness a human being must have experienced to have chosen such a horrific death. I wondered further if anyone cared.

***

The vet

On Christmas Eve 1987 your author was serving as a training officer for a forty year-old "rookie" officer. The rookie was in his last week of training before "graduating" to a permanent patrol assignment. The mature rookie was highly competent and gaining rapid respect from his veteran peers. We were dispatched to a trespassing call at a downtown rented hotel room. Radio asked if I required another unit for backup. Confident in the abilities of my highly capable trainee, I directed the student officer to decline such offer.

We thus arrived at the Seattle Apartment Hotel. Once a very fashionable hotel in the 1940's, the building had long prior fallen into disrepair. A slumlord had gained ownership over the years and run-down rooms were rented by the half-month to drug dealers and the down and out. The slumlord greeted us at the lobby. He was the epitome of compassion. The renter of the hotel room had run out of money the day prior and could not pay for his hotel room on Christmas Eve. The slumlord thus wanted the man tossed onto the streets with no place to stay. We expressed our extreme displeasure with the slumlord's principles. He demanded that the law be enforced and we thus had no choice.

The student officer and I agreed that we would find the man housing, food, and whatever necessities required. We further agreed to pay for such ourselves were service to prove to be unavailable on such short notice. We found no answer to our knocking at the unit door. We directed the slumlord to use his master key to unlock the door.

The student officer stood to one side of the door, as trained, while I stood to the other. He slowly pushed the door open and called out to the renter—a Mr. Donaldson. There was no answer from within. We could hear music playing at a moderate volume. The student officer pushed the door totally open and he was the first to enter the room. He stopped briefly in the entrance and I nudged him to the side.

The student officer was already amazed at the sight within the room. The entire unit had been somehow converted into a quasi-jungle. Windows were blocked out by bamboo curtains. The floor of the room was covered in six inches of sand and dirt. A small palm tree sat in the center of the room, looking to be fully alive. A small deck of bamboo was constructed atop the floor. Toward the corner of the spacious room there existed a tiny bamboo hut, complete with a thatched roof and doors.

The music from within the hut continued. The songs changed from one 60's song to another. Jimi Hendrix music changed to Steppenwolf, and then Jefferson Airplane. We ducked beneath the roof of the hut while again calling for Mr. Donaldson. There was no response.

We walked toward the flimsy door of the hut. The student officer raised the bamboo latch and opened the door outward toward us. Within the hut sat the renter. He was propped against a wall with his legs crossed. His arms lay peacefully upon his lap. The renter was dressed in a full Marine dress uniform, including a white formal hat. He had stripes upon his sleeves, indicating his rank as Sergeant. In front of him lay ornate open jewelry- type boxes containing numerous medals. They were arranged in perfect rows for his viewing. To the man's left stood an I.V. rack. Upon the rack was an attached medical pouch that was nearly empty. Unknown deadly medication was slowly dripping from the pouch into the I.V. Our eyes followed the I.V line to the inside of the tenant's left uniform sleeve.

The marine sat completely serene in his staged position, and also completely dead. The music continued to emanate from a 1960's style record player with numerous records stacked within such.

The record player dropped another disc and the music turned to Scarboro Fair by Simon and Garfunkel.

I marveled at what loneliness a human being must have experienced to have chosen such an ending. Yet, my Vietnam Veteran trainee did not marvel.

***

Scatman's buddy

In March of 1982, while a brand new fully commissioned officer in the South Precinct, I was dispatched to a prowler call at a West Seattle low income senior housing complex. Another officer and I searched the rear courtyard of the complex. Having located nothing out of the ordinary we then met with the complainant. An elderly black man greeted us at the front door. He explained that a "burglar" had tried opening his sliding doors with a crowbar. He added that the burglar was "always" trying to pry the door open. Our examination of the door showed no such evidence of any attempts to pry. It became clearly evident that the man had dialed 9-1-1 so as to have some social contact.

As my career continued, I would learn that such a call was a very common occurrence. As my field training officers had often opined, the calls from the lonely are very important responsibilities to the police officers. They, and other respected veterans, offered that the police were the only entity to which the lonely and vulnerable could turn. Armed with such training, I watched my fellow officer depart and sought to attend professionally to the elderly caller.

The gentleman advised me that he was 91 years of age. He identified himself as "Riff." Riff made grand claims to having been famous once upon a time. He claimed he was best friends with the legendary actor and musician Scatman Crothers. Riff continued to boast that he was once close friends with Sammy Davis Junior, Duke Ellington, and Louis Armstrong. His list of legendary "friends" continued incessantly. I nodded, and answered politely, "Wow. I'll be darned," and hoped not to be perceived as condescending.

Riff ultimately asked, "You probably don't believe me,

do you?" I offered that anything was possible. Riff then said, "Hold on, young man. I'll be right back. Sit sit!" His gnarled but graceful hands were animated. I was thus formally seated on the couch within his tiny residence. Riff immediately returned with a piece of home- made apple pie topped with vanilla ice cream. He carried such atop a huge photo album. I was presented with the pie and ice cream. The dessert was delicious, yet his amazing stories were exponentially more so.

Riff opened the album and his past life sprang from the pages. He had grown up a jazz musician and actor in Chicago. He had performed old jazz, new jazz, scat, blues, bebop and then some. He played seven instruments and had graced Carnegie Hall on many occasions. Riff showed pictures of he and Scatman, Duke Ellington, Ella Fitzgerald, even Frank Sinatra. Riff had acted in over a dozen movies. He had performed in scores of television shows, including Chico and the Man and Sanford and Son. He had wined and dined with royalty, and sat in the front row of the Academy Awards on more than one occasion.

He sat down on his electric keyboard and sang an old song, from his days at the "Loop" jazz club in 1940's Chicago. His voice was gravelly, and his fingers showed wear, but he most assuredly still had the touch. I knew I was in the presence of greatness, in the most inordinate of settings.

With time becoming an issue, I needed to excuse myself. While I wondered about Riff's loneliness, I did not ask. He volunteered that he had two daughters. He stated that his carousing peripatetic lifestyle had long ago estranged him from his wife and girls. He had not heard from either of his daughters in nearly 25 years. He had sent nearly all of his earnings to his ex-wife, and subsequently his daughters over the years. He did not care about money. A tiny apartment would suffice for a home. He knew that the daughters had his address, as the checks had all been cashed. As he related such fact, he began to cry. It was his hope that the daughters would come visit him before he died.

I marveled at what loneliness a human being must have experienced due to his once exciting choices. I wondered if the choices had been worth the cost.

***

Chapter side note: Officer Gregg Pote. A stand- up comic in uniform.

Scores of Seattle Police officers shall attest to one fact regarding Officer Gregg Pote — that the man truly missed his calling. Gregg Pote is a comic genius in every sense of the word. He is a short and chubby man, now of fifty-five years of age, with piercing blue eyes peering out of oversized glasses. His bushy mustache makes his sea-lion appearance complete. While Officer Pote was an exceptionally bright and capable police officer, he shall always be renowned for the comic relief he provided — all free of charge.

Even when he was making no attempt to be humorous, Officer Pote often evoked laughter. He could disable a person with laughter, merely by facial gestures or innumerable imitations of animals or children. A mere word uttered or a half-hour recitation of scores of famous monologues could evoke uncontrollable laughter. He had a photographic memory for comedy.

In a vocation rife with doom, gloom, and gore, the troops quickly came to adore a man who could bring levity to any situation. Pote was clearly such a man. Whether you call him

Kent and I, partners for life. Near end of respective careers.

Sgt. Alvin "Big Daddy" Little & partner John Carlson of "Run SPD."

Officer John Abraham, AKA "the Blue Angel."

East Wenatchee Gun Store murder evidence and drug seizure.

CHAPLAIN
JOHN OAS
October 11, 1946 - April 8, 2013

Saturday, April 20, 2013 1:00 pm
Criminal Justice Training Academy
19010 1st Ave. S. – Burien, WA 98148

The great Chaplain John Oas - confidante and friend to hundreds.

Congressman Marion Zioncheck - the friendly ghost
(*Public domain photo*)

Officer John Patrick Sullivan - A cop's cop.

Ms. Renee Hopkins

Thomas Davis - psychopathic killer (Look at the eyes).
(*Photo courtesy Washington State Dept. of Corrections.*)

Valerie Chard - killer and Davis follower.
(*Photo courtesy Washington State Dept. of Corrections.*)

Captain Larry Farrar (right) at time of retirement

Sisson's Gun Store murder scene
(*Photo courtesy Douglas County Sheriff's office*)

Pote, Po-tay, or his nickname of "Butt Plug," Gregg will always be an endearing soul.

Pote was responsible for my being chastised by supervisors for my insensitivity at a fatality accident scene. Yet, it could not be helped. I was the initial responding officer to a multi-car accident inside the Battery Street Tunnel in downtown Seattle. Numerous vehicles were upside down, on their sides, or in flames. A major north-south highway running beneath the city was paralyzed. As the first arriving patrol officer, I was astounded to survey the carnage and pandemonium. Fire department crews were springing into the tunnel, media helicopters were whirring overhead, and fellow patrol units could be seen establishing traffic control positions north of the tunnel. In a word, I was overwhelmed.

I was busy directing units on traffic control, requesting a supervisor, and summoning Accident Investigation Section detectives to the scene. The daunting task of piecing together the events that had cost lives had just begun. As I stood scribbling notes, and surveying the scene, Officer Pote walked up to a nearby guardrail. Since Pote was a seasoned "veteran" of six whole years of police experience at the time, to my measly two years, I was relieved to see the senior officer. Pote jabbed his thumbs deeply into his gun-belt on each side of his belly. He rocked on his heels several times and nodded his head repeatedly while looking from side to side at the wreckage. He uttered but one word of wisdom. Pote said, "Bitchin." With that, he turned and walked away.

Nearly in shock from the scope of the carnage in front of me, my sub-conscious kicked into self-preservation mode. Strangely, I began uncontrollable laughter. Regrettably, the impulsive nervous laughter occurred just at the point where several news crews were focusing upon the accident and the tall policeman knee deep in the wreckage.

Later, my Sergeant was more than happy to point out how unprofessional I looked at the accident scene on the local news. Sergeant Butler asked me how I could have laughed at such an event. I provided him a one word answer—"Pote." With that, Sergeant Butler's anger immediately faded. He nodded, and said, "Ohhh." Clearly, Sergeant Butler understood.

Pote's gallows humor was legendary. He was quick to observe the comical—at least in a twisted cop's view of circumstances. Case in point, a floating dead Asian male, found off the beach of Discovery Park. As we pulled the badly decomposed corpse from the water, minus numerous devoured body parts, it was Pote whom noted: "Huh, that's ironic...the fish are eating a raw Japanese guy."

Of course, it would have to be Pote who was dispatched first to a burglary alarm at the "Dong Clinic" in the Chinatown part of downtown. He must have repeated the word "Dong" fifty times over the airwaves during his time at the doctor's office.

He was always glad to share his good fortune when stumbling upon some couple engaged in a public sex act. We knew that he would call for backup.

Officer Pote's life would forever change one spring day in 1984. He arrived at a bank robbery alarm near Seattle Pacific University. The suspect within the bank immediately opened fire on Pote through the tinted bank windows, using an assault rifle. A bullet tore through the officer's left armpit area, narrowly missing his heart. A fierce gun battle followed between the suspect and Officers Pote and Clay Monson. Ultimately, a .357 magnum round from Officer Pote's revolver found the side of the shooter's head. Officers Pote and Monson were rushed to

Harborview Medical Center. Pote suffered from the gunshot wound, while Officer Monson was painfully wounded from ballistic glass fragments.

The suspect was eventually treated for massive brain damage at Harvorview Medical Center for several weeks. As per department policy, uniformed police officers were required to guard the prisoner-turned-patient until his release from the hospital. Early during such process, the ever absent-minded Sergeant Draglund assigned a healing Officer Pote to guard the patient. Without breaking form for a moment, Officer Pote accepted such order. The officer told the Sergeant he would be happy to guard the bank robber whom had shot him. He pulled out his massive handgun and advised the roll call, "I can't wait to show this to the guy and ask, do you remember this?"

According to witnesses, even while pinned down from a hail of automatic gunfire at the robbery scene, Officer Pote could be heard screaming at the suspect, "Bull-*shiiiiit!*"

Officer Pote is now retired. His final assignment was to a telephonic reporting unit within the 9-1-1 center. It could be said that his zeal for patrol work was never the same, after experiencing the near-death experience at Seafirst Bank. S.P.D. now misses having their personal John Candy within their ranks.

***

Chapter 11: Lifestyles of the rich and famous

His and her grace

During a career as a big-city police officer, almost all of us will come in contact with many celebrities and powerful individuals. Wherever "important" people go, the police shall be there for their protection. Some officers get more opportunities than others, depending on specialty assignments and other reasons. For myself, usually the "other reason" was that the important people felt more comfortable having a six foot six and a half, 230 pound man in uniform standing beside them — or in front of them in the case of politicians. I often observed that I was the designated "bullet-catcher." Off-duty jobs also entailed Hollywood movie set assignments for myself.

It was thus that one assignment entailed standing at the front of a receiving line for the arrival of Queen Elizabeth. All officers were ordered to wear their finest full uniforms and hats in anticipation of the arrival of her highness at Boeing Field, Seattle in the summer of 1983. The royal airplane touched down exactly on time, and the gentlemen with accents and huge bulges beneath their suit jackets began to become animated while "blending in" with the crowds.

Dozens of camera crews were assembled on the tarmac. Our governor, U.S. Senators, Mayor, and local members of Congress displayed a jousting match that would have made medieval knights proud. If only the public could see how childishly they can behave while seeking attention. We had to keep straight faces while a local former football hero-turned Congressman Norm Dicks actually applied copious amounts of rouge on his vast cheeks before prancing in front of the cameras. His pompousness, ever willing to express how important he was to the cops, resembled a bad mall Santa Claus.

While the plane had been on the ground for nearly forty-five minutes, there was no sign of the Queen. She had apparently entered a nearby hangar and was going through some sort of traditional protocol. We surmised that she was polishing her crown. We became increasingly bored. Our only source of stimulation was a British subject in the crowd whom engaged officers in conversation while awaiting his beloved Queen. The officers immediately bonded with the man. He was extraordinarily charming and pleasant. Plus, he reeled off scores of hilarious dirty jokes, one after another. It was all we could do to keep straight faces while he continued his impressive monologue.

Eventually, after military marching bands played incessant anthems and cameras flashed, the Queen's entourage could be seen. The officers snapped to attention in their receiving lines. The tallest of our crowd, I could narrate her approach to other officers via radio. I could see the armed British secret service moving jointly moving with U.S. Secret Service agents, yet I still could not see the Queen. The group would take a step and stop, then take another. The progress was seemingly painstaking. Finally, they walked past our positions. The guards separated, and I looked downward for the Queen... and downward, and downward. She seemed to be incredibly tiny. I guess I had expected a giant. But, like a true lady, she extended her tiny hand to each of us. We fumbled our ways through bows and watched her walk away.

The British impromptu comedian finally commented, "Well, I'd best be off... best of life to you lads." We said goodbye via our smiles. The man then walked up to the Queen, took her arm, and stated, "Coming dear." The security details did not blink. Indeed, the comic was none other than Prince Phillip, husband of the Queen. He presented a fascinating contrast to the stoic and regal queen. The good prince was easily one of the boys.

***

Have it your way, Liza.

One spring day in 1985 I was working a daytime downtown patrol shift on a busy Friday afternoon. It was raining miserably at rush hour. Thus traffic was at a near stand-still. I was slowed in traffic in front of the famously ostentatious Four Seasons Hotel. From out of the plaza area of the hotel a middle-aged woman called out and waved to me. She was walking rapidly toward my car. I noted that her brunette hair was flying haphazardly in the wind. She was strutting in very high heels, and was dressed in a fur coat and evening dress. She was getting pummeled by rain and wind. Perplexed, I stopped my car as I heard the strange woman calling out, "Officer! Officer!" at an impressive volume. I dreaded what the apparently crazy woman had in store for me, as I logged out on radio.

Suspicious of the crazy woman's intent, I rolled down the passenger window and allowed her to lean into the car. She laughed and thanked me for stopping. Her voice was strangely familiar. She laughed further and stated, "This is probably gonna sound crazy, but I'm an actress. I have a show to do in a couple hours and I'm starving! I wouldn't feed this hotel's food to my dog."

Still cautious, I inquired of the strange woman what it was that she thought the police could do for her. She responded that she had summoned a cab, and that no such cab appeared. She offered that she prayed that New York cabbies would club Seattle cabbies to death someday. She further stated that she had an uncontrollable craving for Burger King's Big Whopper burger. Grudgingly, I finally offered that she seat herself in the passenger seat of the patrol car, and out of the weather.

I finally commented to the comical woman that she was familiar, but that I could not place her. She responded, "Oh great, I must be washed up. Could ya tell the tabloids that and have em leave me alone?" Then it clicked... Liza Minelli! I apologized for not recognizing her, and she only laughed more. She offered that I could make up for the personal affront by getting her through the traffic and to a local Burger King.

I was delighted to comply. She was hilarious. Liza stated that her craving for the big burger was strange. She then added, "But don't go tellin' those damned tabloids I'm knocked up or something huh?" I told her that I would refrain.

During the fifteen minutes it took to wind through traffic and drive through the drive-up lane at the Lake Union Burger King, Liza was pure entertainment. She told remarkable stories and jokes. She was very fond of Seattle and was loving performing "Cabaret" at the local theater. As her order came due at the drive-up window I produced cash to pay. This led to a heated argument over who would pay the six dollars for a Whopper with cheese and chocolate shake. Liza finally relented after stating, "Hell, you're giant, have a big gun, and I'm in *your* car...you win!" She was absolutely delightful during the short drive back to her hotel.

As I sought to drop Liza back at her hotel, she volunteered to give me an autograph. I thanked her, but advised that the only autographs I cared about were in my ticket-book. With that, Liza laughed heartily. The great lady gave me a kiss on the cheek and told me that I was a "doll and life-saver." Liza patted me on the face before exiting the patrol car. I told her, "Someday I'm gonna put this in a book." Liza answered, "Fine, but just make damned sure you make no mention of my hair today." With that, Liza Minelli strutted away toward the hotel.

***

Yes, Mr. Vice President

During the fall of 1984 the city of Seattle would be graced by visits from the two main candidates vying for the presidency of the United States. Former Vice President Walter "Fritz" Mondale was seeking to unseat standing President Ronald Reagan. At the time, Washington State was believed to be a key swing state in the election. Behind the scenes looks at each candidate provided your author with poignant insight into the stark contrast between the two men.

On the evening prior to Vice President Mondale's campaign speech, he was housed in the Presidential suite of the towering Westin Hotel on the scenic 50th floor. Your author, then a young patrol officer, was assigned to stand next to a Secret Service agent. We were located down the corridor from Mr. Mondale's room. Posts nearer his room entailed the coupling of Secret Service agents and specially trained Seattle Police "Tac Squad" (SWAT) officers. Yet, on each shift of candidate protection, a member of rank and file patrol officers was assigned with another Secret Service agent. The purpose of such assignment was simply to post an individual very familiar with uniformed police peers. Imposters in police uniforms were always a concern. Your author was thrilled to have such an assignment, as the Secret Service agents were always found to be very impressive.

I would soon learn that the assignment was not exactly a coveted detail. I had been chosen because the assignment was incredibly boring. We literally stood in one place for ten straight hours overnight. I was able to visit with the agents, whom rotated every two hours. Their insight and wit was highly enjoyable, as we visited in hushed tones. They did break the monotony.

Suddenly, the presidential candidate burst out of his hotel room. It was around two thirty A.M. He was dressed in his pajamas. Secret Service agents immediately began speaking into their sleeves, advising peers of unexpected "movement." The Vice President paraded down the hall and walked all the way down to our position. He then screamed out, "Would you people shut the f--k up. I'm trying to sleep in there, God Dammit!" I spoke not a word, while the agent offered his sincere apologies. With that, the former Vice President re-entered his hotel room with a slam.

Incredulous, I turned to the agent and whispered, "Did I do something wrong?" The agent advised, "You don't have to whisper, really. Those walls are so fortified you couldn't hear a bomb blast in there. He's just that way."

The next day the big speech occurred. Some thirty thousand people gathered near the scenic and historic Pike Place Market in order to hear the candidate speak. As usual, the very tall young officer was placed near the stage, presumably as a bullet-catcher. The drama of presidential politics was intriguing. Just prior to the arrival of the candidate's limousine and entourage, another limousine and van of advisors pulled up beside the stage.

In anticipation of the arrival of the candidate and the corresponding whirring of network television cameras, the advisors were seen to pull out mass quantities of signs. The political operatives handed many signs to the nearby crowd, positioned near the bank of television cameras. The members of the crowd shrugged and complied with requests to hold and wave the signs toward the cameras. The signs read, "Teachers for Mondale." Others indicated various unions for the candidate, various religions, etc. Clearly, the whole presentation was staged.

The limousine arrived behind the stage, and the former Vice President sat patiently inside the tinted windowed vehicle. We were amazed to see him extending both middle fingers through the window toward the line of police officers with a scowl. No one else, sans his advisors, was in the area.

Finally, the network cameras unanimously presented thumbs-up to the advisors, and the candidate bounced from the limousine, all smiles and pleasantry. Suffice to say, the uniformed officers were less than impressed. Apparently, as history would indicate, neither were the American voters.

***

The Ronnie Right Hand

Not long after the public gathering for former Vice President Mondale, incumbent President Reagan was scheduled to arrive in town. His presentation was to be made at the Seattle Center Arena, to a smaller crowd of 9,000 people. The fanfare around his visit, as with every President, was an awesome spectacle. Secret Service agents arrive in the area a couple weeks prior to a scheduled visit. Arrangements are made to scour every inch of a hotel for security measures. Hundreds of miles of electronic communications lines are installed along travel routes, reminiscent of Super Bowl preparations by media. Every man-hole cover along a travel route is searched and then sealed. Any further tampering would be obvious. The four-ton limousine arrives a day earlier by military cargo plane. It is a rolling, heavily armed fortress.

The actual arrival of a President is impressive. Air Force One is famous for touching down *exactly* on time, right down to the second. The aircraft itself is beautiful and symbolic. The President is greeted by marching bands, banks of television cameras, and a huge entourage of motorcycle police, F.B.I. SWAT, and Secret Service. A military helicopter, obviously armed with missiles and Gatling guns, hovers over the motorcade at all times.

It was thus such a spectacle as President Reagan arrived at Seattle Center for his speech. I was eventually assigned to a back-stage area. My partner, Kent Carpenter and I were separated by assignments. As always, other officers and I were coupled with Secret Service agents. To my surprise, President Reagan and his entourage suddenly emerged behind the stage out of a corridor that was concealed. The President was seen to be cinching his tie and batting his hair. He was immaculate, as always. Music was playing at the front of the stage area and the crowd was becoming animated. Advisors gestured to the President to wait for some unknown reason. Yet, the President began to walk toward the stage entrance area. He then took a sudden turn.

The Secret Service agents seemed perplexed as the President altered his route. He began to walk crisply across the concrete floor straight toward me. I looked out of the corner of my eyes to each side, wondering what it was the President saw. I saw the Secret Service agents glaring at me. I became quite nervous as the President of the United States slowed his walk and stopped directly in front of me. While the Secret Service agents cradled their weaponry through their suit jackets, the President extended his right hand outward to me. I was impressed to see what a big man he was. Ronald Reagan must have stood six feet three inches tall, as he did not have to look upward much toward my six foot six plus self. He was a very sturdily built 220 pounds. He was like John Wayne.

My heart raced as I extended my hand to the President. I knew that the Secret Service was very uncomfortable with the President standing before an armed individual. Yet they could say nothing. The President's and my hands met. Ronald Wilson Reagan gave a handshake like a real man. He was strong and sincere, and pumped my hand heartily. He looked me straight in the eye with his very blue eyes. With his other hand he patted me on the shoulder. He then said, "God bless you boys, keep up the good work."

With that, the President turned and headed toward the stage. He waved his hand toward all of the officers and agents and gave a sincere smile. An advisor told him it was time to go to the stage. He uttered a goodbye to all behind the stage, and stated, "Well, time to go to work." With that, he was gone into the crowd.

Later in the day, I would relate the occurrence to my beloved partner. Kent was extremely jealous. Or so he said. As he commented, "Yeah, they always go to the tall guy." And, indeed, that was true. Yet, I pointed out the other aspect of my height. I was always the first to be spat upon by angry crowds as well. It all, it would seem, is a trade-off.

To this day, I have never washed my right hand—my Ronald Wilson Reagan hand. I can't understand why no one will greet me.

***

Hooray for Hollywood

While working off-duty for several years on movie sets that were abundant in Seattle in the late 80's and early 90's, your author had many occasions to see Hollywood stars at their best and worst. I either became a tremendous fan of certain celebrities, or would not walk across the street to invest in their profits. While the job itself of "guarding" a movie set was entirely boring, watching the goings-on was intriguing. Some directors and actors were artists with a profound level of professionalism toward their craft. Others were spoiled children with far too much money with which to play.

I could finally comprehend the accolades heaped upon a successful director. The responsibilities of a director reminded me of that of a college football coach. They had to be aware of every activity regarding hundreds of employees simultaneously. They also had to see that each activity meshed. It was a huge undertaking. On top of that, the directors had to call the plays from hundreds of different angles and anticipate what the camera would capture. It was amazing how much light had to be bounced off of every conceivable angle in order to create a "dark" room. A bright sunny day, even on a bright sunny day, required thousands of candle powers to appear normal on film. A passing aircraft miles away could ruin sound production. I gained a whole new respect for the flakey big bosses from down south.

By and large, the Hollywood people were eccentric, but very nice people. They took a great deal of pride in their craft and had a discernible joy toward their vocations. The majority of the big actors and actresses were actually quite nice people. For one thing, they did not have to put on airs around uniformed police officers. We'd learned long ago that people are just people. They are no different, other than their paychecks, from any other human being. They still left a significant odor when they exited the restrooms.

Your author never had the honor of meeting the mega-stars of decades past, as did my older peer officers. The "old crusties," as we referred to them, had really met some interesting folks in the 60's and 70's. Part of the fun in police work is the collective stories and observations of the entire force. Their opinions of those met would closely mirror ours. Thus, a reliable scouting report of the "hot shots" was always available.

The most beloved star ever met by members of the department was clearly John Wayne. But John Wayne's co-star, Eddie Albert was highly liked as well. The crusties did not think much of the Beatles, describing them as "smelly drugged out hippies." But they absolutely thought the world of Elvis Presley. They described Elvis as an extremely kind and mannered "kid."

Over a career, one forgets how many stars or powerful persons they've met. I will list many, with my brief impressions of each:

Dan Rather. What an arrogant, obnoxious, rude, jerk. Nuff said.

Katie Courick. Incredibly cold-blooded phony. Was quoted by numerous cops at the Columbine Scene as giggling, "Fresh meat huh? ...if it bleeds, it leads." Seattle cops shared the same impressions.

Tom Brokaw. Very pleasant, humorous, and personable. Extremely mannered and professional at all times.

Tom Selleck. (I got to bodyguard him for a three day volleyball tournament at the University of Washington). A very nice, mannered, intelligent man. He was very grounded and principled. And he was one heck of a volleyball player.

Tom Hanks. (Movie set of Sleepless in Seattle. We took him out for drinks one night). An absolute hoot. As down to earth as you get. He always found something to laugh about.

Paul and Linda McCartney. (We arranged for them to go riding our police horses in a local park before a concert at the Kingdome). They were incredibly gracious and appreciative. You could just see how much they treasured their privacy and the pastoral setting. Very personable people whom loved people one on one, and cringed at crowds. You could see that they adored one another.

Theresa Russell. (Filmed Black Widow with Debra Winger). The daughter of legendary Jane Russell, Theresa never made it big-time in the shows. Far more beautiful in person than the camera can capture. She was highly integrous. She refused to sleep her way to the top in Hollywood. While born with a silver spoon, she never showed such an attitude. She studied acting with profound effort. One of the most wonderful stars I have ever met. I always hope she makes it big.

Debra Winger. (Filmed Black Widow). One of the most spoiled and foul celebrities I have ever met. Had to have two entire trailers for her and her dog, while the extras stood in freezing cold outside such trailers for hours. Foul-mouthed and pampered. The movie company had to spend thousands to fly her dog up to the site on a private jet.

Kiefer Sutherland. (Filmed The Vanishing). While highly regarded by the crew for his acting talents, the guy was a total drunk. The minute his scene was over, he was back in a trailer and drinking. He'd spend hours at a local lounge on Lake Union drinking. He could easily down a fifth of whiskey per day. He had nothing to do with anyone outside of his entourage.

Shaquille O'Neill. Absolutely one of the guys. Shaq

wanted, in the worst of ways, to become a full-time police officer someday. He loved to join us for ride-alongs. The only problem with Shaq is that he wanted to arrest half of the world. His hands are enormous! My hand looked like that of a two-year-old when shaking his.

Julius "Doctor J" Erving. (NBA All-Star game). The good doctor was one of the most gracious sports stars any of us had ever met. He was down to earth, mannered, and intelligent. We absolutely loved him.

Charles Barkley. He's all an act on television. Charles is a staunch conservative in many respects. He is highly respectful of law enforcement, and in fact, donates a great deal of money to police unions and survivor funds. A very nice and bright man.

Alex Rodriguez. Actually a pretty shy young man. He was very mannered, and quite pleasant. A lousy driver. Scraped his Mercedes about four times on a curb while trying to park. But, as he pointed out, it's a little tougher to parallel park with a dozen cops watching you do it. Good sense of humor.

Michelle Pfeiffer. Clearly loved her drugs at the time of filming The Fabulous Baker Boys. She was clearly on the planet Neptune for her entire three weeks in the city. Incredibly skinny, and haggard-looking in person.

Jimmy Smits. (Television movie with Judith Light) Professional in all respects. Handled himself with total class. He was friendly and open with everyone. He stands a good six foot eight.

Kris Kristopherson (Television movie). A very down to earth guy. He could clearly become a penniless cowboy tomorrow and be just as happy. He was very unpretentious and liked to laugh at Hollywood itself as an outsider.

Susan Sarandon. A phony and hypocrite. She spent several days in Seattle after the WTO riots and conducted press conferences, referring to the Seattle Police officers as "Jack booted thugs, Gestapo, and repressive bullies with small penises." She then later joined in a colossal tribute in New York to the officers lost in 9-1-1, with her little red ribbon and crocodile tears for the "fallen heroes." She was a vile human being at all times while we had to baby-sit her and Tim Robbins. Strange, strange people.

Singer-- Tom Jones. Total class act at all times. Had some great jokes.

Singer-- Dan Fogelberg. Smoked a world record amount of pot and put on a terrible show. One weird dude.

Violinist Isaac Stern – I was in awe of the greatest violinist ever, as I drove him to the airport. Very gracious and very funny. And he about crushed my hand during a handshake.

Singer – Luciano Pavarotti. An absolute delight of a man. Had a clear zest for life. Oh, how he did love the ladies, especially my attractive female partner for the day.

Jane Fonda. A vile and cruel human. Slapped a little six-year-old girl in the face for presenting her with a rose, and we were ordered not to arrest her. Violent temper, and a self-importance complex. Ted Turner was no better. Both thought they owned the world – not just the Goodwill Games that they sponsored.

President (Senior) and Mrs. Bush. Humble, gracious, and kind people. Mrs. Bush's cookies she brought to us were great!

President Jimmy Carter – Very soft- spoken, genuine, and kind.

Bill Gates – Very pleasant, great dad, teaching humility and kindness to his kids, and truly loves those computers.

My favorite famous or infamous person (depending on your ideology) I ever met via this vocation would easily be Colonel Oliver North. Vast numbers of officers were summoned to provide security for him while he spoke to a crowd at Seattle Center Coliseum. This was shortly after the Iran/Contra controversy. Thousands listened to Oliver North within the arena, while thousands more protested violently outside the venue. While the city would fund security for marijuana-smoking "Hempfest", parades featuring "Dykes on Bikes," and various flag burnings, Colonel North's security costs would all be billed to he and supporters. We could hear Mr. North's speech over the loud speakers while protesters pelted us with excrement of all sorts, bottles, and red paint. His speech was one of the most inspirational orations we had collectively ever heard.

Long after all the crowds had left, an exhausted Oliver North emerged from within the arena. He was doused in perspiration from the bright lights. His handlers wished to rush him out of the arena, to an airport, and to another venue. Yet, a few officers greeted the Colonel and wished him well. He stopped and visited with each of them. He then proceeded to walk around the arena and personally thank every one of the 85 officers on the scene. He shook each of our hands and had very gracious comments to make. Ultimately, he stood for photographs with each of us. He even autographed a program for my ultra- liberal sister in law whom despised him, sending her his love. Ultimately, each and every officer donated the overtime money gathered straight back to Colonel North. He was a great American.

Finally, while I have never met her, all of the Hollywood people advised me that Bette Midler is the nicest star on the planet. They related stories of extras vomiting on a set, only to have Bette run to grab towels and clean up the mess. Other people would run to volunteer to take over the clean- up detail, only to be told by Bette, "Oh honey, I've cleaned up more barf than you'll ever see."

I hope to meet Bette more than any other.

***

Cop Culture: United or divided?

While, from the outside of the force, cops may appear to be a very united corps, nothing could be further from the truth. All police departments possess deep rifts within such. Much of this is due to the necessary personality for police-work. Type A personalities are a must for police-work. A police officer must be confident, decisive, and willing to place oneself at the fore of any situation. It is thus predictable that groups of type Alpha personalities may beget competition and conflict. It is not dissimilar to a pack of wolves.

The Seattle Police Department is known to be one of the most divided agencies in the state. Some of the reasons become apparent. Others become complex. It is your author's belief that the logistics and demographics of the city of Seattle contribute to the phenomenon. Seattle, being an island of sort, is a huge commuter city. While the population is 600,000, the daytime population swells to an estimated 1.5 million. It is a nice place to make a living, but more difficult in which to live. Housing prices are very high. Busing caused huge problems with the public schools. And horrible traffic, traversing the finite bridge spaces into the city, makes any commute an adventure.

While over 80% of all San Francisco Police officers live in the city, only 12% of all Seattle officers live within the limits. Thus, police officers whom commute from every direction of the city may well live 50-100 miles from their peers. Socializing after work hours becomes problematic.

At least within Seattle P.D., many rifts are results of being our own worst enemies. Substantial rifts exist between black and white, male and female, old and young, detective and patrol, and sworn police employees versus civilian employees. Political favoritism toward one employee creates a domino effect of jealousy and distrust along the lines. And a highly left-leaning major city is indeed rife with politics.

When lives or serious police-work is on the line, 99% of all officers work as a team. Yet, during the mundane daily activities, distrust and competition is often rampant. A saying often voiced among today's troops refers to the need to move one's metal protective chest plate in the bullet proof vest to the back—an obvious reference to the concept of back-stabbing.

***

Chapter 12: The Gang Unit

During the late 1980's and early 1990's, the city of Seattle experienced the inevitability of the gang culture migrating from California, Chicago, and the East Coast. The phenomenon was as predictable as snow melt. The response by the leadership of the Seattle Police Department was no less predictable. The Police Chief was in total denial. In fact, he and his staff were in such denial about the gang phenomenon that the mere use of the dreaded "G" word over radio by officers was grounds for discipline. The word "Gang" became as political as the word abortion. A city, once yearly renowned for being America's "most livable city" by national media, was experiencing substantial growing pains. Street-level officers observed gangs roaming in the vast majority of the city's neighborhoods. The brazen and colorful gangs were recruiting. They were indoctrinating. And they were killing and wounding. All of the rank and file officers predicted that the city would not take action until the wrong, newsworthy, innocent victim lost a life.

The cause celebre` of innocent victims would take the name of Mellissa "Missy" Fernandez. Missy was an attractive and very popular 19-year-old engineering student at the University of Washington. She was a graduate of nearby Ballard High School in Northwest Seattle. On March 23rd, 1994 she was visiting with friends on the grounds of the high school around the lunch hour. She was apparently oblivious to the "bad blood" that existed between two rival gangs. Fights had occurred between the "23rd Street Young Oriental Troop" aka "Y.O.T.'S" and the "Bad Side Posse." Weapons had been brandished, and death threats had been uttered. The Y.O.T.'s were primarily Filipino and Vietnamese in composition, while the B.S.P. was dominated by Samoan members.

On that fateful March 23rd afternoon, Missy Fernandez would find herself standing in- between two moving vehicles in a vast parking lot corridor. The vehicles faced and passed one another slowly, like two wolves seeking dominance. Missy Fernandez somehow found herself wedged between the two gangs. She was known and liked by both groups. Sixteen-year-old passenger Brian Ronquillo, of the Y.O.T's fired at least eight rounds from a nine-millimeter semi-automatic handgun. His intended target was the Bad Side Posse. Instead, Missy Fernandez was struck in the head. She died nearly instantly.

Suddenly a huge human outcry resulted. Media attention poured out regarding the shooting. Previously, numerous incidents involving black victims and suspects in predominantly black neighborhoods had merited only ancillary coverage. Yet a pretty, part-Caucasian victim from an upper middle class family, gunned down in a predominantly white neighborhood became front-page news. Seattle officially had a "gang" problem. The death was as much the fault of the Police Department leadership as that of the gang members themselves. Suddenly, Police command had to take action.

Lieutenant Emmett Kelsie was selected to create a Seattle Police Gang Unit. He was the perfect choice. Lieutenant Kelsie was a 28 year veteran of the Seattle Police Department. He was a fifty-year-old black man. He stood six feet tall with a shaved head. Huge arms and hands hung by his side, and he weighed some 230 pounds. He was mostly comprised of muscle, but also sported a healthy belly region that he often referred to as "the signs of prosperity." Once derided by some officers for alleged "affirmative action promotions," Emmett had ultimately gained the admiration and respect of virtually all peers. He was a very bright, reasoned, and articulate man. He was nicknamed "Cool Papa" by many officers, and his reputation lauded his wisdom, charm, and sense of humor.

By the summer of 1994 the Seattle Police Gang Unit would field four full detective squads. Each squad had six members. There were two staggered night shifts and two staggered day shifts. Three of the squads would be attired in unique Gang Unit attire. They wore evolving models of polo shirts or black Dickies with distinctive gang unit lettering and a unique green and black cobra insignia. Black jeans completed the attire. Lt. Kelsie created the image with great forethought. He sought an image of uniqueness, clearly official, and somewhat intimidating to the gangs. Indeed, they looked like a gang unto themselves, which was part of the intended effect.

One night squad would focus primarily upon black gangs such as Crips, Bloods, and Black Gangster Disciples. The other would specialize in the Asian gangs, such as Young Oriental Troop, Bad Side Posse, 23rd Street Diablos, et al. The Sergeant of the black gang specialists was Martin White. Sergeant White was a seasoned 26-year veteran of the department whom had worked virtually every assignment within the department. He was a tall and highly fit black man of 48 years of age. A former decorated military man, he was known for his fairness to his troops and calm under pressure. He was also an expert on any brand of jazz music.

The eventual Sergeant of the Asian gang specialists would be Roger Rusness. A 45-year-old veteran former patrol officer, Sergeant Rusness was better known as "Buddha." His physical appearance most assuredly did resemble statues of Buddha. A huge and strong half Chinese, half Filipino man, "Buddha" had a photographic memory for hundreds, if not thousands of Seattle Asian gang members. His, and Sergeant White's squads would serve staggered late night shifts and provide a visible deterrent city-wide. Their most important task would be that of gaining profound recognition of the gang culture in the city and it's thousands of "players."

A third similarly attired daytime squad would focus upon the city's schools and the growing gang phenomenon thereabout. Seattle school students were becoming fearful of going to school. Lt. Kelsie selected fifty year-old Sergeant Dianne Newsome to supervise the school squad. Sergeant Newsome was a former school teacher and a mother of three teenage sons. She was well equipped for dealing with youth violence. She offered a unique crime- fighting tactic of bringing gang members' mothers to crime scenes. Scoffed at by peers and the public initially, her unorthodox methods proved highly effective. Hardened gang members would be reduced to frightened children upon the arrival of their mothers.

For these three squads, Lt. Kelsie opined that the greatest protection for gangs was anonymity. It would be his detectives' tasks to eliminate that protective anonymity. In essence the detectives were expected to know what would happen before it happened. They would thus either prevent gang violence, or immediately know which suspects to seek were such to occur.

A final squad of suit and tie true Investigations Detectives was the last piece of the Gang Unit puzzle. Such squad would serve to conduct in-depth investigations of all gang related offenses, from drive-by shootings, to rapes, drug dealing, and car thefts. They were to be tasked with documenting the extensive gang component to thousands of Seattle crime cases. An ingenious Detective Ed Harris would compile the entire gang puzzle into a sophisticated computer intelligence database—something yet to be developed in most departments or companies during that era.

The only mistake Lieutenant Kelsie made in choosing the talent for his squads was allowing your author to interview for the Dectective-Sergeant position for the Investigations Squad. Your author had been promoted to Sergeant two years prior, after thirteen years in patrol and Street Narcotics Anti-Crime team assignments. I was ending my two year commitment to the 9-1-1 center and anxious to resume a position on the streets. A respected peer Sergeant transferring from the initial Gang Unit recommended my consideration for promotion to Lieutenant Kelsie. I had heard from other cynical peers that Lt. Kelsie only truly wanted a minority of some sort for the position. Some even claimed the Lieutenant to be racist. Nonetheless, I considered the recommendation by the earlier Sergeant and sent my paperwork.

I was surprised to receive a call from Lt. Kelsie's secretary inviting me for an invitation. I did not take the opportunity particularly seriously. As so often happens in the Seattle Police Department regarding interviews for "jobs," the openings are often pre-filled. The interviews only serve as a rude window-dressing to a pre-determined outcome. In addition, I had very little formal investigatory experience in detective units prior to applying for such position. I knew I hadn't a chance.

It was thus with such a defeatist attitude that your author sought to be interviewed by Lieutenant Kelsie. I had never met the man in person. I sat nervously upon the leather chair in the Lieutenant's office in an old dilapidated downtown Bitterman Building—a brick building once owned by the Police Guild, across from the County Courthouse. The Lieutenant stared at me with his hands behind his head for a moment and smiled. He took in a deep breath and exhaled slowly. I felt I was being sized-up, and hoped that my tie wasn't crooked.

Finally, Lieutenant Kelsie asked me, "Are you thirsty?" I answered that I was indeed thirsty. With that, he said, "Walk with me, my man." We walked three blocks to the nearby 76-story Columbia Center. All during the walk Lieutenant Kelsie explained to me what his philosophies and goals were for the Gang Unit. I was bought a cup of coffee at Starbucks and said nothing about hating coffee. The coffee break turned into a lunch break. I was invited to remove my tie and get comfortable. The conversation spanned from the Lieutenant's experience as a young man from Mississippi who joined the Air Force at seventeen, to his nearly thirty years with SPD.

We eventually walked back to the Gang Unit office as the Lieutenant explained his views on race, politics, troubled youths, the courts, et al. Each of my philosophies and beliefs were examined. By the end of the day, I had conversed for nearly eight hours with Emmett Kelsie about virtually every aspect of life, family, core beliefs, and police-work. It was a relaxed and highly enjoyable visit with a very wise, humorous, and gracious man. It did not feel like I had been grilled for an entire day.

I was shocked to receive a call from Lieutenant Kelsie's secretary, Tonya Porter, the next day. I was to meet again with the Lieutenant that afternoon. I figured the rejection was at least swift and merciful. Upon my return I could hear the Lieutenant laughing inside his office with a high pitched giggle that was to prove infectious. The other detectives filed out of the Lieutenant's office and he immediately extended his huge right hand. As he shook my hand he smiled and stated, "Congratulations, Detective-Sergeant. Welcome to the Gang Unit." With that, a fascinating three-year adventure would commence. For the first time in my life I would have weekends off and regular hours — well, until the shootings started. And, for the next fourteen years of my career in detective units, with each Friday leading to a coveted *real* weekend or holiday with family, I would whisper to myself, "Thank You Emmett." I would work for the best boss, and most diverse and talented unit, I have ever experienced in my life.

***

The West Seattle Bridge Killings

On September 17th, 1997 at 2:38 A.M. on a Wednesday my home phone rang. As usual, I snarled out of a slumber at who could be calling at such an un-Godly hour. Fortunately, for that reason, the phone had been placed next to my wife Mahala. Mahala reminded me, in my drowsiness, that the call would undoubtedly be work-related. With that I managed to mumble a half-sincere, "Martin, can I help you?" As would always then occur, a staccato oration would follow from an insultingly chipper 9-1-1 center Chief Dispatcher: "Sergeant Martin, this is Brian Oesterriecher, Seattle Police Radio…sir, we have a drive-by shooting on the West Seattle Bridge…five people are hit…Fire is there…William Sector Patrol and Sergeant are on the scene… homicide is going, and they want to talk to you on Frequency 7." As was common practice for myself at that time of the day, I then responded with an erudite, "Huh?" I was awake enough to understand the second round.

A quick radio conversation then followed which confirmed all that I had been told over the phone. I quickly dressed in my suit and tie and trench coat that were stored conveniently for such an event. The trench coat just seemed to fit the image. I thus had the privilege of choosing which of my detectives I wished to deprive of any substantive sleep. Given the seriousness of the circumstances, I chose to wake four of my detectives. Unlike the necessarily wide-awake Chief Dispatcher Oesterreicher, I had a different approach to "the call." As was my practice, I would call each detective quickly, advise them that it was a wake-up call for a call-out, and remind them that I would call back in five minutes when they were awake. Each would have a cup of coffee started and a notebook ready upon my follow-up call.

As always, my wife was appalled as I grabbed my bottle of Jolt Cola from the refrigerator and began singing, "Another One Bites The Dust" while headed off to work. (Please see previous section on "gallows humor.")

My squad arrived nearly in sync with one another upon the bridge. While we had all responded to countless shooting scenes, the setting immediately struck us as surreal. A very busy elevated arterial was brought to a standstill. Patrol vehicles had each end of the freeway closed-off. The flashing lights could be seen for miles. Media helicopters buzzed overhead. Several patrol officers and a patrol Sergeant had the scene cordoned off with yellow crime scene tape.

Already on the scene was the legendary Homicide Sergeant "Big Don" Cameron and two of his trusted detectives. This indicated that the shooting was fatal. Per department policy, in any fatal shooting the Gang Unit would serve a back-up and advisory role to the Homicide Unit. Yet, we would always go well beyond such parameters, as our trust was gained. Sergeant Cameron had often served as a trainer to me in the past, when first assigned crime scene responsibilities. Rather than take a disdainful demeanor to the younger Sergeant from a conceivably competing unit, Don had always been gracious. I admired the huge bear of a man greatly. He had forgotten more about homicides than most others would ever dream of learning.

Sergeant Cameron directed me to walk with him to a car that was parked at the curb lane of the freeway and surrounded by crime scene tape. The vehicle was surrounded by massive pools of coagulating blood. There was broken glass glittering upon the blood and pavement. A flat driver's rear tire was visible, with a jack partially extended beneath the vehicle's under-carriage. Clearly, the victims had been changing a flat tire.

Both doors of the compact were open and additional massive pools of blood within the vehicle could be seen. The interior was shredded by bullets. It immediately reminded me of Bonnie and Clyde's final resting place. Beneath the driver's door, wedged partially beneath the vehicle, lay the first body. Nineteen year-old Son Hoang-Vu Le had obviously panicked under a hail of gunfire and sought to crawl beneath the small car. From first glance, he had been struck by at least seven gunshots. He lay contorted in a fetal and very final position beneath the vehicle. One bullet had removed the majority of the top of his head. Fire department paramedics had not even attempted treatment. As I and my detectives continued to bend over, stare, and shake our heads, Sergeant Cameron said, "Oh, that's nothin', come see *this* one." He directed us to the front of the vehicle. Lying in front of the bumper was what remained of the second body. The body of 20 year-old Mr. Visa Khamovongsa was literally cut in half from gun-fire. The numbers of bullet wounds were innumerable. I commented that in all my life experiences I had never seen a body cut in half by bullets.

Virtually simultaneously, Sergeant Cameron and my Detective Larry Brotherton responded, "I have." Both of them nodded at the other, "Vietnam."

We would learn that three other victims had been badly

injured by gunfire. They had been trapped within the back seat of the vehicle and tried desperately to escape. Two sisters — 21 year-old Jennifer Chung and 17 year-old Christina, along with 17 year-old friend, Suzie Park, were seated in a cramped position when the fusillade of bullets erupted. Eleven bullets pierced Suzie Park. Jennifer Chung was struck in the eye and instantly blinded. Christina Chung had a bullet permanently lodged in her leg. All three were at Harborview Medical Center in serious to critical condition.

Both detective units worked for many hours, and into the following evening completing processing of the crime scene. The numbers of bullet strikes would be found to go well into three digits. Clearly, the shooters had used automatic weapons. The drive-by nature of the murders indicated a strong likelihood of gang involvement.

A lengthy three month investigation would follow. While the Homicide Unit performed admirably with evidence collection, witness interviews, and tip-line follow-ups, it would be the Gang Unit that produced the substantive lead. It was only via word of mouth in the gang community that the bragging of two purported gang members came to the fore. Competing Asian gang members related to Sergeant Rusness, aka "Buddha," and other detectives that they knew second-hand of the involvement of "Cisco" and "Yu-Bad" in the shootings. To the Gang Unit, monikers were gold. The Asian specialists quickly produced the names of Marvin Francisco and Emerson Yumul to the Homicide Unit. They explained that both were known to be loose affiliates of the Young Oriental Troop gang. Once they so advised Sergeant Cameron, he simply remarked, "What the hell are you waiting for? Bring em in."

The Investigations detectives and Intelligence Detective Ed Harris quickly obtained all known addresses for the suspects, as well as known associates. The Gang Unit, as a team, produced the suspects in the homicide office within twenty-four hours. Their usual hangouts were well known to the Gang Unit detectives. As with most gang members, each postured mightily within the view of the other that they would not speak. They claimed that their gang bonds could not be broken. Yet, as is also commonplace with such a culture, they each quickly sought to turn on the other during interviews out of sight of their peer.

Ultimately, both would admit that the motive for the profound act of violence was a simple misunderstanding. They had mistaken the youths on the side of the road, repairing a flat tire, for other gang members. They thought the group had driven by earlier in the night and extended middle fingers. They each implicated the other for firing the dozens of rounds from a fully automatic Uzi type firearm. Evidence and further follow-up would implicate Francisco as the actual shooter. Yumul was the driver. Other gang members may have been passengers, but that could never be confirmed.

In reality, the innocent victims were guilty only of celebrating the 20th birthday of Visa Khamvongsa. It would be his last. They were at the wrong place at the wrong time.

Ultimately, suspect Emerson Yumul would testify against his partner, Marvin Francisco. He would state that he was the driver of the vehicle, while Francisco opened fire with the machine gun. Yumul would receive a reduced sentence of 20 years minimum for one count of first-degree murder. Marvin Francisco would receive a sentence of life in prison without the possibility of parole for two first-degree murder convictions and three aggravated assaults.

To this day, Jennifer Chung, now blind in one eye, visits the crypt of her boyfriend Visa Khamvongsa on a weekly basis.

Her sister Christina has had over a dozen surgeries to repair internal organ damage and still suffers from double vision. She walks with a profound limp from the one remaining bullet in her leg. Fate, it would seem, turned so quickly deadly, based only upon a gang, a middle finger, and a flattened tire.

***

The downfall of the Young Oriental Troop

As the violence of the Young Oriental Troop (Y.O.T's) grew in scope in the Western Washington area, so too did their thirst for guns. Such a thirst would lead to a fateful friendship, of sorts, with non-gang members. This relationship would forever alter numerous lives. It would directly cost American taxpayers nearly a million dollars.

The cost to victims and their families would prove immeasurable.

On February 19, 1997, an East Wenatchee Washington gun store was robbed. The owner was brutally murdered during the robbery. Usually such an occurrence would merit a footnote, at best, to the Gang Unit of Seattle P.D. Yet the case would have numerous correlations to the Y.O.T. problem in Seattle.

During the early morning hours of the date following the homicide, Officer Dennis Carlson of the Lake Forest Park Washington Police Department telephoned the S.P.D. Gang Unit. He asked to speak with a Gang Unit investigator to "run something by you."

Detective David Murray, of your author's squad was a renowned early bird, and answered the call with his usual jovial demeanor. As I arrived in the office shortly thereafter to start the day, Detective Murray snapped his fingers repeatedly. He was indicating that I should pick up the other line and listen in on the conversation. Numerous excited voices were on the line. All were indicating that Lake Forrest Park Police had in their custody one of three suspects in the East Wenatchee murder. Douglas County Sheriff's investigators were also present with Lake Forest Park P.D. It was believed that Kirkland Washington Police would soon produce the other two suspects from a stake-out in their jurisdiction.

The small town officers were very professional in their presentations, yet the excitement generated by such incidents in their small and friendly jurisdictions was very evident. They soon advised that all suspects were in custody.

Initially, we did not understand why we were being contacted. We snobbishly felt that the small agencies were possibly seeking advice on case investigation. Yet, the callers would prove to be competent and confident of their abilities. What they wished to relate was the knowledge of a gang component to the incidents. Officer Carlson advised that the detained driver of the suspect vehicle, 18-year-old suspect Valerie Chard, had been clearly terrified at the scene of the arrest. She had eventually related to the arresting officers that the guns had been taken in order to sell them to the "Y.O.T's in Seattle." Nearly half of the estimated one hundred stolen guns were found in the trunk of Chard's vehicle. She offered that the sale of the other half had already occurred at the seedy Rest Inn Motel in Seattle the previous night. The officer advised us that the young woman then insisted upon seeing an attorney and would speak no more. She indicated that "Tommy" would be angry with her for talking to the cops.

Kirkland Police would ultimately a stake out a Motel 6 in their jurisdiction. They arrested 21-year-old Thomas Davis as the leader in the homicide. He was being held in the King County Jail. He was accompanied by 17-year-old accomplice Miranda Johnson.

We were to learn that an alert Deputy Wagg of the Douglas County Sheriff's office had found a license number of a vehicle scrawled on a pad by the cash register of the gun store. The license number would turn out to be that of suspect Valerie Chard's vehicle. The deputies had also recovered small fragments of a potato at the crime scene. This would prove important in a subsequent trial. The collaborative police-work of three small agencies would prove to be extremely impressive.

Detective Murray advised the law enforcement colleagues that we were very familiar with the identities of the "Y.O.T.'s" and offered any and all future assistance. He offered that the SPD Gang Unit would most assuredly be in touch. As he hung up the phone, Detective Murray turned to me and asked, with his famous crooked smile, "Well, Sergeant Sir, now what do you wanna do?" I responded, "Well, this is conspiracy to commit robbery and murder, involving multiple agencies, David." Detective Murray maintained his smile and added a slight laugh, "And I say again, Sir, what *do* you wanna do?" A light bulb went off in my head. I smiled at the detective and advised, "Stand-by, I think I know where to go."

Only recently I had met the new Supervisory Agent of the Seattle office of the Bureau of Alcohol Tobacco and Firearms. His name was Dan Kumor. We had met at a formal gathering in the Seattle Federal Building as our federal counterparts wanted to introduce the new local management and supervision of the BATF. Department heads from each agency made quite a show of the meeting. High ranking special agents in charge, or "SAC'S" as referred to by the agency, wished to express their willingness to work closely with SPD. It was their belief that they could specifically assist the SPD Gang Unit in combating the surge in gang gun violence.

At the conclusion of the formal meeting and the obligatory handshakes of respective command staff, Agent Kumor and I visited. We hit it off right away, and I asked him, "Do you like beer?" His response was a hearty, "Hell yeah." We arranged to meet at a much less ostentatious setting a few evenings later.

Dan Kumor was a highly decorated ATF agent whom had recently been promoted to unit Supervisory Agent. He was a thirty year-old athletic and handsome man. He stood six feet two inches tall and was a perfectly fit 200 pounds. His sandy blonde hair, blue eyes, and slightly freckled face gave him the gift of eternal youth. He had once played college hockey and still enjoyed maiming opponents in recreational hockey leagues. Other agents referred to him a "the chick magnet," yet decried that he was married to his job. Agent Kumor's speech and abrupt demeanor quickly identified him as a native New Yorker. He and I were very alike in personality. We preferred cutting the B.S. of governmental red- tape and doing some real police-work. Talk was cheap. We preferred doing something. We pledged that sometime soon the two units would work closely together. It looked to be a perfect marriage of resources — the unlimited funding, training, and technology of the "feds" coupled with the unlimited street experience and knowledge of the "locals."

Armed with such knowledge, I thus knew immediately whom to call regarding the Y.O.T./Sisson gun homicide investigation. Mr. Kumor could hardly disguise his delight at receiving such a call. The local ATF unit had become largely bound with administrative duties and un-cooperation from the local departments prior to the change of management. The BATF would soon find that the new supervisor would move the unit in a rapid forward motion reminiscent of Kumor's famous New York style of driving.

The first meeting with Agent Kumor and two of his employees occurred in the supervisor's office of the SPD Gang Unit. I summoned the experienced and affable Detective Murray to join the meeting as the lead detective. He would be joined by immaculately-dressed Detective Carlos "C-Rob" Blanco. The two of my detectives were selected for the meeting because of their extensive knowledge, experience, and unquestioned reliability and trustworthiness. Besides, Detective Murray had taken the initial phone call.

The ATF agents arrived at the Gang Unit office exactly at the agreed-upon time of nine o'clock A.M. They were polite enough to not chortle at the Spartan surroundings of the old and poorly maintained brick Bitterman Building that was our home. Agent Kumor immediately had to comment that the three large bullet holes in my desk window and in the wall behind my desk were "quite fetching." I explained to him that we believed some of our street gang clientele did not appreciate our unit. Dan chose to seat himself atop the desk of a night Sergeant, across the room and far from the yet to be repaired window. His agents seated themselves similarly. My detectives offered to hold the hands of the feds, and the bantering began.

Agent Kumor introduced his two lead agents — Agent Ben Silva and Agent Doug Crow. Agent Silva could have been mistaken for Fidel Castro. A thirty-nine year-old Puerto Rican man, he stood five feet ten inches tall and was extremely muscular. His face was lost behind a huge beard. Ben clearly had worked innumerable undercover operations. It was obvious he had been around the block a few times. He looked like a Special Forces commando, and I believed he probably had been. Doug Crow stood as the exact opposite to Ben Silva. Doug was tall and thin and quite serious, in contrast to the constantly joking Ben Silva. Doug was a firearms and explosive expert. They appeared to be outstanding choices for a joint operation. Ben Silva had the street level undercover experience, and Doug Crow had the technical knowledge. Agent Crow took voluminous notes of issues at-hand and the gang phenomenon, while Ben seemed to intuitively comprehend the entire picture.

It was the agreement of all parties present that a clear conspiracy to commit heinous crimes had been created by the murderous youths and the Y.O.T.'s. A strategy was soon developed. The two units would meet at the Douglas County Jail in the near future in order to question the three youths held for the murder of Darrel Eugene Sisson. It was our stated hope that the Y.O.T.'s could be infiltrated. It was also our hope to gain insight into the arrangement to purchase the weapons from the killers and use such for widespread violence. It was an ambitious law enforcement operations plan. We did not dread the difficult investigation. What we did dread was gaining approval from department management for an expensive operation to follow.

The meeting adjourned after two hours amicably. I could see that my detectives clearly related well with their ATF counterparts. Ben Silva was already known by some in SPD for his tenacity, spirit of cooperation, and outright craziness. Doug Crow showed that he was bright and reasoned. The only dispute between the two meeting parties was the location of any subsequent meetings. Kumor insisted that the 24th floor of the Federal Building had fewer bullet holes than our current spaces. Reluctantly, we couldn't argue with such logic.

I knew that visiting with my Lieutenant Kelsie would be enjoyable. The wise and learned man listened intently to every word of discussion from my detectives and myself. He sat on the corner of his cluttered desk and repeated, "Uh huh" to all that was said, with his huge hands clasped together. He asked few questions until the end of the discussion. It was clear that every shred of information was committed to memory. He promised that the unit would take rapid action toward implementing an operation, and immediately approved our travels and lodging in Wenatchee Washington. He pledged that arrangements for a joint operation would be well in place upon our return from the small Central Washington town.

Detective Murray and I thus arranged to meet with an agent of ATF in Wenatchee. Agent Scott McKenna was selected by Agent Kumor to join in the interview. Scott had a law degree and fit the part. He was perfectly attired at all times and very well spoken. He was said to be an outstanding interviewer. Detective Murray and I were each provided a department car and gasoline cards, plus expense money. We agreed to meet at the Douglas County Jail at noon the following day. Known for my promptness, I arrived in Wenatchee with plenty of time to spare, after crossing a snowy Blewett Pass. Also known for my ability to get lost in my own driveway, I ended up across the vast Columbia River from the main portion of the city in the exact *opposite* direction of the jail. I thus arrived at the jail plenty late.

After passing through several security checks, I was finally ushered into the maximum-security portion of the jail. Upon my arrival, I was greeted by the ever-smiling Detective Murray. Dave greeted me with a respectful, "Glad you could make it, sir." Deservedly embarrassed, I had to refrain from displaying a childish aw-shucks. Detective Murray advised that the first interview with suspect Valerie Chard had just ended. I felt like an idiot. The attractive, but overweight brunette of 19 years, clad in red jail jump suit with nose and lip piercings, was being escorted back to her cell. Dave looked down upon his tape recorder and extensive notes and patted them. Before he could say a word I knew that he was pleased with what Ms. Chard had shared with he and Agent McKenna.

I listened to the forty-five minute taped interview of Valerie Chard. The young woman was fairly contrite. Yet, it was clear that she was cooperating so as to broker a prosecutorial deal. Her lawyer was clear on that count. She was honest only so much as to benefit herself. But she was primarily honest nonetheless.

Chard advised that she had been running with gang members since the age of fourteen. She had a criminal history of drug abuse, burglaries, and auto theft. Chard admitted to always being "attracted to bad boys." She claimed she had been a victim of child molestation during the majority of her childhood. She advised that she met her latest live-in boyfriend, co-defendant Thomas Davis when he was nineteen years-old. Davis had recently served a year in juvenile prison in Eastern Washington State for a series of automobile thefts, check frauds, and burglaries. He was a "bad boy" and she found him to be highly charismatic. She said that she was flattered that such a "good looking guy" would be willing to be boyfriend to a "fat girl like me." Almost reminiscent of Manson disciples, Chard advised that she would do "anything for him to keep him." She also stated that she was simultaneously afraid of Davis because she knew he had previously killed another person.

Ms. Chard related that a seventeen-year-old Miranda Johnson was a mutual friend, also enamored with Davis. Valerie liked her as a friend, but was worried that Miranda sought to compete for the attentions of her boyfriend. Living from flophouse to flophouse, Johnson was a street person. She was involved in drugs, thefts, and prostitution. She was said to have been summoned to join in the robbery plan and quickly agreed with Davis' convincing plea.

Valerie Chard proceeded to advise Detective Murray that she had participated in stealing the murder weapon from her father earlier in the year. She knew that her Dad kept a loaded .22 automatic in his desk in his Lake Forest Park Washington apartment. Her father had taught her how to fire the weapon at one point in the woods of Snohomish County. She stated that sometime in early 1997 Thomas Davis instructed her to steal the firearm in order to facilitate a gun store robbery. Chard stated that she had initially balked at the idea. But she relented when Davis drove her to the home of her father in a stolen car. Davis went through Chard's father's closet, collected several rifles and found the handgun in a desk. Chard acted as a lookout.

Chard related that Davis told her that he had arranged with his Y.O.T. gang friends to purchase many guns, to be obtained via the planned gun store robbery. Davis had told Chard and gang friends that he had found an "easy hit" in an Eastern Washington town. He had cased the store in question earlier that month and then coerced the girls into joining him on a second reconnaissance visit to the store.

Valerie Chard stated that she slept with Davis overnight at a friend's apartment after stealing her father's guns. They awakened early the following morning. Chard was instructed to be the driver of her own Green Mercury Marquis. The two picked up Miranda Johnson in Seattle and the trio headed toward Wenatchee. Davis sat in the front passenger seat and Miranda Johnson sat in the back seat. The trio drove to Sissons Gun Sports shop in East Wenatchee Washington. The small store was an adjunct to a residence and was located across a large lawn from the home of Darrel Sisson. The three youths walked throughout the store admiring the firearms without conversing with the owner. Ultimately, Mr. Sisson asked the strange-looking youths to either purchase something or leave. He was obviously leery of the goateed and greasy long-haired Davis, and the two girls with tattoos, goth attire, and piercings. They surely did not match the conservative Central Washington neighborhood. Ultimately, the trio left the store without confrontation.

Chard advised us that Davis went over the plans to rob the store the next day. They spent the night in the car driving around and smoking marijuana. They slept for a while in a nearby park after Davis had summoned oral sex from Chard. The following morning Davis instructed the girls to buy a bag of potatoes. He informed the girls that potatoes functioned as excellent silencers for handguns. As Chard would advise us, she knew at that moment that Davis intended to fire the weapon. He threatened to kill the girls were they not to fully cooperate.

The next morning the trio arrived at the Gun Store near opening time. It was a sunny and crisp morning and the neighborhood seemed largely emptied. Miranda Johnson waited in the back of the parked vehicle, instructed to honk the horn were anyone else to approach. Davis affixed a potato to the stolen .22 automatic and hid such in his light jacket. He and Valerie Chard entered the store. Valerie acted, as previously instructed, and engaged Darrel Sisson in conversation as he stood behind a glass gun case. She was to provide distraction. Davis quickly approached and pulled the handgun from his jacket. With the potato silencer still affixed, Davis was said to fire the weapon into the head of Darrel Sisson without hesitation. Chard stated that Sisson froze for a moment and displayed, "kinda a freaky look on his face." Davis then was said to fire another round into the face of the gun store owner. Darrel Sisson fell hard onto the concrete floor and blood poured freely from his head.

Valerie Chard further advised that she assisted Davis in emptying the store of vast caches of weapons. She said "Tommy" was clearly pleased with her, and kissed her. He was said to eventually make a whooping sound and masturbation gestures. Valerie Chard admitted that, at one point, she heard Darrel Sisson make some sort of gurgling noise. She became vague in stating, "I think it was me" whom grabbed a nearby hatchet and bludgeoned the victim in the face. She laughed about the act like a mischievous school girl. She did admit that she might have performed such an act so as to impress Tommy. But she would never completely admit to such an horrific act.

Ultimately, Chard drove the trio back to Western Washington after loading the guns in the trunk of the vehicle. Chard advised that Davis, Miranda Johnson, and she sold approximately half of the 100 stolen firearms upon their return to Seattle on the night of the murder. The purchasers, as previously arranged, were the Y.O.T. gang members. She claimed that the asking price for the weapons was only five thousand dollars.

The final descriptive oration of the murder from Valerie Chard was to state that "Tommy" had chosen to lie down on the floor, face to face with the dying victim, just before leaving the crime scene.

As I finished the tape, I could see why Detective Murray was so pleased with the first round of suspect questioning. He had listened and cajoled in perfect proportions. Agent McKenna had added insightful input as well. I still wished to kick myself for missing the opportunity to partake.

We sought next to interview Miranda Johnson. She was contained in a solitary cell far from any possible interactions with Valerie Chard. Ms. Johnson was willing to join us at a nearby interview pod and sit down. While she must have been quite an attractive young lady at one time, her emaciated face, greasy long brown hair, piercings, and gang tattoos on her hands indicated a life gone awry. All she would state was, "F--k you... you send Tommy here to tell me it's OK to talk to you and I will... tell Tommy I love him."

Jailers advised that her lawyers had it made it clear to the 17-year-old that she would have greater legal leeway in a courtroom due to her age. The motivation to cooperate had thus been largely removed.

Our tour thus moved to the male portion of the jail. Ringleader Thomas David Davis was our ultimate target of interest. Well equipped with Davis' criminal history, we expected little cooperation from the young hardened criminal. Surprisingly, Davis was willing to vacate his cell and meet with us. My first reaction to Davis was to think, "*This* greaseball is the prince charming to the girls?" The little man was nothing but trash. I picked up immediately that Davis had the trademark ego of a psychopath. He reminded me of an earlier contact with an infamous serial killer, about whom I still cannot further expound. Both psychopaths, like many others, craved attention and power. They thought themselves the intellectual superior of others and so deluded themselves. They were clever, but nothing more. Yet, they possessed the ability to give seasoned cops nightmares for life, knowing explicitly what the animals had done to their victims. These crime details the cops would take to their graves, ensuring that tortured victim families would not learn of them.

Thomas Davis largely refused to speak of the incident in question. While he did not desire an attorney, he was well aware of his constitutional rights. Davis craved any and all information about his mini-harem, Chard and Johnson. He would thus receive rewards from us for any cooperation with vague information about the co-defendants. We made it clear that we controlled the interview and not he. He would only provide the faintest pieces of information about the murder and robbery. He would readily admit to his fondness for the Seattle gangs, and a particular affinity for the Young Oriental Troop.

The interview was thus nearing an inconsequential ending when I turned back to the individual. I'm not sure exactly why, but I asked Davis, "Why did you lay down next to the dude?"

Before he could think, Davis answered, "I like to hear peoples' last breaths."

Once again, I am not sure why I asked, but I followed with, "People?" "Have you heard other last breaths?"

Davis said, "Maybe some girl...maybe I killed her." He would not give further answers until Detective Murray asked, "Why did you maybe kill her?"

Davis said, "Maybe cause I always wondered what it's like to kill somebody."

With that, Davis instructed jailers to return him to his cell. Detective Murray, Agent McKenna and I then gestured a common law enforcement sign. We made rubbing gestures toward the raising hairs on our forearms.

We soon learned that Snohomish County Washington Sheriff's Detectives would seek to interview Davis about a homicide earlier that year in their jurisdiction. Apparently Davis and a gang of friends were bragging of having gone looking to commit armed robberies of local churches, when they happened upon an adult female hitchhiker. They further had bragged of holding guns to the head of the middle-aged woman. They bragged of having her beg for her life while kneeling in front of them.

A woman had been found in a ditch by a highway. She had been shot in the face with a shotgun blast and twice run over by a car. The detectives had photographed a mysterious ear print in the mud next to the face of the victim.

The ATF agent and the two Seattle cops thus returned to Seattle, impassioned to go after the Y.O.T.'s.

Lieutenant Kelsie, as always, was true to his word. He had appraised our chain of command — from Captain Daniel Oliver, to Chief John Pirak, to Chief Norman Stamper. All had signed off to committing extensive funds and personnel to bringing down the Asian gang that was responsible for profound violence in our state. Gang Unit intelligence information indicated that the same gang was also responsible for funding gun store robberies in Utah.

I soon heard from Agent Kumor that he had received even more substantial commitments from the BATF. Enormous funds for multi-agency surveillance and undercover operations were approved for the mission. Approval for the federal side of things had been received from entities as high as the cabinet level. Agent Kumor, in subsequent meetings, offered that he could produce a quality infiltrator/informant in order to observe the Y.O.T. from the inside. He was convinced that the informant could gain the trust of the Seattle gang. Sergeant Roger "Buddha" Rusness was sought repeatedly to share his enormous wealth of knowledge regarding all Seattle Asian gang members.

The overall operations plan for dismantling the gang would be as follows:

- Plant an informant within the gang in order to gain their trust.
- Monitor the informant intently for reliability, and for his own safety.

- Eventually plant recording devices upon the informant, once the trust of the gang was gained. Seek to gain admissions of guilt by the gang members. Seek to use the informant to purchase the stolen weapons from the homicide.

- Intently surveil the activities of the gang, once familiarity with their crime sprees was obtained. Utilize combinations of SPD gang detectives and ATF agents on stake-outs, so as to use the talents and knowledge of each wisely.

- Identify each member of the gang. Photograph, record, document activities.

- Hope like hell we don't waste a fortune in tax dollars on a fruitless venture.

Agent Kumor invited me to the ATF office in the Federal Building in order to review the qualifications of his informant. The informant was a gang member from another state. I cannot advise further on his roots for his safety. He had been arrested by federal agents for serious federal offenses and convicted for such in court. He was facing a minimum of twenty years in federal prison for his crimes. As federal law enforcement is adept at doing, they had managed to convince the lad that he needed to become ATF's special friend. Quan Choi* (name altered for obvious reasons) was a perfect choice. He was a clever and highly experienced Asian gang member, whose familiarity with those gangs spanned two continents. He was bright, articulate, and very confident. He did not wish to spend most of his adult life in a solitary cell in a federal penitentiary. A deal was further pending to secure an early release for an incarcerated beloved family member of his. Other family members would not face pending deportation. Quan Choi was highly motivated to assist law enforcement. And he was clearly adept at the art of bargaining.

Quan Choi was given a very nice hotel room in Seattle

with a view of Elliott Bay to enjoy. He was also accompanied by two huge ATF agents in an adjoining room, so as to keep an eye on him. He enjoyed quality food and beverages, and cable TV. He was then instructed to become a gang member in Seattle.

Quan Choi was given a fancy vehicle and directed to a local known Y.O.T. gang hangout. He was followed at all times by ATF agents and SPD gang detectives in undercover vehicles. A location tracker was placed within his vehicle. The government did not wish to lose their investment. He was coached to simply imbed himself with Y.O.T's on a gradual basis. He would sing karaoke, play pool, gamble, and bowl. He could drink, but he could not abuse drugs.

A few weeks passed wherein Quan Choi would provide daily reports to the task force. Having come from a larger city, Quan Choi commented that he found the Y.O.T. to be "small time" compared to gangs of his past. He had bragged to the new gang of his past and quickly engendered prestige with new peers. As time followed, the Y.O.T.'s would almost come to revere Quan Choi as a leader of much larger and more ruthless gangs out of state. They believed that he sought to recruit and train the Seattle Asian gangs so as to gain pre-eminence on the West Coast. The fish had thus taken the bait.

Ultimately, Quan Choi would wear a wire in every meeting with the gang members. They had long since ceased to search him upon his arrival. The girls of the gang sought to party with their new member and he was invited to perform crimes in the area, such as auto thefts and drug deals. Finally, the gang would speak of the robbery and availability of guns.

As all gang members' roles became identified, high-tech surveillance was installed in the area. Several gang houses were unknowingly surrounded by high quality cameras on numerous light poles. Conversations were heard by remote, on tape, and even via high tech listening devices. The gang members bragged of many crime sprees, and mentioned a robbery and killing of a Salt Lake City gun store owner. They often bragged of the stupidity of law enforcement whom they felt were totally unaware of their activities.

It would be learned how the gang had created a network of drug dealing in the region. They sold any drug, from marijuana, to cocaine and opiates. They stole automobiles for transportation of such. Their business thrived due to undercutting competitors in price. It was almost as if they operated a Costco. Bargain drugs of many sorts would come and go, according to market forces.

The Drug Enforcement Agency was eventually summoned to listen in. The agency enthusiastically volunteered to join in the operation. Numerous drug transactions were thus made with the Y.O.T's. Yet, the locations of the crime guns and more information arrived only in microscopic, painstaking bits.

Several months would pass as information was gained frustratingly slowly. There were times when both law enforcement agencies weighed the costs of such a lengthy operation versus the benefit. Some commanders opined that sufficient evidence existed to make drug and property crime arrests. Yet, calmer minds prevailed.

Ultimately a considerable break occurred. Leaders of the Y.O.T.'s finally admitted to the informant that they possessed some fifty high quality weapons. They were willing to display some of such weapons for sale to the informant. A rendezvous point was thus determined by Quan Choi after considerable planning with the task force. Additional Young looking Asian ATF agents were drafted to join the informant for the purchase. The reasoning was two-fold: One, for the safety of the informant at a high-risk transaction; and Two, so that the sale would seem credible. No gang member would seek such a purchase single-handedly with vast quantities of weaponry and cash involved. The transaction would occur under the Alaskan Way viaduct in downtown Seattle. The location provided for *apparent* concealment for the gang members. Yet, law enforcement had readily available surveillance vantage points uphill from the Pike Place Market, in concealment vehicles, and even from a nearby hotel.

The sale was arranged for a late night hour. Infrared cameras and surveillance equipment was at the ready by ATF. Ultimately, the gang members arrived with a small rental truck. A roll-up metal door was opened. Dozens of uzis, SKS assault rifles, Tech 9 machine pistols et al were on display. It was a weaponry smorgasbord. The very professional informant and his new assistants played their parts perfectly. Rather than offering an enormous amount of money for all of the weapons, they sifted through the cache for quality. They were picky buyers. Quan Choi and the undercover agents were well aware of the types of weapons taken during the homicide and robbery and sought to focus thereupon.

Ultimately, 18 high quality weapons were purchased for $15,000 in cash. The happy traders each drove off in their respective directions. We were pleased to discover that Quan Choi and his colleagues had purchased 11 of the homicide weapons. One other gun was reported stolen in an unrelated burglary, and six others had obliterated serial numbers. We were thrilled! The evidentiary connection between the homicide and robbery and a Seattle street gang had been solidly proven. It was time for the fun to begin. Federal arrest warrants would be sought.

U.S. attorney Jim Lord took the lead in procuring federal indictments against eleven members of Seattle's Young Oriental

Troop street gang. Considerable prosecutorial assistance was lent during the process by talented Deputy Prosecuting Attorney Susan Story and other member of the King County Prosecutor's Office. Grand juries were held in secret. ATF agents and SPD members gave testimony. The key witness — informant Quon Choi was questioned for several days. Federal organized crime charges were rendered against each of the eleven prominent members of the Y.O.T's. Such charges ranged from conspiracy to commit murder and robbery, to drug charges and money laundering.

SPD, ATF, and the DEA held a number of large scale meetings at a secret DEA location. It was decided that search warrants upon three key gang dens would be served simultaneously in the early morning hours of an upcoming Sunday. ATF and DEA agents would join forces to hit one residence, while Seattle Police SWAT and the Gang Unit would breach two other fortified homes.

During the same week, Seattle Times reporter Arthur Santana contacted all three agencies. He indicated that he had gained considerable knowledge of the Oriental Troop Street Gang Operation and sought law enforcement input prior to going public with his story. He was even aware of the pending search warrants to be served. Concerned commanders of the respective agencies decided to refer Mr. Santana to U.S. Attorney Jim Lord for comment. Mr. Lord pleaded with the reporter to keep his information temporarily private.

Commanders of each agency expressed to Mr. Santana that going public with his story could endanger the lives of those serving the search warrants. They stressed that giving the heavily armed gang members prior warning of the approaching law enforcement personnel could lead to tragedy. Mr. Santana ultimately volunteered to keep his story under wraps until all gang members were rounded up. He simply asked for exclusivity of prior information so that his story would break first. U.S. attorneys and law enforcement brass on all sides promised to share considerable information with Mr. Santana at the conclusion of the operation.

The nearby forces of McChord Air Force Base volunteered to conduct fly-overs of the residences of the gang members to be breached. Extremely high-tech infrared photography equipment was used in order to map the interior of the residences. Rooms, furniture, walls, and even weapons showed up on detailed subsequent maps of the homes. The intelligence function was priceless. In addition, our informant gave detailed descriptors of the residences, hiding places for guns and drugs, and even places gang members chose to sleep within the homes. We were confident of the future search warrant successes.

At five o'clock A.M. on a Sunday morning three Seattle gang houses were paid simultaneous visits. Federal Agents in military gear surrounded a North Seattle split- level house. The front and rear doors were shattered in sync and entry was gained. Several slumbering gang members were secured very quickly by Uzi brandishing federal agents.

At the same exact time, two Seattle Police SWAT teams with armored personnel carriers hit two South Seattle residences. Gang Unit detectives were summoned to enter the homes immediately following the initial entries. We secured dozens of gang members on living room floors, on their stomachs, with hands "flex-cuffed" with plastic ties behind their backs. A couple of the "tough-guy" gang members had actually wet their pants when the SWAT members made entry, using "flash-bang" devices.

The gang members were astonished to see detectives walk through their filthy homes with profound familiarity. We went quickly to the locations of guns, drugs, and money. From the respective homes we were able to locate four more crime guns from the gun store murder/robbery. We also located nearly ten thousand dollars in cash. The cash proved to be that of the federal buy money used to buy crime guns. We tore substantial stashes of hashish, cocaine, and opiates from hidden cavities in walls. The gang members cursed as we walked directly to each place of concealment. They knew they were had.

We had plenty of explaining to do with terrified neighbors of the homes in questions. It was not every day that their neighborhoods were blocked off by police cars. Nor had they witnessed armored personnel carriers roll down their streets with helicopters hovering above and canine units standing by. Most neighbors were alternately alarmed and reassured to find a police invasion of their streets. They were quite pleased to see the scores of gang members being dragged from the houses toward police vans. They all expressed their fears of the gang members for months and prior frustration with the lack of response by law enforcement. They even laughed when our Detective Murray advised, "Well, maybe we *were* doing something huh?"

A series of federal trials would follow for nearly seven months. Eleven of the key members of the Young Oriental Troop were respectively represented by expensive private attorneys. Nonetheless, the vast majority of them pleaded guilty to all charges when the mountains of evidence were displayed. Four others were convicted by federal juries. Seven of the members were convicted of conspiracy to commit robbery, weapons distribution, and drug distribution. They received sentences of 22 years in Federal prison without the possibility of early release. Four of the members were convicted of conspiracy to commit murder and robbery. They were thus sentenced to life in Federal prison without the possibility of parole. Even while being escorted out of the courtrooms to their eternal assignments, the Y.O.T. gang members smiled, and flashed gang signs to their friends in the audience.

We could never prove the connection between the gang and another gun store homicide/robbery in Salt Lake City. Yet, the conspirators were facing lifetimes in prison nonetheless. While scores of Y.O.T. gang members remain free in society, they have yet to re-emerge to any extent, over twenty years later. The remaining gang members were often observed after the conclusion of the operation with amusement by Gang Unit detectives. Detectives watched the gang members tearing their cars apart, searching one another, and staring upward at light poles. They were clearly paranoid of informants, listening devices, and cameras.

Seattle Times Reporter Arthur Santana would be rewarded for his consideration by the U.S. Attorney's office. Arthur received a terse two-line press release that indicated arrests of gang members in a federal/local sting had been made. The rest of the media received the same notice at the same time. Members of the SPD Gang Unit were incensed and embarrassed by the broken promise made to the ethical reporter.

Somehow, inexplicably, Arthur Santana seemed to obtain vast amounts of information about the operation and the preceding homicide investigation. It was almost as if he had a personal relationship with the Gang Unit. Mr. Santana would go on to write an exhaustive Seattle Times series on the entire 18-month series of events. He entitled his story, "The Life of a Gun." Arthur proved to be a gifted writer. His reporting of a very complicated series of events was 100% accurate and detailed. We were very pleased to read that Arthur Santana would win virtually every local, regional, and national journalism award for his story. Such awards would lead to Arthur joining the Washington Post as a crime reporter. We were not surprised to learn that Arthur was one of the first persons to arrive at the Pentagon when attacked on 9-1-1. Arthur was recognized for life-saving efforts within the burning building. He again won awards for his reporting of the tragedy. While most media members merit scorn and hatred from law enforcement, Arthur Santana is regarded as a stellar example of what journalism and integrity should be.

While members of the Seattle Police Department Gang Unit never directly met the family of murdered gun store owner Darrel "Jerry" Sisson, they remain on our minds to this day. We read via Arthur's story that Mr. Sisson was the salt of the earth. He had been born in the state of Kansas, and moved to Central Washington State as a youth. He had picked fruit in area apple orchards. Mr. Sisson eventually gained a job with the state's Department of Fish and Game, where he served over thirty years with distinction. He was married and had one five year-old granddaughter at the time of his death. It was his dream job to open Sisson Shooter's Supplies. He was said to be a leader in the local NRA, a distinguished trap-shooting marksman, and a bit of a practical joker. His entire family is highly regarded in friendly East Wenatchee Washington.

Regrettably, no one from the Seattle Police Gang Unit could attend Mr. Sisson's funeral. We were too busy going after the participants and planners of his murder. By the time the operation had reached its conclusion, some two years had passed. I invited Detective Murray to feel free to visit the family were he to so desire. He advised that he felt too much time had passed and there was no need to re-open the family's scars.

Years later I talked to Dave Murray. He was in the final year of his career. He long ago left the dismantled Gang Unit to work in our Fugitive Unit. He related that rarely does a day pass that he does not think of the murder and investigation, and his profound involvement in all aspects of solving the case. Detective Murray advised that he had just recently disposed of his old case files and notes while beginning the packing of his work belongings for retirement. He was very pleased to hear of my attempts to write this book. Dave is an avid runner. He told me that he has run two half-marathons in Wenatchee Washington, and seriously considered paying a visit upon the Sisson family. Maybe someday he shall.

At the very least, perhaps the family will learn via this book that big city cops across the state did indeed care.

***

Chapter side note: Sergeant Bernie Miller

It is doubtful that a tougher patrol Sergeant ever existed than Sergeant Bernie Miller. The former Army drill Sergeant parlayed his people skills into an illustrious career within the Seattle Police Department. Bernie Miller had the face of a pug dog. His bottom teeth jutted outward in an apparent sneer that was merely exacerbated by a sardonic smile that only occasionally emerged. His quarter inch Army hair cut was always perfect. His tanned skin and perfectly fit physique made it impossible to detect evidence of aging on the man.

In his early years, Officer Miller worked a myriad of patrol assignments in Seattle. He eventually walked a beat in the toughest districts in the city. He quickly made a name for himself as one of the toughest, no-nonsense street cops in Seattle. He was eventually promoted to the Homicide Unit as a detective. Bernie Miller would serve a decade and a half in such capacity, wherein his reputation grew exponentially. Bernie proved to be an exceptional investigator. He had a knack for reading the faces of suspects, and sorting lies from their hours of bravado in a holding cell. He also maintained a "hands-on" rapport with many of the murderous street thugs of Seattle.

As physically tough as Bernie was as a homicide detective, it was his mental toughness that added to his legend. It was said that no site, regardless of the morbidity level, could affect Bernie's stoic demeanor. His mental toughness was astounding.

The legend still circulates that Bernie was able to repulse the most callous of detectives at a particular autopsy. As the story goes, Bernie was known to often eat a baloney sandwich while standing near a given body at the proceedings. On one particular occasion, brain matter was said to have gone airborne from the site of the coroner's cutting. The matter allegedly secured itself upon a corner of Detective Miller's sandwich. Other detectives swear that Detective Bernie Miller merely raised one eyebrow. He then proceeded to pick off the affected corner of his sandwich and throw such into a nearby garbage can. Detective Miller is said to have then finished eating the remainder of his sandwich while witnessing the rest of the autopsy. After working later for Bernie Miller, I find the story highly believable.

Bernie was also renowned for his legendary "picture book." It would seem that he kept a scrapbook of the most revolting and notorious homicide cases with which he had been associated during two different decades. He was proud to present such album for viewing by rookie cops in the police academy, while teaching a block on homicide investigation. The book caused many a vomitous occurrence over the years. It has been claimed that a few rookie officers resigned from the academy, after viewing what was in store for them in the career of law enforcement.

Your author was privileged to eventually work for Patrol Sergeant Bernie Miller, while assigned to the downtown West Precinct. My partner Kent and I found Sergeant Miller to be an extraordinary supervisor and leader. He claimed that never a day in police-work passed that he did not learn something new. Yet, Sergeant Miller was highly skilled at passing his knowledge to we young officers. He taught us to check the base of the skull of any dead body at apparent natural death scenes. We were instructed that was so as to seek a needle puncture. (That would years later allow me to detect a homicide that had been overlooked). We were also taught to wear rubber gloves, in order to feel the skulls of the same bodies for any blunt force trauma. He gave us basic homicide detective skills. Perhaps what impressed us most about his skills was the instant compassion he showed for the families of the deceased. While Sergeant Miller was a very, very tough human being, he always made a point of stressing to grieving family members that the deceased passed away quickly, and without any suffering. Often he lied for the benefit of relieving loved ones.

Sergeant Miller was tough on his officers. He expected them to be reliable and hard working. And he demanded that they set a tone of toughness on the streets. Some of the older officers resented him for perceived meddling into their work. We younger officers were grateful for his leadership. Bernie was always present on the streets. He always made more arrests than any of his troops. Yet, he completed all of his own paperwork. As he insisted, "You catch em... you clean em."

We never saw Bernie lose a fight, regardless of the odds versus multiple suspects. Only once did he sound remotely distressed on a radio broadcast, when he requested additional units and an ambulance. He advised, I'm being jumped by a carload of thugs and a Rotweiller...and I could use some company." We hurried to his location in a tunnel beneath a downtown freeway. We found five thugs in various states of consciousness and bleeding. We further found a huge Rotweiller in even worse condition. Sergeant Miller looked very angry, as we turned to him. We stated that we understood his fury at having been attacked. He jutted out his lower teeth and stated, "Nah, that was fun... but I broke my damned night stick on that one's head!" Sergeant Miller's prized hand-crafted rosewood night-stick was, indeed, broken in half.

Fortunately, Sergeant Miller was able to craft another piece of art for his future months on his beat. He could twirl the stick in a blur in front of and around himself. As stated previously, he was often approached by hippie-type leftists whom advised him that his nightstick twirling was found to be "intimidating." Bernie's reply was always the same. He presented his most sincere smile, continued to twirl his stick faster, donned his patrolman's hat and stated, "Thank you very much."

For all his legendary traits for toughness, Sergeant Miller was an impassioned leader and supervisor. He demanded that his officers walk *through* any passing individuals, and never around them. He taught scores of officers basic self-defense and patrol tactics on his own time. And he demanded camaraderie and loyalty amongst his troops. He was always an impassioned accompaniment with his officers, when challenged by Internal Affairs and Command Staff. And he taught his cops the value of working very very hard, while by the letter of "the book."

Sergeant Bernie Miller, now retired and recently deceased, was an extraordinary patrol Sergeant. It was an honor to work for him.

***

Chapter 13: And they give these people guns and badges?

Many dichotomies are readily apparent within a large police force. But what may be most stark are the split personalities of the officers regarding seriousness and the comical. Perhaps one aspect complements the other. It would appear that the harder the officers laugh, the harder they work. Maybe some academic needs to study the phenomenon. During the first two decades of my law enforcement career, abundant laughter and frivolity was expected, if not demanded. The dangerous job was, nonetheless, incredibly fun. This aspect of the work has faded greatly under absurd recent political scrutinies that are designed to handcuff only the cops. Sadly, I'm now almost astounded to recall the childish, clownish, and downright foolhardy behaviors of peers and *self* in the past. Such behaviors would now find an officer fired at the very least. We thought it was all in good fun. And occasionally in good taste.

***

12th Southwest and Edmonds

Your author was a mere two days graduated from the four-month field training (FTO) program when working a solo West Seattle patrol district. My third and final FTO, Mark Gilbert was designated the Acting Sergeant for the day, while the regular Sergeant was in training. Mark was an incredibly distinguished man whom I admired greatly. I had learned a great deal from him and tried to emulate the man, to a vast extent. But I could *never* emulate his deep basso- profundo speaking voice that was reminiscent of James Earl Jones. Mark was a six foot three, two hundred twenty pound muscular man with a large mustache and deep brown eyes. He looked and acted like he should be in Hollywood. He was renowned for his calm and thoughtful demeanor.

Early into the shift of my second solo day the acting Sergeant's deep voice boomed over the radio… "Two William"… (radio responds)… "Two William, I need to meet with Two William Twelve at 12th Avenue Southwest and Edmonds Street immediately." I immediately bounded into action. By the tone and wording of the acting Sergeant, he had something serious to see me about. My heart rate increased just slightly. I knew where a 12th Avenue Southwest was from my training. I further recognized the existence of Southwest Edmonds Street. I thus drove aggressively toward the area. As I neared what I thought was the location, I could see no such streets.

"Two William" (radio responds again) "Two William, what is William Twelve's location?…I need to see him *immediately*." Now my heart was really pounding as I squeaked on the radio that I was almost there. I was afraid of embarrassing myself in front of my former trainer and current boss, Mark.

I drove several blocks opposite my location, thinking an entrance to the area must exist. But there were no such roadways. I stopped and gathered my map. I also gathered my ambulance guide that assisted greatly in locating difficult addresses. I could see no 12th Southwest and Edmonds on the map!

"Two William," again boomed the voice of Mark Gilbert… ."Radio, this is getting serious, I need William Twelve here immediately!" I nervously responded that I would be there any moment. The responsorials continued for a couple more minutes. I never could find any such streets. I visualized the probable whereabouts of such an intersection far into a series of vacant lots and brush covered foliage. Afraid of consequences, either way, I hit the gas in my shiny patrol vehicle and drove over bushes to the approximated location. I again heard the acting Sergeant summoning me over the radio. I finally stepped out of my car, stood on the door jam and looked outward across the fields. I heard the acting Sergeant's voice again over the radio, but I also heard his live voice. I turned behind me and to the driver's side of my patrol car.

There, underneath profound camouflage of weeds, brush, and limbs, was buried a patrol car--that of Acting Sergeant Mark Gilbert! He was laughing hysterically and came out to shake my hand. As I walked toward him incensed and relieved, I was struck in the back by a dirt clod. I turned to find Mark's best friend, and usual partner, Bill Kirk had hidden his patrol car similarly in another space. Bill said, "Welcome to William Sector, rookie!" The location, it would be learned, was actually in the middle of a vast game preserve. I believed I had just become one of the boys, as revenge was immediately on my mind.

***

West Precinct Terrorism: A captain under siege

In the early 1980's, the West (Downtown) Precinct of the Seattle Police Department was highly laden with very experienced officers. In fact, the vast majority of seasoned beat cops and patrol officers were at or near retirement age. During that era, those particular officers could retire after twenty years of service. Most officers stayed for twenty-five years. Such choice was primarily financial, of course. However, the penultimate motivator for many of the seasoned officers staying a few extra years was the joy of working while encompassed by an "untouchable status." They legally could not be terminated absent a felony conviction. The "old crusties" were often heard to utter to high ranking department officials, "What are ya gonna do, make me retire?" Scant few rookie officers were allowed to work within the precinct. And those rookies, like your author, were well aware of the precinct mantra, "Rookie, keep your eyes and ears open and your mouth shut." And, oh my, the eyes and ears were in for a treat.

West Precinct roll calls of the era entailed huge cadres of seasoned officers, supplemented by the few young officers. At one time the Second Watch (day shift) roll calls of the downtown West Precinct would have surpassed the staffing levels of all but a few *departments* in the state of Washington. Whereas today's roll-calls are fortunate to see *four* officers available for deployment, well over forty officers once staffed the downtown daytime corridor. This array of officers filling a roll-call room to its seams thus provided a surreal environment each late morning. The roll call Sergeant could expect numerous cat-calls, off-color jokes, and boastful demands from beat cops to hurry the presentation so as not to cut into their "drinking time." Officers whom were conspicuously absent from roll call would be said to be "in court." Sometimes the Sergeants received pelting by paper products upon their entries into the room. Ultimately, the necessary information would be imparted by the Sergeants and a modicum of earnest reciprocal respect would be exchanged.

A young and aspiring Lieutenant, recently promoted and transferred to the West Precinct, was aghast at the daily spectacle. He was so unimpressed with the situation that he chose to reveal his observations to the precinct commander — Captain Jim Deshane. The Captain apparently advised the

Lieutenant that he was well aware of the irreverent nature of the roll calls. He had confidence in his huge cadre of talented officers. He added that he was often present at such roll calls and found such to be a largely acceptable forum of camaraderie and humor. The rookie Lieutenant was incensed at the Captain's reply and apparently stormed upward in the elevator to the tenth floor of the Public Safety Building. He immediately reported the "issues" to the Chief of Police—the seemingly tyrannical Chief Patrick Fitzsimons.

A former military officer, Chief Fitzsimons immediately sought to instill control and dominance over his downtown precinct. He called for a full stand-up military inspection of the troops the following day. Threats of discipline, to include unpaid suspensions, were filtered downward. The Captain was indeed concerned, and stressed the need for compliance by his officers.

It was thus that some forty-five officers gathered in a timely manner within the hot, stuffy, and smoky room. All arrived early for the roll-call in their finest formal uniforms.

Four lines or "ranks" of officers stood in columns within the room. They were called to Atten-hut! by the Sergeants and snapped to rigid military stances. The Chief of Police entered the room with great fanfare, accompanied by his personal Lieutenant, known by the troops as his "food taster." The pair marched in perfect Hitler style. The harried precinct Captain followed the Chief, accompanied by the young "climber" Lieutenant.

The young officers were placed in the front row of the ranks. We thus stood in fear of the intimidating five foot seven Chief of all Police. Our knees shook as he and his entourage walked slowly past each officer. The Chief demanded the presentation of weapons from chosen young officers, including your author. Our .357 magnum revolvers were detached from our holsters, opened to safe position, and turned to the Chief in perfect military fashion. The weapons were inspected for dust or dirt. The Chief's food- taster then mimicked his actions and scrawled notes into a notebook. The food taster was followed by the rookie patrol Lieutenant. The young officers were chided for the polish of their shoes, the length of their hair, and a myriad of other egregious offenses. They were threatened with written reprimands were their failures to be repeated. The Chief received nothing but nervous "Yes Sir(s)" from the young officers.

Chief Fitzsimons' goodwill tour wound through two more ranks of increasingly more experienced officers. He received reluctant compliance to a few inspections orders given to those officers.

He finally came to the final row of twelve beat cops. The beat cops were dressed in their usual knee-length heavy wool coats with ornate hats and night sticks. He ordered a 27 year veteran to open his shin-length wool trench coat and display his gun belt and inner uniform. The grizzled officer simply shook his head. The Chief pointed at the officer and said, "What are you wearing under that coat, officer?"

The beat cop replied, "Nothin'."

The Chief persisted, "Open up the coat, officer, that's an order."

"Negative, Chief," the officer answered.

The Chief continued, "What the hell do you have under that coat, officer, open it up!"

With that, the officer opened the huge coat. True to his word, the officer had *nothing* on beneath the coat.

Aghast, but not to be upstaged, the Chief moved away from the obstinate veteran and continued down the lines. A slight snicker was heard within the ranks. With slightly less aplomb, the Chief dared to ask another beat cop to display his wares beneath his heavy coat. The huge 28 year veteran with handle-bar mustache peeled back his coat. To the Chief's relief the man was fully clothed. Yet, upon closer scrutiny, the Chief found the officer's gun belt accessories to be out of order. Hanging from the officer's belt was a hand grenade. Astutely, the Chief asked of the officer, "What is that?"

The officer immediately responded, "Hand grenade sir." With that, the Chief sought to remove the grenade from the officer's gun belt and separate such from the supposed pin. The huge officer then towered over the Chief and looked downward. He even bent his knees slightly in condescension . The officer then stated, "I wouldn't do that, Chief."

The Chief countered, "It's not real, I was in the Army."

The officer replied, "I really wouldn't do that if I were you, Chief."

The Chief's hand began to shake demonstrably as he weighed his options. The veteran officer stared at him intently. The Chief looked toward nearby officers. The others in the ranks began to show extreme concern. The officer in question had long ago been nicknamed "Psycho" for a reason. Ultimately, the Chief retreated, and stormed out of the room in fury. His entourage quickly followed.

As the crowd of amused officers gathered around the beat cop they asked of him, "Is it real?"

"Yup," was the officer's reply, as he strolled out of the room toward his beat.

The Captain began to worry.

The Captain only requested that the troops not terribly embarrass him in the future. He asked that we keep the roll call room somewhat cleaner. His final timid request was that officers stop wearing "Captain Snodgrass" name tags and generating Internal Investigations rudeness complaints in that name. The veteran cops, who truly loved the Captain, complied. They changed all their name tags to six syllable Slavic sounding names with their true names included.

***

The perils of Sergeant Don Don

One of the truly beloved patrol Sergeants of the West Precinct during the early 1980's was Sergeant Don Draglund. Nicknamed "Don-Don," Sergeant Draglund was a handsome fair-haired blonde and blue- eyed Norwegian. He was a man of some fifty years of age when your author first met him. Sergeant Draglund was a highly gregarious and engaging man with a quick wit and disarming smile. He was a very bright and charming man whom was nearing the end of his career. He had made a distinguished name for himself as a Homicide detective. Don's greatest attribute or weakness was his self-deprecating demeanor. Whatever Don's weaknesses were, they were displayed for all to witness. In the instance of the West Precinct troops, those human frailties served as perfect targets.

Only Don would be confident enough in his masculinity, or merely insane enough, to reveal humorous home issues. Don dared to relate to one member of his squad that his dominant wife had insisted that he sit to urinate, so as not to make any bathroom messes. In telling the tale to one officer, Don may as well have told all 1,600.

It was shortly thereafter that Sergeant Draglund arrived

at work for the day shift. Don was a notorious creature of habit. He inhaled his cigarette out in the parking garage, ate a powdered donut, and then downed two cups of jet black coffee. He then headed for the men's room. He did not even notice the corps of officers following him into the facilities. There, in the first of many stalls was a special placard upon one stall door. A decorative wooden carved sign indicated, "Private Stall-Sergeant Draglund. Do not disturb." Un-fazed, or absent-minded, as always, Sergeant Draglund entered the stall to take care of business. There within the stall were tastefully wall-papered pink walls, with lovely floral borders. And the toilet seat was adorned in lovely pink fur covers.

The good Sergeant, totally red-faced, expressed his supreme gratitude to the officers of the West Precinct roll-call minutes later.

Several months later, Sergeant Draglund was the head of a precinct-level street narcotics operation for one night. He was sitting in for Sergeant Butler whom had taken the night off. We were honored to have "Don Don" lead the festivities for the night. Sergeant Draglund proved to be highly alert and astute the entire long night of operations. We were impressed with his knowledge and experience regarding detailed street operations.

The last responsibilities for the late night were to serve a narcotics search warrant at a drug den apartment building. Sergeant Draglund was highly impressed with the precision shown by our squad in forcing entry into the room at gunpoint, controlling suspects, and locating a substantial cache of cocaine and firearms.

The questioning of drug dealers and the evidence located in the apartment generated an immediate need to request another search warrant nearby. The only means by which to obtain such a warrant was by telephone to awaken some slumbering judge. We were aware in advance that Sergeant Draglund was very well-versed in the process by which to obtain a telephonic search warrant. But, unfortunately, there were no telephones within the drug den. Cell phones would not exist for another decade. We thus requested of Sergeant Draglund that he locate a nearby business wherein he could use a telephone.

Sergeant Draglund was happy to assist with the search warrant process. Since he was unfamiliar with the neighborhood, we directed him to a recommended business. We advised that the only friendly business in the neighborhood was a bar across the street.

It was a cold and rainy night, and we did not wish for the Sergeant to become chilled. We therefore slid an official SPD Anti- Crime Team "Raid Jacket" over his arms and shoulders and sent him across the street.

The bar to which we directed Don Don was an uproarious gay bar. The back of the good Sergeant's jacket had special identification. The jacket back was complete with a pink sequined heart. Beneath the heart read, "Princess — love me." It was no more than ten minutes that passed before Sarge returned to our location, panting. Clueless, Don Don exclaimed, "That's no good for a search warrant call, boys, all I got was a bunch of weirdos grabbing me."

***

Over a few years, Don took all of the practical jokes with good humor and appreciation — save for one. For some reason he was quite offended by the mannequin tied beneath his patrol car one morning. He offered that we nearly caused him a heart attack thinking he had just killed someone. He had dragged the supposed "body" down Third Avenue for several blocks before leaping from his patrol car to examine the carnage.

Grand theft motorcycle

Our usual Sergeant was a previously mentioned Steve Butler. Given that he was our permanent supervisor, Sergeant Butler was treated with a great deal more respect than poor Sergeant Don Don. Perhaps there were a *few* exceptions.

Sergeant Butler had a habit of always placing his patrol Sergeant's hat upon a roll-call podium in such a way that the inner lining faced his audience. We had seen him address public gatherings with his hat so positioned as well. Thus armed with such knowledge, his squad sought to steal his hat briefly for decorations. The ever absent-minded Sarge, nicknamed "Two-Nebulous" never noticed that someone had placed a highly pornographic photograph inside the lining of the hat. This act of sabotage had occurred shortly before the good Sergeant was to venture from the precinct and give a crime presentation to a group of senior citizens at a local Rotary Club.

For the first and only time in recollection, Sergeant Butler returned to the precinct and addressed his squad of young officers with fury. He believed we had crossed the line of decency and decorum. He had tolerated our sending a call girl to his home. He had countenanced our placing a wino his brand new pickup truck for a day. But we had gone too far on that occasion. We therefore pledged no more such egregious offenses toward our beloved boss.

A few weeks later, we somehow forgot our promise. The Sergeant had recently purchased a motorcycle for his mode of transportation. He offered that he was confident we could not hide a wino on his motorcycle. He had even chortled that he had finally out-foxed his mischievous but highly productive young squad.

Prior to the completion of another particularly interesting day shift, numerous officers were deployed throughout the precinct on a mission. Officers carried portable radios and spread out in the parking garage, and within the building itself. They stationed themselves as lookouts. It was almost as if they were familiar with performing such an onerous task. The strongest officer from our squad, a former college all conference tight end, joined forces with a member of another squad. The other officer – one Dennis Tichi – was the strongest policeman anyone had ever met.

Dennis was comfortable hoisting two bales of hay with each hand from his youth on a farm. A 600-pound motorcycle between he and the other officer would prove child's play.

The two muscle men waited until Sergeant Butler had just brought his gear out to his bike. This was a predictable routine for the Sarge. He would return within the precinct to sign out and re-appear in seconds. Lookouts narrated his whereabouts at all times. His expensive motorcycle was then hoisted into a nearby elevator and taken away to an upstairs office.

All of the officers then happened to loiter on "G-Deck" of the Public Safety Building parking area. We anticipated the arrival of Steve Butler. Just like clockwork, the good Sarge arrived on the deck with his helmet secured atop his head. He reached for his bike and found nothing. He then looked around the area of his bike in a 360-degree radius and still found nothing. The Sarge removed his helmet and stood quizzically. Officer Tichi just happened to be standing nearby and asked, "Everything OK, Sarge?" All other nearby officers stifled laughter.

Sergeant Butler simply answered, "Oh yeah. Just forgot my glasses." With that, he walked back into the precinct and sat himself for a few minutes at his desk. He was seen to shake his head and then rise. He returned to the location of his motorcycle.

He then walked in circles, scratched his head, and checked other motorcycle parking spots on the deck. Sarge then returned to his desk and sat down. He was heard to telephone home from his desk and ask his wife, "Carol did I take my motorcycle to work today?" He hung up the phone, "OK, thanks." He ran his fingers through his graying red hair and again placed his helmet atop his head. He walked forcefully and angrily toward the G-deck area yet again.

By then the two muscle men officers had already replaced the motorcycle to its original position. All of the loitering officers stifled laughter as we watched the Sarge walk over to his prized possession. With a shrug, he seated himself on the motorcycle, started such, and drove out into the night. To this day, none of us know if our absent-minded "Two Nebulous" even realized that his motorcycle had been stolen.

***

Oops

Perhaps the only other memorable exception to the patience exhibited by Sergeants Butler and Draglund toward the mischievous young officers was a lights and siren issue.

At one time, both the East and West Patrol precincts were housed jointly in the aging Public Safety Building. The cold and dusty G-deck parking area of the building predictably resembled the tarmac of O'Hare International. Dozens of patrol cars came and went from the cramped quarters, seemingly in perfect harmony.

A preferred practical joke of the patrol officers was to set the lights and sirens of the vehicles to engage immediately upon turning an ignition key. A continuous cacophony could thus be heard on any given morning, and it was accepted as good fun amongst the troops. Yet, every opportunity for good-hearted fun must eventually come to an end. It was thus with such a time-honored tradition of practical jokes one lovely Sunday morning.

That given Sunday, unknown officers set out to booby-trap yet another parked vehicle. However, they did not give thought to the relative I.Q. of the officer assigned to drive the vehicle. While she would later become regarded as "the stupidest cop in history," during her brief career, the officer's amazing gifts of mental ineptness were not yet fully chronicled.

The first anyone knew of the practical joke gone awry was when the rear bumper of the patrol vehicle crashed with profound impact into the cinder-block walls. The force even served to propel two blocks inward. The lights still flashed and the siren still raged. And the engine continued to race. Nearby officers were seated, typing police reports on typewriters. They made heroic efforts to run out onto the deck, secure the vehicle, and remove the panicked officer from the damaged vehicle.

The Sergeants were immensely relieved to learn that numerous officers had the skills to very quickly repair both the patrol car and the precinct wall. The following day, an irate patrol major could find no evidence whatsoever of any such incident. He examined the wall and patrol car in question and found both to be completely unscathed. The Sergeants dismissed the Major's concerns as mere "precinct rumors" and wished the Major well upon his departure. They then addressed the roll calls and loudly informed the troops that another tradition had abruptly come to an end.

***

Dumb and dumber: We are indeed human

During the Field Training portion of the program numerous recommendations were made regarding a particular rookie student officer (guess who). Such recommendations ranged from, "If this individual is retained I shall resign my commission immediately," to "If this individual is retained, she shall someday cost the department millions of dollars in lawsuits." Yet, all of such observations by experienced and respected training officers were overlooked by the department's command staff. Such recommendations were summarily erased from any record. The Chief of Police wished to greatly increase the numbers of female officers employed by the department so as to show his "progressive" action. Apparently, the roughly 3.5 billion women whom inhabited the earth in the early 80's did not provide ample alternatives to her retention. Thus, the world's dumbest cop embarked upon a stellar career with the Seattle Police Department. She shall hereafter be referred to as "Officer Einstein."

One glorious day, Officer Einstein sought to drive her blue and white patrol car through the city's privately-owned car wash. Located in the northern industrial district of downtown Seattle at 7th Avenue South and South Charles Street, the Charles Street facilities were very handy. The city had wisely chosen to employ its own mechanics and engineers. They thus designed a very high quality car wash for all city vehicles.

The Charles Street car wash was a very sophisticated and complex undertaking. Drivers of patrol cars, or other city vehicles had to perform the following confusing tasks:

- Drive to the car wash.
- Line up the front tires with the three foot wide, very gradually narrowing metal rails.
- Brake slightly while idling forward.

- Take your hands off the wheel.
- Keep your windows rolled up.
- And, finally, perhaps the most difficult task....sit there while the vehicle eases through the brushes and power washers of the facility.

Officer Einstein sought to employ her venerable knowledge and wisdom to attempt the challenging and treacherous journey. Her heroism was laudable. Yet, inexplicably, the mechanical beast devoured her beautiful patrol car. Somehow the vehicle was thrashed about so greatly by the beast that the patrol car ended up at 90 degrees perpendicular within the car wash. Wisely, the exasperated young officer broadcast via her police radio that she needed "Help, Help, Help!"

The cavalry of worried patrol officers hurriedly responded en masse to the sight. Included were two patrol Sergeants. The young officer suddenly emerged from within the car wash, doused in water and foaming bubbles. She was barely recognizable. A sage old Sergeant immediately said, "Where the hell is your car?" Officer Einstein merely quaked in a tearful display and pointed behind herself toward the inner sanctum of the car wash.

Ultimately city engineers were summoned to the site in order to determine how to extricate the lost patrol vehicle. Tow trucks were requested. They were summarily dismissed as impractical. The vehicle was literally being wedged between two concrete cinder block walls, sideways in placement. In the end, the only resolution to the predicament was to jack-hammer one of the two walls nearly to oblivion.

A heavily damaged $30,000 dollar patrol vehicle was removed. A $250,000 dollar car wash was rendered useless. The former field training officers' warnings had quickly proven to be prophetic. Yet, this incident would prove to be only the beginning. In fact, a few years later, the same officer would become famous for seeking to conceal damage she caused to a patrol car. Officer Einstein chose to fool trained observer Sergeants by covering the crinkled door with innumerable bottles of whiteout. Somehow her nefarious plan was uncovered by her supervisor — in approximately forty-five seconds.

***

The adventures of "Airplane Bob"

A certain middle-aged officer with only two years of experience officer wielded a reputation for being devoid of any known thread of common sense. He was a smallish and wiry man, wearing Coke bottle glasses. He lacked a single strand of hair on his head. He consistently stood with a hunched-over posture. The officer had been quickly nicknamed "Elmer Fudd" by the world's funniest policeman — Gregg Pote. The nickname very accurately depicted the poor gentleman.

The first observation of Officer Fudd by your author occurred at a labor strike at a nearby Boeing Plant. Machinists within the enormous facility bordering on the South Seattle city limits were angered by stalled contract negotiations. They planned large-scale demonstrations at the South Seattle plant, among others. While the plant was technically outside of the city limits of Seattle, it was believed by Seattle city officials that a ripple effect could impact the city. It was thus decided that mass numbers of Seattle Police patrol officers would supplement beleaguered Boeing security and King County Sheriff deputies.

An astute South Precinct Captain Don Marquardt was assigned as incident commander of the SPD response to the quasi-strike actions. A former SWAT commander, the distinguished white-haired veteran Captain was well equipped to make shrewd management decisions. He thus amassed nearly fifty uniformed officers, clad with riot helmets and long wooden riot batons. His instructions to the assembled troops prior to deployment were clear and explicit. The SPD officers were to adopt a strict policy of neutrality in the conflict between management and labor. They were to provide a calming barrier between the two parties. They were not to communicate with either party sans approval by himself or a higher department authority. And, finally, the Captain emphatically stressed that *under no circumstances* were any SPD officers to break ranks with the riot lines and engage any criminal acts. Were such actions to occur, the Captain himself would order such actions. He re-emphasized that all officers would stay in line under any circumstances.

The day drew long, as heated verbal exchanges were witnessed between the labor parties and Boeing management. Levels of civility seemed to plummet as the hot summer day dragged on. Minor acts of un-civility by the union members were occasionally seen. They taunted personnel whom crossed picket lines and even committed minor acts of vandalism. A few renegade union members were seen on hangar rooftops throwing garbage and water balloons in the general direction of the assembled police ranks. Yet, the professional and well-instructed SPD officers held their ranks. The South Precinct Captain beamed with pride at the poise of his troops.

The Captain's demeanor instantly changed as he followed the upward glances of several SPD officers in the ranks. His jaw suddenly dropped. In the distance, upon the building rooftops, was none other than Officer Fudd. Like an enraged bull, the officer was leaping from building top to building top in impassioned pursuit of the rooftop garbage throwers.

The scene resembled that of a Wily Coyote in pursuit of

the Road Runner. I would have sworn the chase left a dust trail behind the two contestants. Soon, Officer Fudd and his prey were far out of sight in directions unknown. The Captain seemed stunned. He barked at the troops to remain in line and walked out of earshot. He spoke animatedly and drove his vehicle out of sight.

Approximately fifteen minutes later, the Captain returned to the ranks. He inquired if anyone had seen Officer Fudd. He was advised by a Sergeant that no such sighting had occurred. The Captain cursed under his breath.

Suddenly, a perspiration-soaked Officer Fudd approached our location from behind a nearby building. He was dragging a hand-cuffed striker toward us. The striker and the officer were both bloodied, with numerous scrapes. Their clothing was torn and disheveled.

Officer Fudd announced to the Captain that he was reporting in, and, "The situation is under control, sir." The Captain's non muffled response consisted entirely of creative groupings of four letter words. So ended my first sighting of the legendary new officer. He immediately struck me as a cartoon character suddenly loosed upon real life.

Approximately two years hence from the Boeing strike incident, I was seated in a "write-up room" of the West Precinct typing a report. Captain Bill Taylor was visiting with Sergeants and a nearby Lieutenant, as he was known to do each morning. Bill Taylor was a fifty-something year old, tall and distinguished individual. He held a law degree, among his many academic achievements. Captain Taylor was the latest in a long line of tremendously respected downtown precinct Captains. The troops thought the world of the calm and circumspect leader.

A call came in to the Sergeants' desk area, as the Captain

stood visiting. A Sergeant answered such call promptly. He stood silently as he listened intently on the phone for a considerable period of time. The Sergeant ultimately turned to Captain Taylor, "Uh, Cap this one's all yours." Captain Taylor sighed heavily, obviously sensing a downturn in the quality of his morning. He answered politely and identified himself. Much like the Sergeant, Captain Taylor nodded and offered numerous "Uh huh(s)" to the caller. He finally hung up the phone and clenched his shaking hands. His face turned crimson, as he muttered, "Shit!" Never known to utter a single word of profanity in view of his troops, this was cause for immediate attention from myself and nearby officers.

A partial story would be shared at the time by the Captain. Complete details would quickly follow within the facility. It would be learned that the caller was an irate Sky Marshall from Sea-Tac International Airport. He had called the West Precinct commander out of courtesy to the Seattle Police Department. He advised that, held in his secure facility, was an officer of the Seattle P.D.

It would seem that Officer Elmer Fudd himself had sought to take a flight out of town on a personal vacation. The officer, clad in street clothes, had chosen to walk through the metal detectors at the airport with his duty .357 magnum revolver protruding conspicuously from the back of his waist-band. In doing so he had set off every sensor known to mankind. Alarmed security crews sought to detain the armed man. As the story was told, Officer Fudd retrieved a wallet and badge from his pocket and brusquely identified himself as a Seattle Police officer. He loudly claimed immunity from any further attention. It did not matter to him that he was violating federal law. Perplexed security personnel strode rapidly beside the officer, insisting that he stop. Yet, Officer Fudd strode past the check-in gate and past more confronting airline personnel.

Ultimately, Officer Fudd entered the aircraft with his firearm ever more visible and seated himself within the plane. Polite, yet insistent flight crew members sought to remove him from the plane. He was later quoted as responding, "F — k you, I'm a Seattle Police Officer." As the story continues, the pilot of the airliner eventually approached the seated Fudd. He was quoted as advising Fudd, "I don't care who you are, you will not bring a firearm on my plane." True to form, Office Fudd remained dogmatically seated.

As legend would have it, the only means by which the officer would vacate his seated position was upon the forceful invitation of two federal sky marshals.

Only by the remarkable coaxing of Captain Taylor, who drove to the airport, did the Officer avoid booking into a federal jail. The Captain had to personally retrieve Officer Fudd and drive him back to his precinct.

It was thus that Officer Fudd's nickname morphed. Of course, it was comedian Officer Pote, yet again, whom drafted the new moniker. Officer Fudd would forever be referred to as "Airplane Bob." Other choice alternatives to the nickname evolved, as the troops sometimes referred to the character as "Wild Billy-Bob" or "Cobalt." Amazingly, the man would go on to eventual promotion to the rank of Sergeant. Yet, the legend of his decision-making prowess continued to this retirement date.

***

Dumb and dumber — Officer Einstein's ultimate cost

On April 13, 1995 your author was working as a rookie Sergeant in the 9-1-1 basement center of the Public Safety Building. At around 6:45 P.M. the Chief Dispatcher of the center was monitoring four radio frequencies for each respective patrol precinct in the city. The Chief Dispatcher was a 32-year cop and veteran of the "Comm Center." His name was Gary Greene. Gary motioned across the room to me. He held up four fingers and pointed towards his ear. I knew the signal to indicate that I should put on my console headset and tune to frequency 4 – The North Precinct. Like Officer Greene, I immediately recognized an exasperated voice of Officer Einstein over the airway. The officer was screaming over the radio that she needed paramedics to respond to a back yard area of North 45th Street and Fremont Way North. As was protocol, the radio dispatcher requested the nature of the request. I could hear the officer hesitate before responding…."Radio, just tell em we have a man with a, a, a… puncture-wound." It took considerable radio exchanges before Officer Einstein would admit she had shot a man.

A subsequent police investigation would come to an unprecedented department conclusion. A review board concluded that the officer had unlawfully shot a man fleeing from a domestic dispute. The man had been accused of pushing his wife. He had chosen to flee from responding officers and ran past Officer Einstein. Despite her claims of a struggle, evidence refuted such claims. The review board ruled that the officer had chosen to shoot the man in the back as he passed her. There was no legal justification for such a choice. The officer's version of the incident changed as often as the Seattle weather.

Ultimately, the cost to the taxpayers for the Seattle Police Department retaining a personable but clearly incompetent officer was 2.3 million dollars – the amount of a law- suit settlement. The man whom Officer Einstein shot had suffered an entry wound to his heart, a lost lung, and a subsequent stroke. The past training officers' admonishments had come to sickening fruition. It was no longer humorous.

***

Cop Culture — The "Racial Profiling" myth

The following is an amended re-print of an editorial written by your author for the Seattle Police Officer's Guild "Guardian" monthly newspaper. I should point out that I repeatedly mailed such editorial to all local newspapers and every television station. Not a single media entity would even acknowledge receiving such — much less dare print a contrary opinion to their own.

As I peruse the local and national publications of journalistic impartiality I see with alarming regularity the political usage of this powerful term. The context of such verbiage leads one to believe that a possibility of widespread racist police-work reminiscent of Nazi Germany clearly exists in America. More specifically, our local civic leaders revile my Seattle peers as participants in such activities. Our union leaders have attended seminars sponsored by our Black Law Enforcement Union in efforts to address this issue. Central Washington Police Chiefs have held marches against such practices.

My question is, has such an allegation been validated or does the mere accusation become fact? Do we police officers dare stigmatization by attempting to refute such claims or merely remain silent and lend credence to such?

The tendency of police officers is to rely upon assumptions in quotidian endeavors. We base these upon personal experience and that of our peers. While such assumptions are often inaccurate, we know that they are more often than not, true. I will cite some examples that fall outside the realm of politics:

- Most alarms are false.
- Most street criminals are young.

- Most street criminals are male.
- Most fleeing suspects take a right turn to begin with.
- Burglars don't answer the phone.
- Drunks will want to fight.

We look at police-work much as a baseball player would the opponent. Instantaneous decisions are based upon assumptions and guesses. The decision cannot wait as the pitch comes your way. Will the pitcher throw a curveball on a 2-2 count? Well, he has the last three times. We haven't the time for academic review.

After a while the officer forms a guess as to criminality of those on the *streets*. Does the person with the glassy eyes, Mohawk, and cigarette hanging out of the mouth strike you more as suspicious than the person in the three piece suit? There are fairly clear patterns to criminals as the arrests mount. We can sort those patterns by race, as well as a myriad of other factors.

More controversial assumptions have been made by me in 27 years of police-work, and I invite a contrary opinion:
- Most serial rapists are white.
- Most marijuana grow-house operators are white.
- Most LSD dealers are white.
- Most heroin dealers are Hispanic.
- Most crack dealers are black.
- Gangs employ a disproportionate number of ethnic minorities.

The allegations that traffic stops are based primarily on race perplex me. How many times can an officer focus upon the color of the light, license tabs, etc., the travelling vehicle, *and* the race of the driver? If such is a practice, their eyesight clearly surpasses my 20/10 vision. Rarely did I know if Ted Bundy or

E.T. was going to poke a head out of that window. All too-often, it was the driver or occupants who brought race to the fore. An air of persecution complexes often are evident, seemingly as a ploy to make the officers defensive or reluctant. One must wonder if King County Sheriff's Deputy Steven Cox exhibited a reluctance to search an African American suspect for just such reluctance. He was ultimately murdered by the suspect, who pulled his gun from a pocket and opened fire.

It is claimed that our officers stop vehicles at will to terrorize certain groups "for no reason at all." Who are these hate-mongers? Would their peers who chose to work in Seattle for its civility allow this? It is further claimed by some that a disproportionate number of the incarcerated are prima- facia evidence of police bias. Do our officers not try to arrest white suspects as diligently? Do they release these victimizers with a wink? Perhaps these numbers are merely reflective of another problem, far beyond the control of police officers. I cannot imagine working with an officer bent upon oppression of any sort.

My contention is that we in police-work concentrate primarily on street-level crimes, rather than those in the boardrooms. The reasons for this strategy are many:

For one, street-level crime is more readily identifiable. It often entails acts of profound violence which are witnessed by many and reported in the media. Many street level criminals tend to dress or behave in easily recognizable manners.

Street level crime is easier to investigate and prosecute due to the lack of sophistication of the offenders. Our law enforcement laziness at many levels precludes other efforts.

Affluent criminals function with the protection of wealth and the corresponding legal representation (O.J. Simpson? John and Patsy Ramsey?)

Affluent criminals have strong political connections who can "turn down the heat." (Pardon me, Mr. President?) No one gets caught in the crossfire of insider trading.

The driving social impetus of money and power compels us to enforce only a portion of the criminal pie. That portion, sadly, entails a disproportionate number of minority individuals. The statistics are a mere indicator of this phenomenon. That social impetus is a political animal far beyond the control of our officers. Yet the blame is placed upon the wrong shoulders. Scapegoating will solve nothing.

While society solves its problem of socio-economic corruption, let us address what we can. Video/audio tapes upon all police vehicles would prove invaluable in encouraging accountability of all officers. Conversely, such may accurately record and depict the behaviors of those contacted. A state law would need to be enacted to allow such an invasion of the privacy of **both** the officer and the contacted party. No party should possess special rights nor be denied equal rights. Were the officer to be out of line, sanctions should be levied. Were the other party to have broken a law or otherwise embarrassed themselves, may the recording prove evidence thereof.

I am confident that the overwhelming majority of my peers, of all walks of life, perform their duties with class and excellence. We are all blue and huge beneficiaries of the diversity of our ranks. We have nothing to hide and I welcome all observers. I believe many eyes would be opened if they dare to look.

Chapter 14: Sometimes the bad guys lose

Most police officers will volunteer their perceptions that criminals always seem to benefit from incredibly beneficial fate. All too often criminals can evade the most ardent of detection efforts. Their speeding fleeing vehicles will penetrate a red light at a crowded intersection and emerge on the other side, totally unscathed. Numerous smashed patrol cars will be scattered in the wake. A suspect will fire an errant round toward distant cops and the bullet will find the intended target. After a while, the cops ascribe to the Billy Joel song title, "Only the good die young." Sadly, on only rare occasions the stars do line up against the thugs. Still, it is those moments that re-instill our faith that the pursuit of justice is a worthwhile venture.

***

Jessie James meets the bag

On a mid- spring day in 1982 a radio alert tone came across the air. A Chief Dispatcher indicated that a bank robbery had just occurred at Seattle First National Bank on 15th Avenue Northwest, in the northern portion of Seattle. Numerous patrol units, including your author, sped toward the area. We set up a wide net of containment, known as "quadrants" for several blocks around the bank. Some officers entered the bank, while others began driving adjoining blocks. The officers within the bank indicated via radio that the armed suspect had successfully completed the robbery. They advised that he had pointed a large caliber handgun in the face of a terrified young teller. He had obtained thousands of dollars in cash. After providing a suspect description, the officers broadcast that the teller had managed to hide a dye pack within the cash. (Note: A dye pack is a tiny implant into a piece of currency that has an explosive charge. The charge is designed to emit vast amounts of luminescent green dye. It is hoped that suspect will later be found "green-handed.")

The search for the frightening suspect continued in earnest, but seemingly to no avail. Yet, approximately twenty minutes later, two officers calmly advised that they most certainly had had located the suspect in a nearby alley. They were asked over the radio by a patrol Sergeant how they could be so certain. Laughter could be heard from the arresting officers as they indicated that the dye pack had indeed exploded, as designed — within the front pants of the suspect!

As the future eunuch suspect was taken via aid car to Harborview Medical Center, numerous officers opined that he had already been rehabilitated.

***

Crimes in the dark can be hazardous to your health

During the mid-1980s gasoline prices took a demonstrable upward swing in price. The commodity became more expensive and less abundant. Predictably, gas thefts soon became epidemic in Seattle, like most other cities. It was thus not surprising that other officers and myself were dispatched to the Crown Hill area of North Seattle to another gas siphoning in progress. Those types of dispatched calls were commonplace. While not exactly the crime of the century, residents in the upper middle-class neighborhood took such offenses seriously. Therefore, so, too did the Seattle Police department.

Ever pleased to be able to capture thieves of any sort, three different patrol units pulled up to the scene virtually simultaneously. The victim vehicle was said to be a white Ford F-250 pickup, complete with a very large camper atop. Our patrol car spotlights illuminated the truck and camper from all sides, as we exited our patrol cars with flashlights alighted.

Initially, we could locate no signs of a theft, or a suspect. The gas cap was found to be untouched. Yet, we soon heard nearly imperceptible moaning coming from a human being. We eventually located the source of the moaning. Lying prone beneath the chassis of the truck was a twenty year- old white male suspect retching continuously. He had sought to cover his mouth upon the approach of officers, but he could not stop the convulsions. Nearby Officer Rod Hamlet's unmistakable laughter could be heard. Officer Hamlet was a close facsimile to James Earl Jones in appearance and voice. His shoulders shook with his deep bass laughter.

The enormously strong Officer Hamlet reached beneath the truck and grabbed the suspect's foot. The officer easily pulled the young man from beneath the vehicle and shone his flashlight on the suspect's face. Rod smiled toward me with his famous gapped front teeth grin and commented, "Man, Steve, I've never seen a white man this green."

As Officer Hamlet lifted the vomitous young man to his feet, he turned him to face the pickup truck. The officer then commented to the young thief, "Son, next time you go to siphon gas, you might not want to put your hose in a septic tank." Officer Hamlet shone his flashlight upon the opened waste release valve, with the siphon hose still very much intact.

All officers on the scene opined that the young thief had perhaps already received ample punishment for his heinous act. He was released from the scene after being identified. The young thief staggered away from the scene, still experiencing profound "dry heaves" as he departed.

Astoundingly, the police report drafted would make national news the following day. It would appear that America had a similar sense of humor to the police.

***

Poor customer service?

Daytime North end patrol officers were dispatched to a report of a masked armed man entering Shoreline Savings bank at 12300 Lake City Way Northeast. The call came during a week of numerous violent bank robberies in the city. Within moments, numerous units arrived in the vicinity, including me. As per procedure, all patrol officers encircled the bank and remained outside. A Chief Dispatcher then telephoned within the bank to determine the circumstances within the establishment. This procedure is for the safety of responding officers and the persons within the bank. It is intended to avoid creating a hostage situation were the suspect to still be present within the institution.

Within a few minutes, Radio advised that the manager of the bank stated that no tellers had experienced any problems. Another officer and I then entered the bank to confirm the situation in person with the manager. We performed a perfunctory scan of the premises and questioned the manager and his tellers. All advised that they had no idea why a 9-1-1 caller would claim to have seen an alleged bandit.

Meanwhile, other officers outside the bank radioed to us. They stated that they were interviewing two witnesses who insisted that their claims were true. We thus repeated our questions to all bank personnel. The answer remained a steadfast negative to any problems. We finally decided to review bank camera tapes. We were escorted by the lead teller to a rear office of the bank to view the camera's recollection of occurrences within the establishment. The lead teller was clearly frustrated with our wasting her time. She advised that the bank had been very busy and she needed to update her accounting. Nonetheless, she sat with us impatiently.

We forwarded the tape to the approximate time of the 9-1-1 calls in question. We immediately noted a large white man with a blue bandana around his neck. He had concealed a powerful handgun in his front waistband while entering the bank. The suspect had patiently waited his turn in a lengthy line. He was in the line of our lead teller. As the bandit finally moved to the front of the line he approached the teller window and lifted the bandana across his face. The bank robber began to pull his firearm from his waistband. At exactly the same time, the teller could be seen to grab a "teller window closed" sign and place it in her window. Just as the robber fully withdrew his handgun, the teller could be seen mouthing unknown words. She quickly turned away from the teller window and walked toward the employee break room.

A stunned bank robber stood for a few moments at the teller window. He clearly did not know how to react. Finally, the robber shrugged, pulled down his bandana, stuffed the gun in his waist band, and walked out of the bank.

As we watched the tape in fascination, the lead teller gasped and covered her mouth. The middle aged woman said, "Oh my gawwwwd!"

We asked the teller what she had said to the robber. She responded, "I didn't even see the gun or mask....I was so frazzled from how busy we were I just told the next customer

I was going on my break and move to the next window." She followed her statement with another, "Oh my gawwwwd." She nearly fainted.

We later advised the bank manager that we did not know whether to commend the teller for her heroism or recommend discipline for her poor customer service. Regardless, the masked bandit was eventually apprehended. An experienced bank robber, the suspect knew that he was "had." The robber readily alluded to the rude treatment from the lead teller of Shoreline Savings. We were advised by detectives and F.B.I. agents that even *he* laughed at the situation.

***

Mr. Burglar meets Mr. Winchester

A radio broadcast rang out on a warm summer day in 1985 of a burglary in progress at a home on picturesque Queen Anne hill. The owner of a beautiful Tudor house, overlooking downtown and the Space Needle, was on the line with 9-1-1. Dispatch related a narration of the burglary. It was said that a shadow of the burglar had been viewed circling the entire house by the elderly complainant. The caller related that he had called out to the prowler to "get the hell out of here." But the prowler had not been dissuaded from his affront. The narration continued in real-time as the burglar returned to the front door of the home. Mere seconds had passed as other patrol units and myself sped toward the location, lights and sirens engaged. Yet, the broadcast situation changed by the second.

The caller advised that a large and muscular black male was cursing him and attempting to kick the front door of his home into shards of wood and glass. The caller advised that he could see the outline of a knife through the overhead window of the front door. Seconds later, the caller advised that the suspect had broken the glass window of his door with his hand, and was trying the interior door knob. As we continued to speed toward the address, radio related that they had heard a gunshot from the residence.

Radio went silent for moments. Ten seconds passed until the dispatcher advised that she had re-connected with the caller. The caller advised that he had fired one blast from his shotgun in the general direction of the suspect. Radio informed that the 9-1-1 operator in question had heard a distant voice screaming, "Sheeeeit!"

Multiple units arrived at the residence, almost in unison. Unit 2-Queen-3, Officers Maser and Tichi first emerged from their vehicle. The tandem was legendary for their savvy and toughness from decades past. Officer Dennis Tichi was the strongest human being ever known to the patrol bureau, and Officer Maser was known for his tenacity. I followed the veteran officers toward the residence. Our guns were drawn. We quickly noted a broken six inch by eight inch window atop the front door of the lovely home. Blood was dripping noticeably from the window opening. Officer Maser radioed to dispatch to inform the home owner to drop his shotgun and allow police into his home.

Quickly, a silver-haired 65 year-old gentleman opened the badly damaged door. He was shaking demonstrably. The gentleman politely allowed us into the home. Officer Tichi began to mute a laugh as he looked downward at the door jam. His partner and I immediately joined his downward glance. Sitting on the inside of the doorway was a bloody hand. No knife was found. The home owner related how he had separated the burglar's hand from his body with the shotgun blast. But it was already obvious.

Nearby roving patrol units very quickly located the burglary suspect. He was located in a nearby alley. The suspect was bleeding badly and lacking a right hand. Officers searched the entire bloody trail of the suspect, aided by a canine unit. Yet, a knife was never found.

Several days later, Officers Tichi and Maser related to their peers that they had been summoned to the office of the Chief of Police. It was stated that the Police Chief had furiously grilled the officers, for considerable time, regarding the incident in question. The Chief held in his hands the written statement from the Queen Anne home owner. Apparently, the home owner had drafted a statement of a quality usually reserved for a sage attorney or police officer. In such statement, the home owner related how he was in fear for his life during the incident. He penned that he was certain that the burglary suspect was armed, and that the suspect had verbalized an intent to cause him serious physical harm. The home owner even added that he was a disabled senior citizen left with no other reasonable options but to open fire upon the burglar with his hunting shotgun. The Chief apparently insisted that the officers had dictated the statement in question to the home owner.

Apparently, the revered senior officers merely shrugged their shoulders at the Chief of Police. They expressed how equally amazed they were at the erudite and descriptive statement given by the "poor little old man."

Eventually, the matter was dropped. This was a similar fate to the burglar's hand. Burglary detectives later offered that they believed the suspect had victimized dozens of homes. They were confident that it was he whom had seriously assaulted several elderly victims within those homes. It was hoped that the suspect had been rehabilitated.

***

The one that didn't get away

On another date, your author was again working a patrol unit in the northern downtown environs of Seattle, known as David Sector. A report of a home invasion robbery was broadcast. An armed individual had broken into a Queen Anne home and demanded cash at gunpoint. The victims had provided a detailed description of the suspect and his vehicle, as the suspect fled the home with cash. Arriving patrol officers updated the call with extensive details of the incident. A license number for the escape- vehicle was broadcast by those investigating officers. The home in question was approximately three miles north of my location.

A couple minutes later, I saw the suspect vehicle driving eastbound on Denny Way, a street beneath the shadow of the historic Space Needle. I sought to trail the vehicle from an inconspicuous distance while radioing the sighting. Stupidly, I drew too near the suspect vehicle, and was detected by the suspect. The suspect immediately braked his older Chevrolet and pulled a skidding 180 degree turn. He sped westbound and past my vehicle, concealed by traffic. I was slow to react to the maneuver, and the suspect vehicle gained considerable distance. I nearly lost sight of the vehicle as I engaged my lights and siren, and advised radio that I was in pursuit.

Luckily, my less than powerful Dodge Diplomat was faster than the suspect's aging vehicle. I eventually gained some distance. The suspect vehicle turned northbound on Elliott Avenue West. The chase entered a highly-congested rush hour traffic. Yet, the suspect vehicle deftly flew through the traffic as if Moses himself were parting the Red Sea. I fell hopelessly behind in the chase. I did what I could to maintain a visual of the suspect vehicle, while narrating my losing endeavor. Other patrol vehicles drew to my rear in a sort of formation of pursuing patrol cars. Yet, more skilled drivers in the adjoining patrol cars could not gain ground on the suspect. He continued to dart through the dense traffic unscathed. My backup patrol vehicles dropped behind me.

The suspect vehicle continued northbound on the arterial, as Elliott Avenue West became 15th Avenue West. It was rapidly disappearing from view. Yet, my colleagues and I forged hopelessly onward. I was pleased to see traffic lining the curb lane of the arterial, paying heed to a lunatic suspect driver and the squadron of wailing patrol cars in pursuit.

It appeared that the chase was over, as the suspect vehicle could no longer be seen. At nearly the moment I was to broadcast a lost cause, a spiritual vision emerged before me. I could almost hear harp music. There on 15th Avenue West was the suspect vehicle, suddenly stopped. The suspect driver had no choice in the matter. Before him stood the historic Ballard draw bridge. And the bridge was rising rapidly skyward. The driver had the choice of jumping into the frigid Lake Washington Canal, or merely awaiting the officers, running his direction. He chose to stand out of his vehicle and place his hands on the trunk.

A jogging Officer Greg Pote, renowned for his humor, commented, "Oh... this is gonna be fuuuuun.!" It is highly doubtful that the suspect agreed, as his face was implanted securely into the metal grating of the bridge.

We were soon to learn that the operator of the draw-bridge was listening to the police scanner. He made a habit of doing so during his tedious job. He had listened intently to the progress of the chase. He further had waited until the last moment to engage the draw bridge. I could have kissed the wiry middle-aged man, but I did not wish to become the brunt of Officer Pote's hilarious sarcasm.

***

Chapter side note: Lieutenant Emmett Kelsie

Emmett Kelsie was simply the finest boss I have ever had in my life. It is my belief that every manager should aspire to his qualities. As more and more individuals lament the poor management in their respective vocations, America could benefit greatly by producing managers of Lt. Kelsie's caliber. For the rest of my life, I will aspire to emulate his manner of handling people and a company's mission. He did both with distinction.

Lt Kelsie could be described in one word — wise. He took the time to know his employees very thoroughly before selecting them for a position. He had a shrewd gift for finding talent. He knew how to make a unit stronger by diversity. He chose the finest from every walk of life and melded the differing talents.

Lt. Kelsie also maintained a very key awareness of the buttons to push on his employees. He knew how to motivate them. Emmett never held a formal meeting. Instead, at the beginning of each day, he loosened his tie, demanded the same of his people, and placed his feet upon a desk for a "rap session." The dominance of rank was immediately dropped. He wanted to know what his peoples' concerns and needs were before the day began. He studiously took notes and listened intently. He would then advise his employees how he would address each issue. Nothing was ever forgotten. He encouraged innovative strategies by each of his people. He invited criticisms of himself, and dissenting opinions. Mere complaints were discouraged unless a better idea was provided. As each employee provided insight, he then communicated how such strategies could be melded to fit many needs. A group plan was therefore formulated.

At the end of such highly informal meetings, Lt. Kelsie would invariably cinch his tie, so as to indicate he was again wearing a rank hat. At that time, he would provide each employee with a set of simple and specific philosophies under which we would operate. We were otherwise encouraged to freely seek individual means to follow such philosophies.

Emmett had one other demand of his troops—that they have fun. There was never a day when "Cool Papa" was not heard to laugh heartily, with a high-pitched giggle. Emmett was a diplomat with any member of society. He could speak with academic elite as if he were once a Rhodes Scholar. He could provide politicians with educated and frank information and evoke supportive responses. And he could speak with troubled gang members like a stern, yet caring grandfather.

Emmett created a means to combat gang crime within the black community without ever drawing acrimony from his constituency. In essence, his detectives had to do more homework than the average street cop. Were they to confront a group of young black males wearing L.A. Raiders garb, sagging pants, and black bandanas hanging from pockets, there was more to the impetus of the confrontations than met the eye. Emmett developed a policy by which gangs were approached. We maintained extensive databases of information on the thousands of Seattle gang members. Often, they were foolishly cavalier enough to freely admit gang membership at a given time. That was documented. Group violence was documented. Gang tattoos were photographed and recorded. For those reasons, when new youths were seen with known gang members, we had a solid reason to stop and identify them.

Emmett knew that eliminating anonymity of gang members was the ultimate key. They could not disappear into their peer crowds. The moment a known gang walked down the street, they were identified and greeted by name by Gang Unit detectives. They knew that the Gang Unit had a very good idea of who would cause a problem before the problem occurred. All gang member monikers were copiously recorded. Thus, the minute a shooting in the Puget Sound area occurred, a mere mention of a nickname involved was the genesis for profound investigatory leads.

Emmett received innumerable commendations for his unit by members of the NAACP and Urban League. The ultimate praise came to his detectives on the streets of Seattle. We literally received standing ovations from apartment buildings of people, as we made the black community safe and fair. It was possible to do both. Were the wisdom of Lt. Kelsie brought into Seattle Politics, it is my belief that many racial chasms could be healed.

Emmett was both a unit manager and a father figure to many within the Gang Unit. To this day, while now retired, Emmett maintains relationships with his former employees. He proudly attends promotions and weddings, much like a father. I will always miss his smile, two-handed handshake, and…ultimately, his infectious laugh.

***

Chapter 15: Kenton Phillip Carpenter: A partnership for life.

In the world of police-work, a patrol partner may surpass a spouse in overall importance. Indeed, more of one's waking hours are spent with that partner than any other human being. The partner is relied upon for companionship, support, and literally life itself. They are positioned three feet to your side, almost as would be a Siamese twin. It is accordingly hoped that a high degree of compatibility may be found. Often, the partnership is an arranged "marriage" by a patrol supervisor. A "two man car" was once a main-stay of the SPD patrol bureau. Yet, in this modern era of budget cuts and efficiency studies, such an arrangement has gone the way of the dinosaurs.

I was paired with 25 year-old Kenton Phillip Carpenter. While Kent was a year my senior in age, I held a *huge* advantage in police experience. I wielded three entire years of experience to Kent's one. It was hence a prospect of the blind leading the blind, although we both thought we knew it all. I didn't know what to think of the guy initially. Our first tour of duty together commenced with him pointing to a nearby billboard for an airlines featuring a stunning Asian woman and commenting, "Yeah, that was an old girlfriend of mine. I had lots of girlfriends."

I commented, "Yeah, sure she is." I'll be darned but not two minutes later a stunningly beautiful Asian woman matching the billboard approached our passing car and summoned Kenton. She embraced him warmly and wished him well. He completed the day by telling stories of his innumerable romantic conquests during college and beyond. Being a shy man whom married his first girlfriend, I certainly enjoyed his stories.

The nearly five-year experience would prove to be an extraordinary honor for me. In the subsequent third of a century, I have learned that a man could have no greater friend in this world than Kent. The patrol partnership has long since ended. (Kent traded me in for a dog and I traded him in for stripes.) Yet, the friendship shall grow until we are in our graves.

In the initial weeks of the assignment as conjoined twins, I held some reservations about the marriage. Kent was brash and combative. The handsome, mustachioed blonde-haired young man looked like he could be a surfer. He reminded many people of Kevin Costner. Yet, his demeanor on the streets was one of a 25 year grizzled veteran. His fiery temper often emerged in his younger days. I, on the other hand, was a taciturn six-foot-six bean pole. We made quite a pair as I towered over Kent. Initially, each of us harbored our doubts as to the abilities of the other in a street fight.

Our doubts were quickly alleviated when confronted with a group of drugged and aggressive assault suspects on a metro bus in Pioneer Square. Without any particular communication, we moved in virtual sync as we toppled the thugs like bowling balls. All I saw was bodies flying in my periphery. I sent my share airborne off of the bus walls. Quickly, the four young thugs were brought under control, panting and bruised upon the bus floor. Kent looked over at his docile giant partner and nodded. He smiled and said, "This could be the start of a beautiful relationship." Indeed it was, as we jointly rode a five-year roller coaster ride of every emotion and experience imaginable. We have laughed and cried together for over thirty years. And the memories in that patrol assignment have proven to be priceless. I only hope that I may relate the following halfway accurately. Otherwise, I will never hear the end of it from my now retired partner…

***

Dropping in on a party

On a particularly dull and tedious Saturday afternoon we were dispatched to the historic and ornate Moore Hotel, at 1906 Second Avenue. We were dispatched to a dead body (D.O.A) found in a tenth floor room. This was a very common call for patrol, as many of the formerly grand hotels were occupied by full-time elderly residents. While the hundred year-old building was losing some luster from years of neglect, the grand ballroom and lounge remained a gathering place for many of the city's elite.

We arrived shortly thereafter at the hotel. We were greeted by the hotel manager at the front entrance. The manager was an impeccably dressed woman in her mid-thirties, complete with a black bow tie. She immediately sought to usher us away from the grand ballroom area. While she did not overtly say so, it was clear that she did not wish for uniformed police officers to be viewed by a large gathering of New Years' Eve revelers in the ballroom and lounge. We were content to comply. While we felt like lepers, we realized that our mere presence in many places instilled a sense of doom and dread in onlookers.

We were escorted to a nearby side elevator and ascended to the tenth floor of the building. The manager unlocked the door of the room. Within the room, we found a portly elderly gentleman in his boxer shorts in a chair. He had obviously died while watching television. There were no signs of foul play. We summoned a coroner, as is customary. The coroner arrived within fifteen minutes. He was a grizzled older man, who walked hunched over from severe back pain. Kent and I looked at one another and knew we owned the job of hoisting the 230 pounds of dead body onto a gurney. After a count of one… two…three, we were able to lift the rigid body onto the white sheeted gurney. We exhaled demonstrably for a moment. The coroner thanked us profusely for the assistance. He wrapped the body with two white sheets and strapped it down snuggly with three seatbelts, from chest down to ankles. Relief set in, as we knew the physics of rolling a gurney were undaunting. The apparatus was designed to easily roll hundreds of pounds.

Thinking we were artificially gracious, we even volunteered to roll the body down the hallway of the hotel toward the main elevator. The hotel manager and coroner provided an entourage. As the door of the elevator opened, our sense of relief immediately disappeared. The manager said, "Oh, you won't fit in *that*." We had forgotten that the ornately bronzed elevator was tiny. There was barely room for four people to stand upright within it. A dead body on a gurney wouldn't come close to fitting.

Not to be disheartened, we asked the manager for alternatives to our quandary. She offered that we could use the stairs of the hotel. Kent said, "Ten flights of stairs?... Oh, I don't think so." The manager then directed us to a remote service elevator that traveled to a side room of the downstairs ballroom. The elevator door opened and our delight diminished yet again. The elevator was actually narrower than the previous elevator. At least we could avoid the growing holiday celebrations below via that route.

We scratched our chins and pondered our predicament. A very handy and clever man, Kent offered a solution. He calculated that we could tilt, twist and turn the body and gurney, much like a couch being carried into a bedroom. We could then stand the body upright in the elevator, because there was a very high ceiling in the lift. He even took measurements with his hands. We consequently sought to cinch the body ever more tightly into the gurney by tightening the seatbelts to maximum capacity.

We were very pleased to find that Kent's calculations were accurate, as we succeeded in tilting the body within the elevator. There was barely room for my partner and me to squeeze within the elevator, as we sought to hold the heavy body in place. We tried to breathe faintly so as not to inhale the overwhelming essence of DOA.

We were quite relieved to hear the ding of the elevator door as we had reached the lobby of the hotel. Yet, the possibility of backing the body out of the elevator, while contorted within such, proved problematic. We each grunted and groaned in discomfort as our faces were pressed against the sheets and the dead man. We tried to communicate with one another and synchronize the twisting of ourselves and our payload that had somehow shifted in transit.

Somehow, inexplicably, the body and gurney seemed to spin on its own volition outward from the elevator. I thought Kent was holding him. Apparently, Kent's belief was just the opposite. In extremely slow motion, we lost the battle with gravity. The body fell from our clutching efforts and tumbled from the elevator. Regrettably, since the elevator abutted a series of cutback grand stairways of the grand ballroom, the body fell downward in the stairwell. Amazingly, the body rolled and tumbled like a downhill skier out of control. A sideways roll was followed by a head over heels catapult action.

Thankfully, the avalanche eventually came to a stop, and peace was restored. Yet, the body had slid from the gurney.

The dead man lay face up…in the middle of the vast gathering of holiday partiers within the ballroom! We were not sure who gasped more loudly, the hotel manager or the half intoxicated party crowd.

I do not recall which of us commented first, but my partner and I nearly simultaneously pointed at one another and said, "I thought *you* had him." Once again, I do not recall who started first, but we began to giggle. The giggles turned to laughs. And the laughs turned to hysterical, tears-falling roars. The coroner shared our sense of humor. Yet, the hotel manager never seemed to agree.

***

That handsome young man

Another fine afternoon in downtown Seattle, Kent and I were dispatched to another vintage hotel. The dispatcher indicated that we were to remove an intoxicated and belligerent man from the bar. As always, we commented to one another, "Well, isn't the bar a place for drunk people to be?" We also invariably commented, "Well, who got the man drunk in the first place?" Ever the humble public servants, we responded to the call as directed, and tucked our opinions in our back pockets.

We arrived shortly thereafter and entered the bar area. An attractive female bartender pointed to a brightly festooned middle-aged gentleman at the end of the bar. She merely said, "That one… he needs to leave… I 86'ed him." With that, we approached the gentleman with one of us on each side of him. The man said not a word, stared directly ahead of him, and away from us. Kent stood on the man's left side, while I was on his right side. I politely advised the man, "Sir, you need to leave with us." He merely muttered incoherently and stared forward. Kent then spoke into his left ear while placing his hand upon the man's left shoulder. The man shrugged my partner's hand away and uttered muffled profanities. Kent again placed his hand on the shoulder while I drew nearer the man. My partner again invited the man to leave the premises with us.

At that, the intoxicated man angrily spun around on his bar stool and stood to face my partner. I grew tense, anticipating a fight. The drunk began to raise his voice at my partner, and then suddenly gasped. He said, "Oh my God... I so thorry (lisp)... I had nooooo idea." The man's irate demeanor immediately changed to that of delight. He smiled at my partner and gently brushed his hand against Kent's shoulder. He said, "Oh, my, you're thuch a handsome young man." The drunk added, "You can take me anywhere you want." The drunk used a napkin to fan his own blushing face and continued his flirtation.

Of course, by then I was in uncontrollable laughter. My serious and ultra-conservative partner was turning four shades of red. Ultimately, Kent said to the drunk, "Partner... I'm not your type." Ultimately, we were able to extricate the trespassing drunk from the premises without any problems. Indeed, he would follow absolutely any order my partner would have chosen to issue to the man.

All these years later, Kent still identifies himself when phoning me as, "That handsome young man."

***

The commendation not earned

During the Christmas season of 1986, the downtown business association of Seattle attempted to hire mass quantities of off-duty SPD officers. The officers were hired to work uniformed "Christmas Beats" in the major shopping areas. The intent was to convey an extra sense of security downtown. It was believed that out of area shoppers would thereby choose to patronize the businesses. The West Precinct commander agreed to support those efforts by allowing the officers to take unmarked vehicles to and from the venues. An officer could work an eight-hour regular patrol shift, and amend that with four additional hours, compensated by the businesses. Patrol officers clamored for the opportunity. The officers could get an extra four hours of pay per shift. All that was required was strolling in pairs through the small malls and massive department stores, escorting shoppers to their vehicles, and showing a consistent uniformed presence. The atmosphere was festive and cheerful, with vast arrays of Christmas scenes. The décor was replete with ice rinks, carousels, artificial snow, and caroling choirs.

Kent and I were very content to work one such shift on a Friday night. Nonetheless, we were plenty tired at the end of the extra four hours on our feet. We entered our parked unmarked Dodge Omni to drive the four miles back to the precinct. I was the driver. I chose to drive southbound down one- way 5th Avenue. As we neared Pike Street, a radio alert tone rang across the air. An armed robbery had just occurred at a local convenience store, approximately 12 blocks northwest of our location. The detailed broadcast suspect descriptions were as follows: Two black males in their early twenties; one around five foot ten and thin, the other around five foot eight; each suspect was said to have a large afro; the taller of the two wore a purple and gold Los Angeles Lakers puffy jacket and sweat pants; the shorter wore a green Seattle Supersonics puffy jacket and sweat pants.

As was usually the case, Kent was the more ardent crimefighter than I. He turned to me and vocalized that I should opt to turn the vehicle around and begin a search for suspects. I stubbornly continued to drive southbound. I told Kent we had just finished working twelve hours at the end of our work week, and that it was time for going home. I added that ample night shift patrol officers were available to crush crime. As our quasi-argument continued, Kent looked to his right out of the vehicle window and animatedly pointed. He said, "That's them!" As I glanced in the direction he was pointed I instantly answered, "No it's not."

Despite my efforts toward indifference and outright laziness, I could not help but hit the brakes on the car. I cursed while doing so, as we both knew we were looking at several more hours of police-work to follow. There, to our right, a few feet away and closing, were two individuals perfectly matching the suspect descriptions. They were sprinting from the direction of the robbery and looking back in the direction of the crime.

The suspect in the Lakers jacket literally glanced off of the hood of our unmarked vehicle. Both suspects showed surprise to see two uniformed police officers rapidly exiting the unmarked vehicle. Kent and I simultaneously drew out .357 magnums from our holsters and ordered the suspects to freeze. As expected, the suspects merely changed gears in a sprint away from us. The chase was on.

Stupidly, the two suspects decided to stay together while fleeing. As a result, my partner and I could remain together. We were running and screaming into our portable radios that we were in pursuit. The suspects, clad in their sweat pants, were slowly out-distancing us. We were at a distinct disadvantage, with our cumbersome patrol uniforms and jingling keys. The robbers bounded like deer eastbound from us and began to smirk while looking backward. They turned northbound, down an alley. It was at that point that *our* smirks emerged. We were well aware that the two robbers had run down a narrow dead-end alley.

The slower, and taller, of the two suspects slowed momentarily in indecision. Consequently, we were able to tackle him in a heap upon the cobblestone surface. I quickly applied the cuffs, while verbally freeing Kent to seek the outstanding suspect. As I dragged the suspect to a standing position, I attempted to join Kent's visual search for bad-guy number two. Kent was pacing like a bloodhound in the tightly enclosed end of the alley. The poorly lit area was surrounded by multi-storied industrial buildings. There was nowhere to run. We both noted a large green industrial dumpster behind a nearby building. Kent nodded at me, and I nodded acknowledgement, while maintaining a one-handed grip on my suspect.

Guns drawn, we slowly approached the dumpster. I held fast to my suspect and walked him with us. Kent shone his powerful flashlight beneath and beyond the dumpster. No suspect was seen. Kent then began to smile broadly. He pointed the barrel of his revolver at the top of the dumpster and slowly lifted the lid. Two large eyes peered outward from the dumpster toward us.

My partner pointed the barrel of the gun toward the forehead of the suspect. Kent calmly and slowly said to the suspect, "Do you want to *live*?" For some reason, merely hearing Kent's utterance caused me to start laughing. The dumpster suspect could be heard hyperventilating. As I continued to laugh, Kent spoke out of the corner of his mouth while maintaining visual and weapon focus upon the suspect. He told me, "Shut up already." With that, I could not help but laugh harder.

The dumpster suspect called out, "Please, don't kill me man. Don't kill me." My handcuffed suspect then called out to his partner, "Damn, bro these mother---kers are crazy…do what he say." The dumpster suspect was more than happy to follow my partner's terse instructions on extending his life expectancy. I was finally able to control my laugher.

We were therefore able to apprehend a set of brothers for an armed robbery—Mr. Rocky and Stoney Rivers. (Real names!) Our twelve-hour shift morphed into a 16-hour shift.

The following week, Captain Gene Hunt of the West Precinct presented a letter of commendation to two young officers during roll call. He praised my partner and me for our devotion to duty, and willingness to put in the extra effort to make downtown safe. To the eternal credit of my beloved partner, Kent, he said not a word about my actual efforts that night. I have often told him, he deserved both commendations.

The experience of working with Kent Carpenter would span five years. We would experience many laughs, and a few tears. From my principled and talented partner I would learn a great deal about police-work in the big city. More importantly, from my relationship with the man for now thirty-five years, I would learn the meaning of friendship. A man could have no finer friend in the world than that handsome young man with whom Sergeant Butler once paired me. It has been an honor and privilege.

***

Cop Culture: The media—the ultimate enemy

I highly doubt that the readers can locate a single American law enforcement officer whom has any faith in the media. Each respective set of cops will claim to have the most "liberal" media in their particular city. In cop vernacular, "liberal" is equivalent to a hybrid blend of Satanism and mental retardation. Seattle cops can capably argue to being cursed by some of the most liberally slanted media members in America.

While all media are expected to view law enforcement with caution and scrutiny, it is the blatantly obvious bias that infuriates Seattle cops. It is abundantly clear that the local papers seek to print negative slams upon the police in order to sell papers. Similarly, television stations bolster ratings at our expense. No efforts to record and print positives ever seem to occur. Officers deliver babies, run into burning buildings to retrieve victims, dodge bullets at bank robberies, and perform life-saving CPR on overdose victims, for example. Yet the media never reports these positives. It is often said, within the ranks of Seattle cops, that the only time the local media says a positive word about a local police officer is when that officer is killed in the line of duty.

Conversely, fire fighters are virtually never reviled in the media. And, I assure you, they have more than their fair shares of personal and professional foibles. Clearly, they are media darlings, and do not receive the same treatment as the evil cops.

Similarly, never do the reporters report on the reporters. Were their only interests to lie in newspaper sales, or station ratings, one would think that the market would wish to hear of celebrity scandals within the media. Case and point the following: A Local TV news icon has had innumerable shoplift arrests over many years at the Southcenter Mall , and elsewhere in downtown Seattle. In fact, she was once banned by court decree from the mall. Yet, the most foul-mouthed, sexually obsessed person I have ever met, is depicted by the media as the sweetest lady in history. We in S.P.D. better know her as "Klepto-nympho Joan*." A local "Community-Helper*" reporter on a competing station is known as a saint to the public. Yet, her involvement in a bizarre gay lovers' triangle suicide never made the news. Reporters caught on SPD film buying cocaine, summoning prostitutes, or those arrested for lewd public sex acts in bathrooms, get the same treatment. No air time or print. They are thus known as the ultimate hypocrites, in always citing the "peoples' right to know."

While the bias exists in the choices of stories to report, the greater abomination often lies in how they are reported. Clever splicing and recording can totally change a story to fill their respective needs. In just such a manner, local television station KIRO (CBS affiliate) once ran a series of scathing stories regarding our anti-crime teams. These followed an accidental shooting of a drug dealer during a search warrant entry into a pitch-dark drug den. KIRO expounded to the point of showing ACT team written statements after numerous search warrants. Said SPD statements were shown claiming that we had waited an estimated seven seconds after announcing a search warrant entry, for the safety of all. KIRO showed several videotapes that they filmed of the corresponding warrant entries. In their tapes, the "lying" cops immediately entered the drug dens without legal announcement or waiting several seconds. The public and local politicians were outraged. What station KIRO never admitted to, was editing 8 seconds out of each tape. This was only learned after our department legal unit subpoenaed the original tapes. In other walks of life, this would be called "fraud." Yet, no retractions were ever aired.

This is not dissimilar in intent to a national broadcast run by ABC's Prime Time Live program that derided Chicago Police for "racial profiling." A close friend within that department advised me of how the department was ultimately awarded millions from ABC for deceptive slanderous reporting. The network's convincing videos showed repeated unmerited stops of young black men, for merely driving within the city. They stated that each time the poor youth drove, a police stop followed. In actuality, hundreds of hours of footage had to be filmed to find any such stops. And these occurrences only began to happen after the following efforts by ABC's Dianne Sawyer, et al: License plates were removed from the vehicles; drivers were instructed to burn rubber and break traction in the vehicles near police stations; and, finally, realistic-looking toy guns were placed within view in the rear windows of the vehicles. Thus, ABC had their pre-conceived story of oppression. They quietly paid their monies and never retracted the story. The deliberate damage was done.

Moreover, the frustration lies with reporters who know the truth, and find the truth to be too dull. They will arrive at a homicide scene and ask, "Is it true that man killed the other in a fight over a quarter?" When told no, the same reporter can be seen turning to the camera and stating, "Police sources have just confirmed that the suspect killed the victim in a fight over a quarter."

The most infuriating constant media stunt shall forever be the following scenario: "Cops shoot and kill black man, who *allegedly* robbed the bank and shot at them." We often ask ourselves, are the" alleged bullets" fired at us by the robber less of a threat?

This is not to say that true quality journalism no longer exists. Two notable examples are Mr. Mike Barber of the Seattle Post Intelligencer, and the great Arthur Santana of the Seattle Times. Each won well-deserved innumerable prestigious awards for journalism. Yet, they never stooped to contrived laziness for their stories. They were respectful and insightful. And they could write like Charles Dickens. Sadly, each chose to leave their respective local publications. They seemed to know that such honesty and integrity was not welcome by their editors.

In the radio world, we are honored in Seattle to have such a quality local journalists as John Carlson on talk radio KVI. John is the son of a retired Seattle Police officer, recently deceased. He is insightful and honest to a fault. It is often believed by the cops that talk radio is the only conduit for relating our side of the story. We know that we shall receive honest support from such a person. And when they criticize us, we know that such criticisms are merited and balanced.

I would invite the readers to approach any reporting with the following perspective: That the vast majority of these news "services" operate for profit. In order to make profits, they must excited you, appall, you, or intrigue you. With millions, or billions of dollars on the line, do you the think the truth is more important? They are selling you a used car.

My wife, Mahala, is exactly right on where the media needs to go. We need at least one more national network-- G.N.N. The Good News Network. There are millions of positives to report in the world. There are still heroes everywhere. Yet they are totally overlooked. The sky is not truly falling. Manhattan is not destined to be submerged in five years. And America is not headed into a century long depression. The world is blessed with heroes and innovation. They just don't sell papers.

***

Chapter 16: Things that make you go 'Hmmmm'

In December of 1993 the Police Department made a huge mistake and promoted your author to Sergeant, after 13 years on the streets. My first assignment was that of the 9-1-1 center. The assignment was quite an education. I was astounded to observe how so ridiculously few employees within the center could hold lives in their hands. The underpaid and underappreciated operators fielded nearly 600,000 bizarre and troubling calls per year 24/7. They were simply amazing.

What was the most troubling aspect of the 9-1-1 center of the times was the fact that the employees worked in a poisonous facility. Housed in a lower level basement of the old Public Safety Building, the facility resembled a dungeon. More troubling than the lack of daylight within the submarine-like setting, was the environment itself. For years, the police department received fines from OSHA et al, demanding to immediately close the facility as condemned. Yet, the police department merely tore down the posted condemnation notices and paid the fines. The city knew that a 9-1-1 center could not be closed by the state or federal government. Employees were subjected to the following hazardous conditions: Intense asbestos exposure; chemical fumes from an adjacent crime lab; carbon monoxide from an adjacent parking garage; lead exposure from a previous gun range in the basement; daily exposure to rat excrement from the collapsing ceilings; and exposure to spores drawn from human excrement — as artificial air ducts from the outside world were placed directly above the favorite fecal deposit site for downtown bums. The incidence of cancer among the employees of that facility was found to be sixteen times that of the national average. Yet, the stories of the dispatchers has gone unheard by media, the courts, or the government. I will forever hold the employees of that facility and era in extremely high regard.

***

A highly political shooting to 9-1-1?

On a Friday night in February, 1994 a highly concerned 9-1-1 operator approached me at my console in the 9-1-1 center with her headset unplugged. She stated that she had on the line a call from someone claiming to be the mayor of Seattle. The caller indicated to the operator that he had been shot in the arm. The operator requested my input on how to handle the bizarre circumstances. I immediately attempted to determine the authenticity of the call. I returned to the operator's console and made efforts to confirm the automatically traced address of the call by reviewing my files of the mayor's phone number and address. The caller had quickly disconnected. Nonetheless, the computer records matched those of the police confidential file.

The Chief dispatcher of the unit advised me that he was on the phone with a very high ranking Police Department member. That particular call had been fielded on a non-recorded land line. My Chief dispatcher advised that he had been ordered by the department official to disregard the call in question.

Another of my dispatchers had been directed to contact the Seattle Fire Department on a non-recorded line. A fire dispatcher had advised her that the Fire Department would transport the mayor far outside the city limits to a quiet and private Valley Medical Center in Kent Washington. The mayor's injuries were said to be a gunshot wound to his wrist. The fire department dispatcher quickly advised my police department dispatcher that a very high-ranking Fire Department official had just called in and advised all of their communications center employees to disregard the call in question. We were thus totally baffled as to the totality of the circumstances at the mayor's home.

Per orders of the Chief of Police, the SPD Communications Center was directed to make no further inquiries into the alleged shooting. As a result, life went on as usual. But a mystery remained.

The following night I returned for the subsequent shift. The mysterious shooting remained a hot topic of discussion in the 9-1-1 center. Many aspects of the incident remained a hot topic of discussion within the department as a whole. Gossip, rumors, and legitimate informational discourse followed. Consensus among many members of the police department and fire department was fairly clear. It was believed the mayor of Seattle had been shot. He was supposedly shot in the wrist. And the shooter was believed to be the mayor's wife. There were wild claims of a case of the mayor having been found in bed with another woman. Still wilder claims were that he was found in bed with another man.

Cops working within the Comm Center came to the conclusion that the shooting was bona-fide. All of us believed that the mayor's wife had grazed him in the wrist with a single gunshot. We held serious doubts as to the additional purported facts of the case.

Out of profound curiosity toward the case, my Chief dispatcher, who was a veteran cop, and I endeavored to review records of the 9-1-1 call in question. As with any big city 9-1-1 center at the time, extensive steps were always taken to maintain all call records. Any call of that sort would be maintained in a computer "Ali-Ani" (Address, location indicated/Address, name indicated) system. There would also be two reel-to-reel tape recordings of any call. Additionally, a ticker- tape type of printer system would scrawl the phone number of the call, just in case all computers failed.

We earnestly tried to locate the call records. We were surprised to discover that no computer record of the 9-1-1 call existed. Yet, we knew that computer records were not infallible. We further attempted to listen to the tapes of the call. No such recording existed on either tape. Yet, one minute 45 seconds of tape seemed to be missing. The tape *sounded* perfectly uninterrupted or un-spliced. Yet, digital internal clock mechanisms of the taping machinery indicated a nearly imperceptible anomaly in the timing of the event. Lastly, we checked the manual ticker tape printout of the call. Thousands of phone numbers and exact times were found on the cash-register type roll of paper. Yet, no such phone number or time was located. Strangely, on a busy Friday night at the height of 9-1-1 call-loads, there were no records of any 9-1-1 calls having been received for nearly a minute of time. That was simply impossible.

My highly veteran cop and chief dispatcher turned to me and made a shuddering motion. He said, "Stevie, I think we best let this one lie." I went home to my wife perplexed. I informed her that I could understand how computer records could be altered. I even understood how sections of recording tapes could be edited. But I could not, for the life of me, figure out how a minute of time could be removed from the huge paper ream of calls without a sign of cutting and splicing the paper. I can only guess to this day that someone of extreme technical ability generated a re-printing of thousands of calls — missing the call in question.

I considered doubting the 9-1-1 operator in question. Yet, for 25 years officers had depended upon the highly decorated dispatcher with their lives. Her credibility surpassed that of our mayor and police chief by approximately 5,000 per cent. During the same time span, the mayor of Seattle had been a front-runner for a cabinet assignment within the Clinton Whitehouse. It was an election year. The mayor was said to be favored for a position as Secretary of Education. Yet, approximately 24 hours following the phantom shooting call, the 9-1-1 center received another strange call. A perplexed operator advised that she was holding a call from someone claiming to be the President. She said he sounded intoxicated, but that the 9-1-1 trace only showed an out of state location. The operator indicated that the caller's voice sounded like the President. I tapped into her conversation on my headset. The caller *sounded* like Bill Clinton. His speech was slightly slurred. However, he was very polite and asking to be transferred to the mayor's home phone. The comm center had the capability of doing just that.

I quickly dialed a contracted phone trace service out of Denver Colorado. Within seconds, I was advised that the genesis of the call was traced to the White House. I immediately authorized the operator to punch the programmed transfer button to the Mayor's home. Our phone involvement was immediately terminated.

Strangely, shortly thereafter, President Clinton unexpectedly dropped Seattle's mayor from consideration for a cabinet position.

Many months later, local KVI radio talk show host Mike Siegel would broadcast "rumors" of the shooting of the mayor by his wife. The talk show host intimated that numerous employees of the police department and fire department had informed him of the event. He went on to broadcast that the mayor was shot by a jealous wife, after finding him in bed with a male lover.

An outraged mayor and other media verbally crucified Mr. Siegel. Mr. Siegel refused to disclose his purported sources. Siegel was unemployed shortly thereafter. I felt terrible for the man. Yet, I dared not lend him any support for fear of suffering the same fate. His anonymous source(s) most assuredly did not include me. To this day, I cannot be absolutely certain of the event in question. But I have very strong suspicions. I would bet my house on it.

Sadly, the dispatcher in question died of a strange form of cancer a few years later. (Much like many of her peers).

***

The sports hero rapist

During the early fall of 1989 a young University of Washington co-ed summoned patrol officers to report a rape. She alleged that she had passed- out from excessive alcohol consumption, while attending a fraternity party. She further stated that she awakened to discover obvious indications of sexual intercourse stemming from her time of unconsciousness. She reported that she remembered details of the fraternity party in question. She further recalled joining a young man in his fraternity room before she passed out. She had flashbacks to the man upon her.

Thus, an incident report was drafted. The young lady was taken to Harborview Medical Center for a sexual assault exam. It was evident that some male had sexual intercourse with her. She had clearly alleged date rape. The suspect whom she implicated happened to be an all-American football player for the University of Washington. Being a huge University of

Washington football fan, and from the hometown of the player in question, I instantly recognized his name. He was considered the most important player on the team. Word traveled rapidly throughout the North Precinct of the alleged rape.

Several days following the reporting of the incident, the young lady and her parents drove to the North Precinct. They asked to relate follow-up information to her earlier allegations, including bruises appearing. I was summoned from a nearby roll-call area to take a follow up report and photographs. The young woman and her parents handed me a letter she had just received. The text of the letter was that of an apology from the football player in question. He expressed profound regret for his actions. He admitted to taking sexual advantage of the young woman once she had become unconscious. He stated within the letter that he was highly intoxicated at the time of the incident. He closed with profound apologies for his actions and any trauma he might have caused. This was, essentially, an admission of guilt.

I therefore wrote a brief follow-up report that indicated where and when the alleged victim had received the letter. I used the same incident number of the original report. I obtained the incident number from the department's computer records management system. I then placed the letter in a sealed envelope along with photographs of bruises and drove the letter to the SPD Evidence Section. This was located on the 6th floor of the downtown Public Safety Building. I placed the sealed letter into evidence, with personnel at the evidence window, whom meticulously recorded the transaction. I attached a copy of my follow up report.

Several weeks passed, when I became curious as to the status of the case investigation. I had heard nothing from follow-up investigators. I sought to locate the incident report number from the computer system again. I was amazed to discover that no record of the incident still existed. I figured there must be some kind of computer problems. Therefore, I telephoned our Sexual Assault Unit and talked to a detective. He advised that he was not familiar with the case, but would check the case assignment book. A couple minutes later, the detective advised that they had no record of any such incident. Both incident reports were missing.

A couple days later, I consulted with my Sergeant regarding the strange set of circumstances. He advised me to contact the victim by telephone and seek to confirm the case number provided to her by initial reporting officers. The Sergeant then checked log sheet records of the original responding officers. The case number on the log sheets was the same which I had annotated in my follow up log sheet. Meanwhile, I placed a telephone call to the victim. I left an answering machine message.

The very veteran Sergeant advised that he would "check around the company" regarding the incident in question. My Sergeant and I checked evidence section logs of the day I submitted the letter. There was no record of such a transaction. I left several more calls for the victim, but never received a return call.

Ultimately, my Sergeant advised me that his sources within the department advised him that the case was "handled." He had been further advised to drop any further inquiry into the matter.

During 1989, the star football player for the University of Washington would have a stellar season. All during the 1989 season, a very high-ranking Police Department official could be seen in the press boxes of Husky Stadium. Apparently, he enjoyed each home football game as a guest of the university.

The football player in question would eventually enjoy several years in the National Football League.

To this day, there is absolutely no record in the Seattle Police Department of any rape allegations lodged against the young man.

***

An overdose or murder?

During winter of 1993 I was working a two man patrol unit in North Seattle with a seasoned cop and Vietnam veteran by the name of Jack Napolitano. We were dispatched to an overdose death call at a seedy motel in the 8900 block of Aurora Avenue North known as the Green Lake Motel. During the era in question, the motel was known for prostitution and drug dealing within such. Filthy rooms could be rented by the hour.

We arrived and were greeted by the motel manager. The Korean man spoke broken English. The manager stressed that he wanted us to remove a body from within a second floor unit as quickly as possible, so that he might quickly rent the room again. The manager used his key to allow us into the room in question.

A body lay upon a bare mattress in the back corner of the dimly lit room. We opened the blinds to allow extra light into the room. The twenty foot by fifteen foot single section unit was filthy, as expected. Garbage and wine bottles were strewn across the floor, leading to a dirty toilet area to the rear right of the room. As we approached the body, we noted that he was a white male in his early forties. He had been dead for an estimated 24 hours. He was meticulously dressed in slacks, a white shirt, and a red white and blue tie. The man's slightly graying hair was immaculately groomed.

A syringe was protruding from the inner left forearm of the body. A red Trojan condom package lay partially opened upon the mattress, to the right of the body. The ever-observant Officer Napolitano noted a small Navy insignia upon the man's tie pin. Jack also noted that the man's left wrist had calluses and redness upon such. We sought to locate identification upon the body. We went through a hanging suit jacket and some meticulously packed luggage. There was no wallet, nor any identification of any sort.

My partner immediately unbuttoned the starched and pressed white shirt of the man. He reached around the dead man's neck and found nothing. He then reached deeply down a pant leg of the body. He smiled, as he retrieved a laminated card from an inner flap of the man's pant leg. The card was a Naval officer identification of some sort.

Officer Napolitano had considerable past experience with classified work for the Army. He immediately took serious note of the identification card. He asked me for my assessment of the scene. I advised that my experience with narcotics work would indicate that China White heroin had been the drug in the syringe in question. I offered that China White was known to be highly lethal in unpredictable potencies within Seattle's drug trade. I was confident the man had died of an instant overdose.

Napolitano offered that it was indeed possible that the man died from a massive heroin overdose. However, he advised of the following astute observations: That the man was clearly a Naval attaché; that the man's identification placed him at the nearby Bangor nuclear missile submarine base; that the man's dog tags had been removed; that the man had been carrying something to which his left wrist was handcuffed.

Napolitano advised that it was an impossibility that the dead man had ever previously used heroin. He advised that such an important military attaché would be subject to daily drug testing. Jack was utterly convinced that we were viewing a homicide scene. We thus radioed for a patrol Sergeant and a response from SPD homicide detectives.

Before our Sergeant even arrived, several black suited individuals suddenly arrived at the doorway of the motel room. They provided governmental identification of an unknown nature. The six men advised that the scene was now a federal matter, and that we were invited to leave the scene. We both stubbornly advised that the scene would remain that of the Seattle Police Department until such time as our responding supervisor advised otherwise. The uzis and other weaponry the men in black concealed were obvious. But they did not seem to wish to challenge our authority at that point.

Our squad Sergeant arrived at the scene shortly thereafter. We sought to talk to him in a corner of the motel room. As we were advising the Sergeant of our observations, the radio dispatcher called him. He was advised to tune his radio to an alternate patrol frequency. We listened as the Chief Dispatcher for the Communications Center advised the Sergeant that, per an assistant police chief, we were to leave the scene to federal authorities, and depart immediately. We grudgingly complied.

We expressed our displeasure to the Sergeant at a location away from the incident scene. He voiced his displeasure with the situation, but said the matter must be dropped. We never heard further about the incident.

Officer Napolitano opined that it was his belief the man in question had fallen victim to the actions of the very governmental men whom had relieved us of our duties. Additionally, he surmised that the black suits had responded very rapidly to the scene. He suggested that they seemed to be located conveniently nearby. The men seemed un-surprised as to the circumstances, upon their arrival. My partner was convinced that the man had fallen prey to the "good guys," for reasons forever unknown.

***

The dreaded "C" word

Does corruption exist within the Seattle Police Department? That is a very touchy subject. That is especially so, while drawing a nice police pension and hoping to continue doing so. At this juncture I shall state only this: That 98% of all the rank and file officers of the S.P.D. are as honest as the day is new. They are the salt of the earth, performing a difficult job. That said, do the math on two per-cent times 1,600. There is the inevitability of anomalies. The percentages increase rapidly, the higher up the chain of command one travels.

Have crime statistics been deliberately and illegally falsified for years in order to downplay the problem?

Have caches of drug monies been stolen?

Were drugs ever planted on suspects?

Has expensive jewelry been stolen from dead bodies by cops, inclusive of the site of a notorious quadruple homicide?

Do countless tens of thousands of dollars in Homeland Security and other grant funds fraudulently end up in the pockets of high-ranking department officials to be used for trips to see pyramids, fly mistresses, and obtain apartments for illicit trysts?

Do officers get paid to be at work, while simultaneously outside the city limits working another job or carousing at casinos while complicit supervisors look the other way?

302

Yup.

Do all the ethical officers and leaders have nightmares about corrupt Nazis coming to get them? Absolutely. They know that crooks cover very well for fellow crooks. It is usually those pointing fingers whom are the truly guilty.

***

Chapter side note: Sergeant Alvin "Big Daddy" Little

Alvin Little would serve as the antithesis to all that is liberal in our society. He is a black, conservative, cop's cop. He has never accepted a benefit in his life that he has not fully earned. He finds affirmative action to be an insult to his upbringing. He compares political correctness to a series of excuses by losers. He is absolutely loved and respected by all of his peers — with the exception of the political elite within the department.

Sergeant Little is capable of seeing his peers in only one color. That is blue. He does not stand under the banner "African-American." He only knows that he is an American. He was insulted when local publications depicted photos of him, lauded as "the first African-American member of the Seattle Police Motorcycle Drill Team." He took his only pride in earning a place within an elite team. While politicians and ambitious cops use race as a tool for advancement, under the guise of uniting, Alvin Little practices the art. There is no segment of society within which Alvin cannot travel readily.

Sergeant Little is an extremely articulate speaker. Yet, he can speak street rap with the best of individuals. In fact, he and a motorcycle officer peer formed a two-man rap group in the 1980's that was designed to reach out to local youth. His now famous "Run S.P.D" was a clever parody of the then infamous

Run D.M.C. The hilarious performances of such instant classics as "You be cited!" were cleverly replete with poignant issues for our youth. The team ultimately received acclaim from as far away as the White House. He recently performed a marvelous imitation of Cee Lo Green, replete with the white cat at an uproarious talent show.

Alvin is aptly nicknamed "Big Daddy." He is a huge, six foot three, 260 pound combination of muscle and a couple too many cheeseburgers. He has served with distinction in Patrol, ACT teams, Traffic, Training, and now in Narcotics. He has earned every position and rank. He functions with a passion for serving the public and protecting his "brother officer." Big Daddy can punch a hole in a brick wall with a martial arts move. Yet, he would prefer to seat a toddler on his police motorcycle. In times of trauma, for cops or the public, "Big Daddy" just happens to be nearby to give his time and compassion.

Big Daddy is renowned for his sense of humor. He is Eddie Murphy with a badge. Moreover, he is known as a trusted peer to anyone with a badge. He is indeed a "brother" in the truest sense of the word.

***

Chapter 17: (Dis)order in the courtooms.

Be careful what you ask for, counselor

Officer Douglas Vandergiessen sat on the witness stand in Seattle Municipal Court. The honorable judge George Holifield was presiding. The judge was, and is, a legend in the black community. He is known for his wisdom and fairness. The trial was in regard to a lewd conduct arrest in a local park. The misdemeanor charges entailed an adult male suspect, allegedly masturbating while approaching a young boy. The large, blue-eyed Dutchman cop, with a vast mustache, was known for his professionalism and unending seriousness. He loved being a cop. The defendant sat impeccably dressed in a three-piece suit beside his high-priced defense attorney. The attorney spoke passionately, while making jabbing motions at the seated officer with his pointed finger. Spittle flew from the attorney's mouth as his diatribe continued.

The arrogant attorney questioned the officer's eyesight, upbringing, religion, ethics, schooling, and every other inane subject imaginable. The attorney then leaned toward the face of the officer and smirked. He asked the officer, "Officer, don't you hold *your* penis in *your* hand when *you* urinate?"

The beleaguered officer hesitated. The attorney placed a hand on his hip. He leaned even closer to the testifying officer, and nodded with a smirk toward the jury. The officer inhaled. Finally, the officer shook his head and answered, "No, my doctor advised me not to lift anything over forty pounds."

Judge Holifield literally fell out of his chair. His glasses went sideways on his face, as he landed on the carpeting. The judge was quick to regain control and re-seat himself at the bench. Yet, his voice broke noticeably as he sought to comment, "Counselor, do you have any further questions?"

The red-faced defense attorney knew that his day was to end unsuccessfully.

***

Don't ask the question if you don't know the answer.

A DUI case was in full swing on another day in Seattle Municipal Court. A grizzled veteran motorcycle Officer Michael T. Scott was on the witness stand, being grilled by the defense attorney. The attorney was dissecting the police paperwork, completed by the gravel-voiced former Marine. Michael T. Scott was renowned for his toughness and savvy on the streets of Seattle. But his reports were never to be forwarded for Pulitzer consideration.

The defense attorney scored a point on critiquing the paperwork. Yet, the wily old officer returned serve, with his common sense and sincerity. The volleying continued for an hour and a half. Both the defense and prosecution felt they had scored their respective points with the jury.

Eventually, the smug defense attorney displayed the DUI citation, written by the motorcycle cop. He grilled Officer Scott as to the accuracy of the citation. The sage bike officer was able to expertly explain his vast knowledge of Seattle traffic laws. Finally, the defense attorney turned to the backside of the ticket. A brief narrative was read to the court. And the officer was asked to explain his notations.

Finally, the defense attorney moved in for the kill. He asked Officer Scott, "Officer, do you have a bias toward my client?" Officer Scott responded, "Sir?" The attorney repeated, "Officer, I am asking you if you pre-judged my client?" Again, Officer Scott expressed his confusion as to the line of questioning. The defense attorney then pointed to a small marking at the bottom of the citation back. The annotation read, merely, A/H.

The motorcycle cop explained that the symbol was for later reference in court, to indicate that the motorist was "Argumentative and Hostile." The defense attorney immediately countered, "That's not what you cops indicate by that and you know it, officer...you know good and well what that means." The attorney leaned toward Officer Scott, "Officer, is my client an Ass-Hole?"

Officer Scott smiled amicably at the defense attorney, and turned his glance toward the jury. He said, "Counselor, you know your client better than *I* do." Loud laughter arose from the jury box. The laughter spelled doom for the remainder of the defense attorney's case.

***

Your racist author.

Your author was by no means immune from the torture of rigorous cross-examination by defense attorneys. It is part of the job. Yet, often, unprofessional attorneys make the trial a personal matter.

I was in trial on a drug dealing case. It was one of hundreds of such trials stemming from our Anti-Crime team activities in the late 80's. At the time, the majority of downtown drug dealers were Cuban "Marielito" immigrants, recently flushed from Castro's prisons. There were also occasional Venezuelans,

Nicaraguans or Mexican nationals. They mostly sought to sell "Chiva," which was black tar heroin.

During the trial, my paperwork was dissected for hours. My evidence collection was equally questioned. My experience and training were all reviewed in painstaking detail. All was fair, to that point. The defense attorney seemed frustrated that he could not shake me on the stand.

Yet, the defense attorney had one final question to launch. He said, "Officer, I see case after case of yours coming to court... and they all have a pattern... every one of these poor arrestees are recent Central American or South American immigrants." He continued, "Officer, are you racist against Hispanic people?"

I hesitated only momentarily for effect. I then said, "No, counselor, I don't *believe* I am racist against such Hispanic people... I kind of like my wife from Chile, and my two half-Hispanic daughters... I speak fluent Spanish... and I do volunteer work in the Yakima Valley for underprivileged migrant Hispanic kids, at special Spanish speaking camps."

With that, the great Judge Norman Quinn turned to the defense attorney and stated, "Counselor, I believe you are about done today... and so is your case."

***

A dog day in court.

All rookie officers in the mid 1980's experienced a rite of passage in Seattle Municipal Courts. The infamous Department 1 was one of the most chaotic municipal courtrooms in America on any given day. Mondays were by far the most insane. Street thugs and uniformed cops jammed the dilapidated courtroom well beyond capacity. There was a constant low roar of scores of voices seeking to communicate. Cases were bought and sold, and traded much like the pit in the New York Stock Exchange.

By mid-day, the courtroom would finally quiet. Cases had been assigned throughout the old Public Safety Building and trials would begin. On alternating Mondays, a very special prosecutor would attempt to try a DUI case. Rookie officers would be called to the table with the city attorney to begin brief, whispered collaboration with the prosecutor. Soon, they would notice that she wore enormous hearing aids. Unfortunately, the woman had issues with hearing and speech. The commonplace pre-trial conversations were an impossibility.

As would any prosecutor, the woman would begin to read the police incident reports. Yet, as any given officer approached the prosecutor, they would notice a strange sight. The city's attorney wore a magnifying glass attached to a head wrap. She looked like she was seeking to perform micro-surgery. In her hand, she held another smaller magnifying glass, like a jeweler. When she finally turned toward the approaching officer(s), one could not help but note the similarity to cartoon characters' eyes poring through a looking glass. It was comical. Sadly, the woman was legally blind and hearing impaired. She squinted to read any portion of the legal paperwork, with little success. Her head bobbled helplessly from side to side, seeking to find meaning in the paperwork over which she bowed.

At about the time any given rookie officer realized the scenario, he or she would also notice a horrible odor wafting upward at the prosecutor's table. Often, the officers would look at the prosecutor suspiciously. Immediately thereafter, they would notice the prosecutor's seeing- eye- dog sitting beneath the table. The source of the horrible stench emanated from the smallish part black Labrador, curled passively at the prosecutor's feet. It appeared that the dog had spent a lifetime rolling on dead fish.

Invariably, the young officers would seek to cover their noses covertly with a hand or napkin. Yet, also invariably, the young officers could not help but seek to pet the little doggy. Without fail, the veteran officers, in the rear of the courtroom, would suddenly feel a need to come further forward in the courtroom. They always had front row seats by the time the little dog clamped its fangs into the arm of the young officers. A snarling dog would shake its head angrily from side to side, seeking to tear through the officers' jacket sleeves with its tiny yellow teeth. It was a loudly alarming sound. Once the initiation was completed, the rookie cops would realize they were in for a long day in the courtroom. The futile trial would make the dog bite seem a pleasantry.

Often, the rookie cops would later comment to their peers, that they literally looked for the hidden Candid Cameras. The setting was too surreal to be legitimate. Yet, the city's well-intended efforts to create opportunities for the disabled also enabled many a DUI suspect to walk out of the courtroom singing. I don't recall the prosecutor ever winning a case.

***

The fashion plea.

The absolute opposite scenario also existed in the King County Superior Courts. Officers clamored to show up early for court, to sit next to another prosecutor. Anne Bremner was a brilliant, meticulously prepared, Deputy Prosecuting Attorney for D.A. Norm Maleng's office. Ms. Bremner was conservative, confident, driven, and fiercely loyal to the cops. She was instantly "one of the guys" in the courtroom or beyond such. And, she happened to be enormously, tremendously, phenomenally attractive. In fact, she was just plain "hot." Hundreds of current and former SPD officers will attest that

Anne was the most appealing woman they have ever met. And she never lost a case. Officers could look forward to sitting at the prosecutor's table next to Anne and know that she had the trial well under control. The only challenge lay in paying attention to the case. Distractions always existed due to Anne's $2,000 dollar suit and $500 an ounce perfume.

Incredibly, one particular male defense attorney made a motion to have Anne Bremner ordered to change her attire. He felt the prosecuting attorney's gorgeous appearance would unduly sway the jury. The sage Judge Norman Quinn immediately quipped, "Counselor, I have no objections whatsoever to Ms. Bremner's attire....to be fair, you may wear whatever makes you feel pretty as well." All of us knew that Judge Quinn shared in the pool of hundreds of members of the Anne Bremner fan club.

***

Heroic attorneys.

Contrary to my depictions thus far of defense attorneys, not all of our adversaries in the courtroom are sub-humanoid. However, it is my belief that the overwhelming majority of defense attorneys are insultingly biased over-zealous antitheses to all police officers. When they can't win a case based on merit, they resort to name-calling. That is especially true, in my opinion, of Public Defenders. Most Public Defenders espouse venomously hateful biases toward the police. We are called racists, bullies, ignorant jack-booted thugs. Thus, they attach a label of "biased" to the arresting officers while showing nothing but prejudices on their parts. In some forums this is called... "hypocrisy?" Yet there are exceptions to this observation.

For forty- two years, Mr. Irving Paul prowled the Seattle

Municipal Courts, King County District Courts, and King County Superior Courts. In the latter part of his career, Irving reminded most people of a very tall Albert Einstein. He walked hunched over, with a profound limp. He had been awarded two purple hearts and several heroism medals during his Army service in World War II. Mr. Paul stood some six feet six inches tall. He wore thick black-rimmed glasses. His white hair flowed beyond his shoulders, and his long white beard fell far below his chin. Irving was a brilliant attorney, and could have easily amassed a fortune as a private attorney. He had finished at the top of his law school class at Harvard in the 1940's.

Irving chose, instead, to create the Public Defenders Association of King County. He always loved to represent the down and out, or unjustly accused. Unlike nearly all other Public Defenders, Irving was dearly loved by the rank and file Seattle Police Officers. We all knew him to be fair, intelligent, and reasonable. Irving understood that the vast majority of his clientele were completely and totally guilty of the crimes for which they had been arrested and charged. Yet, he sought to stridently present each individual with a modicum of fairness in the courtrooms. The poor would receive legal representation usually reserved for the fortunate.

Irving was eternally mannered and evocative in his legal presentations. More often than not, Mr. Paul plea-bargained on behalf of his client. Usually, Irving would call a side conference with the arresting officers prior to trial. He would ask in a whisper, "Officers, was my client an a--hole, or did he just mess up?" If we answered the former, he would engage us in a round of dirty jokes, and post no defense to prosecutor demands for lengthy jail sentences. But, more often than not, we would advise that his client had merely shown an error in judgment. We were content to see Irving negotiate the release of his client from jail, after a one night stay. He passionately imparted upon his relieved clients the need to make future better decisions.

Irving trusted 99% of all cops, and 99% of all cops trusted him. His trusted associate, Brenda Navarro also maintained a similar relationship of fairness and dignity. In the rare instance when arresting cops chose to lie in a courtroom, Irving would provide an impassioned defense reminiscent of F. Lee Bailey. His brilliant legal mind would be demonstrably on display.

Irving Paul made life fair for thousands of people, at great monetary and physical costs to himself. He died at 72 years of age, exhausted, but at total peace. Dozens of cops, attorneys, and former clients graced his funeral. The man was, indeed, a hero.

***

Cop Culture: How things ought to be — Assistant Chief John Pirak (Retired)

John Pirak was a highly decorated Vietnam War hero in the Army. He devoted over thirty years to the Seattle Police Department. He rose in the ranks the right way — he performed each assignment and rank with distinction and integrity. At every rank, he was revered by his subordinates. To the day he retired, John took a twenty minute workout break and an afternoon fifteen minute brown bag lunch break. He was never late for work a day in his life, and he never called in sick. John practiced what he preached.

Ultimately, John Pirak ascended to the rank of Assistant Chief of the Seattle Police Department. His humility and greatness were profound. He always made a point of stressing that the party in which he had contact was far more important than he. This occurred, whether he was on or off-duty. Chief

Pirak was renowned for his fairness. He might have applied more discipline than most other assistant chiefs. But were such discipline to be administered, the receiving party knew that they were deserving of such actions.

Chief Pirak was empirically honest. If bad news had to be delivered, he did so quickly and openly. During a down budget cycle years ago, the need for layoffs within the department appeared necessary. Thus, Chief Pirak immediately gathered those employees destined to be affected at the end of the year. He delivered the bad news, and immediately sought to lessen the blow. He prepared glowing recommendation letters for future employment. He arranged for and budgeted a myriad of training classes to better prepare the employees for the eventuality of losing a job. He arranged for resume preparation assistance.

When the end of the year arrived, only scant few layoffs actually had to occur. Yet, numerous employees had already found gainful employment. Others were well prepared to transition quickly into other jobs. Yet others remained with the department. But the overall impression of the department, thanks to John Pirak, was that the agency handled its employees with class. The class of Chief Pirak sometimes stands in stark contrast to current command staff actions—such as *Christmas Eve* layoff notices *via e-mail* in 2002. A lasting impression was also made on that occasion. While Chief Pirak has now been retired for several years, every member of department command staff is measured on the "Pirak Scale." It is a testament to the most respected member of the Seattle Police Department in the last thirty years.

***

Chapter 18: The W.T.O. Riots — The Battle in Seattle

Gordon Graham is a retired California Highway Patrol Captain, of 33 years of law enforcement experience. He added a Master's Degree in risk analysis, and Doctorate in systems analysis, to his hefty resume. Doctor/Captain/or Gordon has provided over 3,000 lectures to law enforcement personnel across the country. His presentations are always received by packed houses. The man is brilliant, sensible, and incredibly witty. He often makes his point by poking fun at police mentalities, from the rank and file to the top. He begins every lecture by repeating a single phrase a dozen times... "Things that go wrong are highly predictable." He finally adds a footnote to the phrase, by screaming at the audience, "If things that go wrong are highly predictable....they are highly *preventable!*"

Yet, even now, his common sense insight often goes ignored in law enforcement. The World Trade Organization (W.T.O) conference in Seattle Washington in November, 1999 was an extreme example of failure to accede to foresight.

In early 1997, Seattle won a competitive bid to host the week-long conference. Then Mayor Paul Schell considered the W.T.O. to be a major coup for the prestige and economy of Seattle. Indeed, world leaders from every major country, and many minor countries, were committed to attending the conference. The intent was to set trade agendas and agreements for globalizing trade and commerce. It was a very boring sounding agenda. Nonetheless, the world summit had economic ramifications that could top a trillion dollars. It was thus a gathering of the economic world elite, with an impact upon millions of jobs worldwide. The mayor was excited to pledge the manpower of the Seattle Police Department to ensure a peaceful setting for the summit.

During 1998 and early 1999 news services constantly featured reports of riots at any city in which the W.T.O. or related conferences convened. Switzerland, Germany, Canada, and Mexico, to name a few countries, saw mass demonstrations turn into full-scale riots. People were hurt or killed, and mass property destruction occurred. The rank and file police officer of Seattle Washington immediately developed lumps in their throats during the two years leading to the Seattle W.T.O. Conference. Cops have always been huge believers in carefully reading handwriting on the wall.

Yet, as invariably remains a tradition for Seattle Police command staff, the ostriches drove their heads into the sand. Very little planning for the event occurred until the year of the event. Mayor Schell stressed to S.P.D command staff that enormous planned demonstrations against the conference, by a myriad of causes, would only provide a peaceful and thoughtful back-drop to the event. He was convinced that an anticipated 30,000 demonstrators in the congested downtown corridor would behave amicably at all times. After all, the setting was Seattle, where the sixties had never departed. Therefore, as was traditional for Seattle Police Command Staff, all department leaders espoused the mayor's words to the rank and file officer, as if gospel.

Some training was provided for officers, some three months prior to the beginning of the conference. On scattered occasions, hundreds of officers were convened in huge hangars at an abandoned Navy base on Sand Point Way. Officers were provided very rudimentary riot gear, to include vintage 1960's poorly fitting riot helmets. Riot batons were inspected and upgraded. Brand new gas masks were at least provided.

Assistant Chief Ed Joiner was designated the ultimate authority over the upcoming events by Chief of Police Norm Stamper. The widely respected veteran commander personally addressed each gathering of the scores of patrol officers, Sergeants, and detectives from an elevated stage, using a bullhorn. He provided insightful analysis into the workings of the economic summit. He advised of where the summit was to be hosted within the downtown Seattle corridor. He advised of which world dignitaries would attend, including the U.S. President and Secretary of State. Itineraries were shared with the officers. Chief Joiner further advised that an estimated 20,000 to 50,000 demonstrators were expected to convene around the economic summit. He even shared some warnings from out of state agencies of anarchist intentions to disrupt the event. Yet, the chief concluded by stressing that he and the city did not anticipate any serious incidents to occur during the event. He reassured us that we would enjoy a profitable and peaceful week on the downtown streets. As the Chief finished his politically scripted oration, the rank and file officers nodded in unison, and muttered, "Uh huhhhh." We looked at one another and rolled our eyes.

Two impassioned Sergeants then provided the bulk of the riot training. Twin brothers Ron and Don Smith had traveled the world to socialize with police officers across the globe. In establishing friendships worldwide, the two Sergeants were often invited to observe the handling of global riots. Impressed by the severity of the events, the Smith brothers took voluminous notes, videos, and photographs. They were gracious enough to relate what they had learned to their own department and thus carve cushy department niches for themselves.

We observed countless videos of demonstrations turning to riots. In such videos, we observed masked marauders hurl rocks, Molotov cocktails, pipe bombs, and bottles, upon business people and amassed police officers. The scenario was repeated at every business summit around the globe.

The twin Sergeants re-asserted what we had already heard from law enforcement peers outside our own agency. They stressed that intelligence reports indicated that mass numbers of anarchists from California, Oregon, and out of the country were planning on creating chaos in Seattle. Other agencies advised that numerous communist groups, such as the Red Brigade and Act-Up were en route to the event in large numbers to join local radical groups. Concerned law enforcement officials from around the country insisted that these plans were not amateurish. They advised that the anarchist groups had extensive training, equipment, and leadership toward a continuing crusade of causing mass havoc and destruction.

During the final weeks leading up to the Seattle summit, we all watched city leaders and department command assure the media that a peaceful gathering would occur. They stressed that the 500 officers assigned to the event would maintain total order and decorum. They even expressed pleasure with the pending expressions of freedom of speech. They predicted the demonstrations would be "healthy." Each of the rank and file police officers advised their family members that we would be soon placed in the middle of chaos. As we told one another, "We're screwed."

Day One

Your author, then a Detective-Sergeant regularly assigned to a juvenile crimes squad, was assigned a corps of 12 officers within the Washington State Convention Center. Rather than being given control over my own squad of detectives, I was given responsibilities over what was predominantly, a cast of total strangers. That made absolutely no sense to me, nor my Sergeant peers throughout the venue.

We were told that the Convention Center would be the central hub for the gathering of thousands of worldwide delegates. While side business deals would most assuredly occur in sequestered hotel rooms and conference rooms, the huge public gatherings would occur in a main gigantic auditorium. We were to simply provide a polite and helpful uniformed presence within the massive sections of curtained-off meeting rooms. We were the protectors of foreign dignitaries.

The majority of my assigned squad consisted of very young and inexperienced officers. The officers were visibly disappointed to be assigned the "boring" detail. They were almost embarrassed to be indoors, warm, safe, and dry. Meanwhile, their peers were assigned the nearby outdoor street corners in full riot gear. They asked me if there would be any chance to gain re-assignment to the "action posts." I had to stifle a laugh, as I assured them they would see all the "action" they would ever want.

The officers did not seem to believe my prognostication during the first day of the event. We stood by as thousands of pleasant, well-dressed participants in the summit hurriedly scurried from one venue to another, notebooks and legal papers in hand. Early in the day, we located six anarchists whom had broken into an alley door and gained entry into the Convention

Center. They carried backpacks containing gas masks, pepper mace, and several pints of human blood. Their intentions were obvious. Each of them proved to be from Eugene Oregon.

We otherwise provided "critical" tactical assistance that first day. We directed thousands of credentialed delegates to the nearest restrooms, and advised of the finest dining locations throughout the city. We were essentially bored. We entertained ourselves by socializing with a nineteen year-old Army Canine Specialist named Sam. Sam was assigned a floppy-eared, clumsy German shepherd mongrel, with exceptionally big feet—named "Kenny." The dog was supposed to be a bomb-sniffer. The personable young man and his worthless dog were the source of considerable ridicule by ATF and FBI bomb dog teams. The elite federal canine teams scoffed at the kid and his clumsy mongrel with the funny name.

Throughout the day, just outside the enormous glass facades of the Washington State Convention Center, we could see hundreds of impassioned demonstrators morphing into thousands. Sporadic violence was already beginning to occur in the downtown corridor. I advised my young officers to get some sleep that night, as our twelve-hour shift ended uneventfully. I knew that would be our last.

Day Two

As we arrived for day two of the summit, we had to drive our personal cars through vast crowds of demonstrators. Some five thousand angry people stood outside the convention center, making it difficult to wind through the gathering and park in a secure underground facility. The members of the masses waved signs and roared. But they did not erupt into violence. It was five o'clock A.M. and already the tension could be felt on the cold late November streets of Seattle.

Lieutenant Richard Schweitzer was assigned the incident commander for the Convention Center venue itself. The Lieutenant was a highly experienced 30 year veteran of the department, whom had excelled in any position to which he had been assigned. He was known as a no-nonsense leader. He was known as a staunch supporter of hard working and honest cops, and the nemesis for the converse. Lt. Schweitzer was renowned for his honesty. Such honesty was usually delivered bluntly. The W.T.O. would be the last serious assignment of Richard Schweitzer's distinguished career.

Lt. Schweitzer gathered the approximately 120 officers and Sergeants in an underground parking garage, far beneath the convention center. He wore his knee length boots from assignments past on a police motorcycle. As always, his uniform was immaculate. The Lieutenant was in perfect physical condition, and resembled a rodeo bull-rider, with his bushy mustache and wind-blown dark hair. He addressed his throng of officers briefly and succinctly. He shouted that he was not good with words. Yet, Lt. Schweitzer provided an oration of profound impact. He advised that, despite what department and city commanders claimed, the event was most assuredly going to "go to shit." He advised that we were about to witness chaos and violence of a magnitude he had once witnessed in the 1960's and 70's. He knew that such events pre-dated any of his gathered officers. He stated that it was possible that lives would be lost in the pending riots. He looked each and every officer and Sergeant in the eyes and stated softly, "And not *one* of those lives will be yours."

All of the officers were initially deployed again within the convention center. My squad of officers assembled around me in a back hallway, perplexed. They wondered why we were not already deployed out on the nearby city streets. I advised them that department command had insisted that we remain within the facility, as security for delegates. The only provision for a change of posting would be that of emergency situations. I advised my young officers that the moment the officers on the streets uttered the magic words, "Help the Officer" over Seattle Police Radio, we would drop any other orders and respond en masse. I further informed the officers that such a call would come very quickly. We thus gathered our riot gear for that eventuality.

I held the microphone speaker of my portable radio to my ear. I heard the first alarming reports from the streets. Lieutenant Steve Paulsen, at the 6th and Pike venue advised that his small corps of thirty-five officers was totally overwhelmed by thousands of angry protesters marching eastbound. Shortly thereafter, he screamed into the radio, "We're losing it!" My officers tensed and wanted to sprint that direction. I slowed them and advised that we would be hearing calls for help in every direction. I knew that only a dozen officers held a post directly to the south of our Convention Center vantage point. We could hear the angry roar of crowds on police radio. And, we could now hear the roar through the windows of the huge facility.

We all heard the telltale high pitched alert tones over Seattle Police Radio, and repeated utterances of "Help the Officer" stemming from innumerable locations. I took a deep breath and tried to force myself to look calm in front of my young officers. I realized that I had rarely had occasion to be involved in riots during my career. Nonetheless, the young officers were looking upward at the six foot six man with bright white stripes on his sleeves. I made an exaggerated waving gesture to my officers and shouted, "OK, sports fans, it's show-time."

As we began to form into two ranks of officers in a quasi-military marching style, I immediately took notice of my long-time friend and fellow Sergeant Mike Brady, across a hallway to my left. Mike was simultaneously glancing to his right toward myself, while he was gathering his squad of officers. Having known and trusted "Brady Bunch" for nearly twenty years, I knew he had my back, and we would have his.

We marched rapidly to the south exits of the Convention Center. As we pushed the door open, the cold November wind poured through the opening. The deafening din of the angry mobs enveloped us. We were immediately pelted with fist-sized rocks and chunks of concrete. We could see that mobs were perched atop freeway overpasses, some sixty feet overhead. And, of course, SPD command hadn't assembled sufficient officers to secure such a strategic location. Almost immediately, a female officer was struck in the side of her riot helmet with concrete. Her knees buckled, and she went down.

Before Sergeant Brady or I could even respond, Lt. Schweitzer approached behind us from out of nowhere, with a small band of eight huge officers. The group encircled the injured officer and carried her rapidly to the safety of the Convention Center. Lt. Schweitzer gestured us to continue moving forward into the crowd. Our two squads quickly joined a beleaguered group of 12 officers and a Sergeant at 7th Avenue and Pike Street. You could see the fear and relief in the squad's eyes, through their riot helmets. We were one block from the Convention Center. My squad inserted itself within the other dozen officers, scattered across 7th Avenue. Sergeant Brady's squad secured each respective opposite side of the police line, so that our adversaries could not penetrate our lines, or circle behind us. We tried, as best we could, to provide safe passage for hundreds of terrified delegates in business attire to their venue. Yet, the crowds tossed blood and excrement upon some members of the delegation. Some spat upon the delegates after climbing street lights.

I was astounded as to the ferocity and size of the crowds. To our south, we faced some five thousand angry demonstrators. Many were dressed in turtle outfits, walking on bizarre stilts, waving swastikas, or banging on metal drums. Others were seen wearing bandit-like masks, carrying baseball bats with pickets loosely taped upon them, and toting conspicuously large denim bags over their shoulders. The crowd was spitting at officers, throwing small rocks, and waving middle fingers under the masks of the officers who were standing at ready attention in the ranks. The taunting was obviously intended to lure an officer into entering the hostile crowd. Yet, not one officer took the bait, as Sergeant Brady and I constantly reminded them to stay in formation.

To our north stood over 20,000 people gathered under the banner of the AFL-CIO, and other labor organizations. They were supplemented by the local Freedom Socialist Party, Communist Red Brigade, and a group of anarchists known as "Act Up." Approximately 120 officers in riot gear stood between that crowd and us. The squads of cops seemed to be dwarfed by the crowd. The massive crowd was beating on drums, blowing into horns, and setting off dozens of air-horns. Their roar resembled that of an NBA playoff game. I dreaded the thought of the two crowds coming through us to join ranks. We could hear the roar of additional thousands to our east, mostly out of our view.

The rocks and concrete continued to rain down upon us from above. I sought to broadcast the occurrence, but radio was too busied with cries for help. I could hear on police radio unknown Lieutenants and Sergeants advising of "shots fired," and "Molotov cocktails thrown." I could constantly hear an overwhelmed Lieutenant Paulsen advising that his troops were retreating, followed by, "We're losing it, radio…we're losing it!" There was absolutely no sense of leadership over the police airwaves from a high-ranking authority.

For many, many hours, the 36 to 50 officers at our location were able to convince the 5,0000 bizarre rioters to our south to not seek to fully challenge our force and authority. We were taunted into the night. We were pelted with rocks, and struck by steel ball- bearings fired with wrist rockets. We sought to jab at the masses with our heavy sticks, in order to keep some distance. Heavily tattooed young women of college age, with lip piercings, ran past the police lines. They carried vast "Super-Soaker" water guns with three-gallon packs on their backs. The young women ran down the police lines as they emptied the tanks into the many facemasks of the standing officers. The stench of human urine was unmistakable, as the matter dripped down our face shields, down our necks, and inside our bulletproof Kevlar vests. Two officers collapsed from exhaustion, and were carried to the safety of the Convention Center. Yet, we held our ground.

Finally, well into the early morning hours, the crowds subsided. We were ultimately relieved by dozens of officers from the night shift. They were shocked to hear our revelations of the first day of the riots. Our backs and feet were killing us, as we wandered to our personal cars, carrying the stench from our assaultors. We drove homeward for four hours of sleep before our return.

I listened to the AM radio on the drive home and learned of some of the extent of the rioting on the first day. I was astounded to hear the mayor and police chief proclaiming that all was well at the event. They each stressed how much they "appreciated" the demonstration of first amendment rights by the demonstrators (rioters). I was incensed and sickened to be working for such imbeciles.

Day Three

The sun rose reluctantly over the Washington State Convention Center on a cold, early December day. Tired officers arrived at five o'clock A.M. to the secure entrance to the underground parking garage, dreading the day to come. Seattle police officers from the overnight shift looked relieved to see their replacements arrive. They were augmented by Secret Service agents and military bomb canine squads. The arriving officers were greeted by more metal ball bearings, launched from wrist rockets from overpasses and rooftops. Numerous windshields of our personal vehicles were shattered. We hurried into the cave-like facility. We then mumbled profanities under our breaths, as we ambled toward the make-shift assembling area.

Lt. Schweitzer appeared, impeccable in appearance, as always. He quickly cut the pleasantries and told us what we already knew — that by far the worst was yet to come. He was unrepentant in his harsh criticisms of the Chief of Police and Mayor. He told the scores of assembled officers that our city was about to be "ruined." He was not telling us anything we did not already know. Yet, it was reassuring to hear the truth from a member of the department's command staff.

My squad was placed, yet again, within the safe confines of the Convention Center. Yet, all of us knew that the assignment would end with another sprint to the aid of fellow officers on the streets. At approximately nine thirty A.M. Chief Norm Stamper appeared in the halls of the Convention Center. He looked well-rested. He was smiling and shaking hands of officers and passing dignitaries. He again uttered comments about the beauty of the event, and how well the week was going. Officers turned away and rolled their eyes. Some officers were amused by the Chief. Others were infuriated.

By ten a.m. the atmosphere had changed. Our radios rang out with numerous reports of overwhelmed squads of officers. Molotov cocktails were said to be raining down on Seattle cops. Property destruction and looting was reportedly rampant. A full state of emergency was announced. Chief Norm Stamper simply stood, smiling at my assembled officers.

Finally, experienced Detective Karen Haverkate broke the silence, and screamed at the Chief, "Why don't you do something?!" The Chief remained standing and smiling, momentarily. Then, without uttering a word, he turned and sprinted down the long concrete back corridor of the building, and out of sight. We never heard his voice on Seattle Police radio at any time. He had simply escaped.

As my squad completed donning riot helmets and gloves, Lt. Schweitzer strode by our location. He assembled mine, and another squad, and directed us to hurry to 7th Avenue and Pike Street. He quickly uttered that we would experience nothing of an organized manner from our department. We were to use our own good judgment to preserve life, and hopefully property.

We opened the glass doors on the West side of the Washington State Convention Center into instant pandemonium. The crowds of 25,000 angry people the previous day had easily doubled. Our two squads marched military style the two blocks to 7th Avenue and Pike Street. We were pelted by rocks, bottles, human excrement, and M-80 firecrackers. The ever-present ball-bearings whizzed past our heads like bullets. Numerous individuals broke through dozens of police lines and sprinted past us. But we did not alter our course, knowing that backup squads were in place behind us to take out the freaks in turtle suits. Or so we hoped.

We arrived quickly to supplement one hundred or so Seattle cops, all clad in riot gear. I could not recognize anyone in the other squads, as we all had donned our gas masks. I finally recognized the nametag of Sergeant Mike Brady. I was again relieved to work beside a trusted friend of many years, as he patted me on the back and nodded. My squad joined the other squads in seeking to control police lines. I could see that the glass windows of all buildings within my view were shattered. Smoke and fire was rising from several burning dumpsters, and rioters were filling the dumpsters with unknown fuels. They were attempting to roll the first of the dumpsters into the police lines. As a half-dozen officers sought to roll the dumpster away from ourselves, I heard an enormous explosion. Scores of officers fell to the pavement, crushed by panicking crowds. Hundreds of rioters ran westbound from the explosion. I thought initially that the dumpster had contained a bomb. Yet, the dumpster remained intact, with flames rising five feet above such.

Another explosion echoed through downtown, louder than the first. I was able to determine the location to be a block to our north. Hundreds of rioters to our north scattered momentarily. The explosions continued for several minutes, and drew nearer with each detonation. We had no idea that the source of the deafening explosions was police concussion grenades. No announcements thereof ever came across our radio frequency. Rioters continued to alight dumpsters, and roll the burning cauldrons toward the cops. And officers alternately rolled the dumpsters away from themselves and the masses. Freaks in slasher movie-type garb, complete with hockey masks, continued to hurl rocks and Molotov cocktails at our officers. Others hurled teargas at police lines, while donning their own gas masks. We could hear windows smashing in the distance. Incessant sounds of banging drums and shrill whistles could be heard. A police helicopter and multiple media copters echoed loudly off of the skyline, overhead.

Simultaneously, tens of thousands of orderly union protestors could be seen standing politely in enormous, several block-long throngs. They looked to be aghast at the sight of the city in flames, smoke, and breaking glass. Some could be seen screaming at looters, as entire department stores were emptied.

Soon, mass quantities of tear gas could be seen exploding near our lines. The explosions endangered rioters and police at the same time. Ultimately, SWAT vans could be seen approaching. There were innumerable explosions, both generated by SWAT teams and parties unknown. In a surreal scene, school children could be seen, guided by teachers, participating in the demonstrations. This scene occurred, even while the chaos increased. Our faces burned from the ever-present tear gas, caking the sweat-soaked exterior of our gas masks. Our faces looked as if they'd been greatly sunburned. We gasped for ample oxygen through our gas masks, while seeking to force the hostile crowds backward. It was like breathing out of a straw while doing aerobics.

For hours we fought back thousands of angry rioters, while being pelted with every projectile and fluid known to exist. The sun fell without notice. The fires from burning dumpsters grew brighter in the darkness. The flashes of police concussion grenades soon resembled a fireworks display. Still, the fights with baseball-bat brandishing thugs waged long into the night. Some of the rioters awkwardly swung medieval-type maces in the direction of our heads. They received strong jabs from riot batons, as well as blows to the knees. They screamed out in pain and anger. We could see Captain Jim Pugel of the West Precinct standing decisively within the chaos. He stood with a bull-horn in his hand, and a portable police radio in the other. Clearly, he had taken command of the riots. We doubted that he had sought the blessing of assistant chiefs in doing so. We took great pride in his leadership and presence, as he strode rapidly toward other sites of skirmishes and into harm's way.

As midnight approached, our officers neared exhaustion. We had been on duty for nearly nineteen hours. We had barely time to locate a restroom. At times the gas masks became stifling, as we struggled for oxygen through the filters. Sweat pooled and sloshed within the masks, yet we dared not open them and allow tear gas within. Our own perspiration steamed up the eye-wear within the masks. A bottle of water was a luxury for scant few over the passing hours. Supplies of food never arrived. Some officers knelt on one knee in order to catch their breath. Yet, the thousands of demonstrators and rioters seemed to lose no energy.

At half past midnight, we knew that our energy level had dropped greatly. I was very concerned for the safety of our officers. They were perspiring enormously, and lowering their protective shields in fatigue. Thrown rocks were nearing faces. Additional college- aged young women emptied super-soakers filled with urine upon the facemasks of the cops. We were becoming surrounded by the angry mobs of rock-throwing, baseball bat swinging anarchist groups. Scattered rifle shots rang out from masked anarchists on building rooftops. I thought to myself that, were approaching assaulters to go unchecked, I would choose the use of my handgun. I no longer cared.

Suddenly, from out of nowhere, dozens and dozens of green-clad riot cops appeared amongst us. Fully clad in gas masks and helmets, the energetic squads of cops immediately set upon the rock-throwing thugs. I could hear whoops of joy coming through the masks of the exhausted Seattle cops. Our officers regained energy immediately. We all noticed, "King County Sheriff" patches on the shoulders of the new arrivals. Suddenly, rioters were falling to the ground from the jabs of riot sticks and the force of angry cops dragging them to the ground. Numerous thugs were dragged behind police lines and hog-tied in plastic "flex" cuffs. We could hear their breath exhaling rapidly from the force of officers' knees upon their backs.

King County Sheriff's Department helicopter, "Guardian One," broadcast via radio that they were eliminating the threat of rooftop snipers. We formed our own opinions as to how that occurred. The score of the ballgame was changing rapidly, in favor of the cops.

A county officer stood shoulder to shoulder with me for hours, repelling approaching rioters with strength and deftness. I was impressed with his stamina and quickness. While attempts were made by rioters to force the burning dumpsters and hurled debris upon police lines, they eventually retreated in defeat. Well into the early morning hours of the next day, the streets became silent. Only small skirmishes could be seen and heard. Scores of violent felons had been removed from the area.

Slowly, the green and blue-clad riot cops began to remove gas masks and helmets. Relieved and grateful Seattle cops patted their County counterparts on the back. Hands were shaken, and smiles returned to faces. I immediately noticed that the man next to me directed the county officers to share part or all of their carried food rations to the starving Seattle Police officers. As the county officer next to me turned around, I noted that he was a silver-haired veteran. He smiled and handed me his full food rations. I desperately gulped the bottle of water he handed me. He looked very familiar to me. I could not see any Sergeant stripes, nor Lieutenant bars upon his collar. Yet, he most assuredly displayed a command presence amongst the county officers. Just as I began to recognize the man, I heard one of his deputies refer to him, as "Sheriff." He was none other than the revered King County Sheriff, Dave Reichert.

As television crews began to near our location, the Sheriff directed his troops to join him in departing. It was very clear that he sought no media attention for his heroic actions, or unselfishness. It was only much later that Seattle officers related the story to the media.

We ultimately freed ourselves to roam a nearby alley for remaining rioters. We located two dozen bandana-masked individuals carrying wrist rockets and denim backpacks. They tried to fire more ball bearings at us as we approached. Yet, we closed the distance rapidly. Veteran officer Jack Napolitano was the first to reach our attackers. A former patrol partner, and respected Vietnam Veteran, Officer Napolitano could be seen smiling beneath his gas mask. Through the muffling of the mask, Officer Napolitano was heard to say to a fighting rioter, "Would you like stick… or spray?" With each word, the officer made ample use of his night-stick and pepper-mace. Our once cocky assaulters may have experienced a degree of discomfort, before becoming fully subdued for arrests.

Numerous squads of officers from innumerable outlying agencies, including the State Patrol, began deploying throughout downtown. We knew that the worst was over. By the same token, we knew that the worst could have been avoided, had the department sought assistance in advance. But the Mayor's office and Chief's Office had shown the costs of arrogance.

Finally, nearing two thirty A.M., we were officially relieved of our positions. We had spent 21 hours on our feet, watching the entire downtown Seattle corridor become a disaster area. The stunning sight resembled an epicenter of a massive earthquake.

I drove home, yet again, for the four hours of possible sleep. I again listened to AM radio accounts of the day. I learned that dozens of city blocks had been reduced to piles of broken glass. Hundreds of rioters had been arrested, and dozens of officers had been injured. Incredibly, no known fatalities had occurred. Finally, I heard the Mayor advise an earlier press conference of the following: That he had personally ordered city officials to summon mass quantities of pizza deliveries at the King County Jail. Hundreds of friends of rioters were provided free pizza dinners, while awaiting bail for jailed thugs. The freed thugs enjoyed the meals, upon their release. Mayor Schell's 500 cops could go without food or water for 21 hours without his concern. Yet, those responsible for millions of dollars in damage, and mass injuries, were deserving of delivered meals—at taxpayer expense. My fury regarding city and department management simply doubled. But that was just the beginning.

Day Four

Upon arrival at the venue at the usual hour of five o'clock a.m., a very different tone to the streets was evident. Mass amounts of riot-uniformed officers from a multitude of agencies lined the downtown corridor. Mayor Schell had finally called a state of emergency overnight, after Secret Service officials expressed their fury at the incompetence of the city of Seattle. National Guard troops were seen at numerous posts, augmenting the police presence. While the Guard was comprised primarily of unarmed young men from retail sales jobs and middle-aged professionals, the presence of the Army uniforms was reassuring. Scattered groups of anarchists could be seen wandering the streets, looking to smash what had already been smashed. Yet, the concealment of large crowds had ended. The streets were largely emptied by mayoral decree.

The somewhat uneventful morning was quickly disturbed by a commotion amongst law enforcement personnel, near the southwest grand entrance to the Washington State Convention Center. Secret Service Agents, ATF Agents, and several Seattle Police Lieutenants sprinted toward a driveway. Curious, my squad and I followed. As law enforcement personnel backed up toward us, we could see an automobile cordoned off by police tape. I asked a nearby Secret Service Agent the nature of such concern. A disgusted agent advised that the vehicle possessed a powerful pair of pipe bombs beneath the chassis. The agent muttered that the vehicle had passed through numerous secure checkpoints without bomb detection. He added that F.B.I., A.T.F., and Washington State Patrol bomb dogs had given no indication of a threat. I then asked the agent who *had* discovered the bombs. He pointed to the far side of the vehicle, as a young man in a green Army jump suit circled around the rear of the vehicle with a leashed dog. The nineteen-year-old raised two fingers toward scene commanders. He was indicating that, indeed, two bombs were attached to the vehicle. He walked his floppy-eared, clumsy German Sheppard away from the vehicle and petted him repeatedly. Skilled bomb specialists slowly removed the explosives. Sam and Kenny would later receive White House level commendations for locating the lethal devices. No one was laughing at the pair anymore.

Prior to our eventual deployment on posts on the streets, Lt. Schweitzer allowed the Convention Center officers to view an internationally televised press conference by the Mayor and Police Chief. We barely paid attention as the Mayor expressed his disappointment in the looting of his city. Yet, he remained steadfast in the wisdom of his event planning. We took profound interest as Police Chief Norm Stamper took the podium. We expected the Chief to laud the efforts of his officers in preventing a single fatality during two days of intense rioting. We further expected him to take some blame for the horrible pre-planning and staffing for the event by he and his "Senior Leadership Team."

Our collective jaws struck the convention center floor as the Chief began to speak. After rambling incoherently about first amendment rights, the Chief spoke about his troops. He apologized profusely for any "over-reactions" by his officers. He then strongly encouraged the public to file Internal Affairs and Civil Rights complaints against any officers perceived to have been heavy-handed during the riots. He made scant mention of any positive actions taken by his troops.

As the Chief continued to drone in front of the blinding lights from dozens of worldwide cameras, we walked furiously out of the building. He glanced sideways, momentarily, as he noticed all uniformed officers abandon him. He had instantly caused an irreparable rift between himself and his officers.

The WTO summit was essentially cancelled. Only small gatherings of insignificant delegates were seen within the convention center. The cavernous halls echoed from public address announcements, heard by virtually no one. As we walked onto the downtown Seattle streets to take numerous posts, we marveled at the spectacle. Countless blocks of the once vibrant downtown business core was a decimated ghost-town. Every window within view was shattered. Broken glass covered every inch of pavement and sidewalks, like six inches of fresh fallen snow. Every business was emptied of contents and demolished. The blood red encircled A of anarchist graffiti was spray-painted upon every building. Dozens of automobiles were overturned, and innumerable dumpsters lay on their sides, still smoldering from fires. A police patrol car was found lying on its side. The windows of the patrol car were shattered, and a shotgun had been torn from the floor boards.

We wandered aimlessly for hours down the eerily empty downtown. We visited with state troopers and officers from outlying agencies. We expressed our embarrassment at the handling of the event by the city. Yet, each officer, from agencies such as Bothell, Tukwila, Renton, et al expressed their respect for the rank and file Seattle Police officer. They were honored to come to our assistance. I had never personally experienced such camaraderie with other agencies, as during the riots. Similarly, the camaraderie amongst often- bickering SPD officers was unparalleled. There was a positive to the negatives.

Ultimately, the Seattle officers co-mingled with themselves. Hugs and handshakes abounded. We were astounded to learn that no life-threatening injuries had occurred during the battles on the streets. Yet, the worldwide event had been ruined, and we knew that we would take nothing but blame and acrimony from media and politicians.

We huddled around battery-powered televisions that unknown officers had supplied. We watched as Dan Rather of CBS News referred to the "total over-reaction" by Seattle cops. We watched actress Susan Sarandon address a press conference. She stated that "Seattle Cops are all jack-booted thugs, with big egos and small penises." We continued to watch for hours, lacking anything else to end the boredom. Local television news reports showed the "brutality" of Seattle and King County Sheriffs. They specifically stressed footage of a King County Sheriff's deputy kicking two "innocent art students from Seattle Central Community College." Angrily, numerous officers immediately recognized the two tattooed 20 year-olds. They were among those whom had emptied numerous super-soakers filled with urine upon our faces. We knew the same reporters had earlier stood- by filming such actions by the girls. Yet no footage nor mentioning of such assaults ever made the broadcast. The super-soaker girls were only referred to as "victims." We hoped to not contract hepatitis from their earlier assaults.

In the end, the largest riots in the city's history would conclude as they began—slowly and quietly. Official estimates of damage to the city exceeded 10 million dollars. The real total dwarfed those claimed. The incident was already being downplayed. The damage to the reputation of the city and its police department was inestimable. Yet, my pride in the professionalism and courage of my fellow officer was unparalleled in my career.

Police Chief Norm Stamper would ultimately resign in weeks to come. To his credit, he took all blame for the horrific planning that had been dominated by the Mayor. He managed to later compliment his officers. He knew that he had overlooked such a statement during the time of greatest poignancy. Mayor Paul Schell would not seek re-election to office the following year. He knew that he stood no chance of regaining his position.

And, a year later, actress Susan Sarandon would lead a star-studded cadre of entertainers in New York City at a gala event. She wore her red ribbon proudly on her evening gown, as she tearfully lauded the heroism of police officers lost during 9-1-1. She continued her performance by stating how much pride she had in all police officers across America. I could have vomited, as my wife Mahala quickly turned off the television.

Now, many years since the W.T.O. riots of 1999, I find it strange to return to the site of that bizarre week. Strangely, when in the area, I continue to hear the roar of 50,000 angry people. I still hear the explosions, banging, and whistling. And I see nothing but shattered glass and looted buildings. Interestingly, I have heard many peers relate the same phenomenon. At the risk of seemingly over-dramatizing the experience, the term Post Traumatic Stress Disorder comes to mind.

There were some positives to be attributed to the W.T.O. experience as well. We were later overwhelmed with the outpouring of appreciation from our community. It was evident that few believed the biased reports of local and national media. Hundreds of thank you letters and cards arrived in the precincts. Our doorsteps were buried in flowers. Most special to us, of all, were hundreds of pizzas delivered to our precincts. They arrived with letters of thanks from listeners to local radio station, KVI AM. Beloved talk show hosts Kirby Wilbur and John Carlson were the first to report the "pizzas to the thugs, starvation to the cops" program, endorsed by Mayor Schell. It meant a lot to us.

The greatest positive from the frightening week was the camaraderie and professionalism displayed by my fellow Seattle Police officers. For the only time in my 32- year career, all pettiness, selfishness, and competitiveness, all too often rife in our department, fell by the wayside. We stood side by side with one another and, literally, held one another up. The courage of 500 cops versus 50,000 angry people was astounding. And two leaders emerged from department management, in the forms of Lieutenant Dick Schweitzer and Captain Jim Pugel (who would ultimately become interim Police Chief).

***

Chapter 19: The Saints

In the profession of law enforcement, one is bombarded with years of negativity. Gore, violence, corruption, incompetence, and humanity at its worst, can greatly affect a perspective. It is, nonetheless, imperative that a balanced perspective is gained over the years. At the conclusion of my three decade-plus adventure, I will still state unequivocally that humankind is basically good. In the same breath, I will also add that humankind is basically corruptible. The glass is always filled to the mid-level.

When I walked away from this profession, I ultimately cherished the memories of some phenomenal souls encountered. I have worked with, and met, innumerable extraordinary human beings in Seattle Washington. I will hope to recount but just a few such persons. I honestly believe there are many living saints within our society. While the media wishes to convince gullible viewers that no heroes remain in society, nothing could be further from the truth. It is just that the truly good are too preoccupied with unselfishness to parade in front of cameras, like a football player after a touchdown. I would invite the cameras to visit an emergency room, police station, urban church, or alternative school some time. The stories are there for the recording.

***

Ms. Harris

In early 1982 I had occasion to return a wayward youth to her home in the Central District of Seattle, Washington. Within a crime-ridden, quasi-ghetto area of the city, sat a large, two story home on two lots. The home had a perfectly maintained white picket fence, neatly manicured lawns, and a crisp new paint job. A swinging bench sat occupied by two young girls on a beautiful white front porch. Other children could be seen playing on an extensive home-made playground on an adjoining lot. The thirteen year-old girl I had in custody looked frightened, as I walked her up the steps of the front porch. I asked her what she was so afraid of. She looked upward at me and said, "I let down Momma Harris."

Before I could even ring the doorbell, the stained glass door was opened. Before me stood a trim black woman of approximately fifty years of age. She was wearing a neatly pressed nursing outfit. She was very physically fit, but I could see fatigue in her eyes. Before I could say a word, she stated, "I saw your car pull up, officer...oh lord, what trouble have we tonight?" She cupped the young lady's chin in her palm gently, and guided the two of us into her parlor. The 75 year-old vast house was as immaculate within as the exterior had foretold. I was amazed at the appearance of the home, considering nearly a dozen young people, from ages 5 to 20 were busily circulating within such.

The woman introduced herself by name, and then advised that "everyone just calls me Ms. Harris, or Momma Harris... you can take your pick young man." She smiled warmly and offered me a piece of pumpkin pie. I declined her offer and sought to explain the shoplifting of a book by the young lady. Only then did she show minute anger toward the girl. Again, she cupped the girl's chin. Yet, this time she did so more firmly, as she raised the girl's eyes toward hers. Ms. Harris waved her finger at the girl's nose. She said, "What did I tell you about books, young lady?"

The girl responded, "That you will buy me any book I want, any time."

Ms. Harris then placed her hands on her hips. She said to the girl, "Then why in the Lord's name would you *steal* yourself a book?"

The girl looked up at Ms. Harris tearfully and said, "Cause I didn't want you to spend your money, Momma Harris… you work so hard for it."

With that, Ms. Harris said to the girl, "Oh girl, you just went and took all the angry outta me…you go on upstairs and do your homework….we *shall* talk later." I ended up conversing with Ms. Harris and many of her "kids" for nearly two hours. I would learn that she had adopted over fifty unwanted children to date, in her life. Without the assistance of a husband long ago lost to cancer, Ms. Harris had given them all a loving, strict, Christian home. While not every kid turned out perfectly (some went to prison), all had the knowledge of what love entailed.

In subsequent years, I would learn the legend of Ms. Harris within the Central District community. She often worked double shifts at a local hospital in order to maintain a lifestyle for her many children. Yet, all of the children were provided with the essentials — three delicious and healthy meals a day, immaculate sensible clothing, and unlimited love and guidance. Ms. Harris had created a "system" of raising children. As each child progressed in age through her guidance and discipline, they would provide mentoring and peer support to the newest, youngest additions to the family. Rules were posted conspicuously throughout the home, and chores were assigned. The penultimate rule was simple, "Give." Ms. Harris gave to the sick, the poor, to her church, and even to the down and out on a street corner. She never thought of herself. It was often said, that the lady never slept.

Were some of the troubled kids to come into legal trouble, Ms. Harris had a set response. She would always offer "no excuses" for the children. She never allowed such thinking. She would then advise the particular incarcerated youth, "I will *always* love you....but, today, you do not love yourself or your God." Most of her kids would turn out to know the meaning of love, and pay the gift forward.

Ms. Harris has now passed away. During her amazing lifetime, she raised countless kids whom had been thrown on the trash heap by society. The kids were of every color, background, and difficult situation. Some of those grown kids remain troubled. Some are just regular folks. Many have become exceptional, in compassion or in talents. On one occasion, a certain weightless Space Shuttle astronaut, briefly flashed a scrawled message on a message board. It simply read, "I love you, Momma Harris." A NASA photograph of the moment was displayed prominently on the wall of Ms. Harris' home — along with hundreds of other family photos.

Another of her kids would grow up to become a commercial artist. He eventually purchased a home, directly to the north of Ms. Harris' cradle of love. I was enormously privileged to be invited into the home. While the very large home had once been a run-down disaster, the artist had nursed the house back to health — and then some. He had eliminated many ceilings of the three story house for openness. Within such, stood the African-American version of the Sistine Chapel. The sight was mind-boggling. Every wall and ceiling of the house was painted in the most dazzling settings I have ever seen. It was an explosion of color. The brush strokes were clearly that of genius. As I looked closer, I could recognize the dozens of scenes, depicting Momma Harris and her scores of children. The varied meanings of the scenes became evident. All were showing how to raise a family.

I advised the man that he could be enormously rich, were he to allow the public and media to view the home. He answered, that he made a sufficient living in his commercial art business. Finally, he added, only family members and invited guests would ever view the astounding interior of the home. He said the home stood as "a shrine to Momma Harris — a true American Saint."

She never made the papers, magazines, or Oprah. But I believe she sits alongside Mother Theresa somewhere, swapping stories and recipes. And, undoubtedly, thinking of someone other than herself.

***

Police Chaplain John Oas

Chaplain John was a tiny five foot seven, curly-haired, mustachioed man. He wore large glasses and showed ample evidence of having eaten at a few too many weddings, over which presided. He, and his equally tiny and delightful wife, Kay, were a blessing for the men and women in uniform in this area for over thirty years. As Chaplain John was often wont to saying, to the crowds at the funerals of fallen officers, "There is not one of you here today that I do not know or love." And the wonder is in the truth of his statement. Chaplain John Oas served as an unpaid clergyman to the 1, 200 men and women of the Seattle Police Department, the 800 Seattle Fire Fighters, and even the members of the Local Bureau of Alcohol, Tobacco, and

Firearms for over three decades. It is astounding that he could make the time to personally know and appreciate every single member of these vast agencies. His tiny office was wallpapered with hundreds of photos of officers, our spouses, and our kids. John could name every subject of a photo.

I was forever amazed to see how John innately knew when he should spend extra time with a heavy-hearted or troubled officer. He seemed to be everywhere at once. As years passed, I learned that he was the confidante of hundreds. Were a friend to be in need, we would all request John's intervention. And he would soon work miracles on the friends. John would go flying in their experimental airplanes, ride horses, or attend a karaoke- fest in order to show the officer he cared. He married hundreds of officers, including my best friend. He baptized our children. He even married my daughter, which made the event even more special.

John was a learned theologian whom led many pilgrimages to Israel. He held great respect by leaders of other religions, and was often welcome in domains where others would not gain entrance. John Oas lent his expertise in crisis intervention on a local, state, and even national scale. He had been there with devastated families for plane crashes, school shootings, and scud missile attacks on our soldiers in Iraq. He led the somber procession of six firefighters' bodies, carried from the burned remains of the Pang Warehouse arson fire in Seattle.

While a man of the cloth, being around thousands of cops and soldiers his whole adult life most definitely rubbed off. I recall one of my earliest occasions meeting John Oas, on a day in which we had all hauled a robbery suspect into a holding cell. The suspect presented himself as a vile and hostile human being. We asked the good Chaplain if he would be willing to speak with the 20 year-old man. John was happy to assist. After about five minutes, Chaplain Oas stepped out of the holding cell, toward the several gathered patrol officers. He said, "I can't help this young man....he's an a—hole." Chaplain John Oas always was, and forever will be, one of us. We lost him suddenly last year and heaven has gained a priceless new member. He will be forever missed in these whereabouts. There is no way to replace him.

***

Officer John Abraham

On any given day, or inconvenient hour, SPD motorcycle Officer John Abraham might have been awakened from his sleep with a call for help. The call would invariably entail a tragedy suffered by a law enforcement family. Since Seattle is blessed with Harborview Medical Center, and legendary Doctor Michael Copass, seriously injured or ill patients arrive from all over the country. Years ago, devastated law enforcement families did not know where to turn for assistance, so far from home. That void was filled by John Abraham from 1991 to 2013.

Officer Abraham was a member of the staff of the Seattle Police Officers Guild for many years. He was a respected patrol and traffic officer for his entire career. He once nearly lost his life, when attacked by a homicide suspect that he arrested. He did not allow the vicious attack to deter him from enjoying a prosperous career. He could be relied upon for good judgment and impassioned, honest police-work. John also devoted himself to a side job within the department, as the police safety officer. He worked a full-time motorcycle traffic position and then lent his insight into assuring and improving safety precautions for all rank and file cops.

John advised that he was first called upon to answer his "calling," when he fielded a request at the Police Guild office to lend assistance to the family of an east coast officer. John learned that the officer was receiving treatment in Seattle for life threatening leukemia. The assistance provided to the family by Officer Abraham surpassed the family's wildest dreams. John did not do anything half-heartedly. He opened his home, his wallet, and his heart to that family during a time of crisis. He did so ever since that time.

Over the years, Officer Abraham formalized the creation of an official Seattle Police Officers Guild sanctioned program known as, "Help the Officer." The name of his program mirrored the three most serious words that may be uttered over Seattle Police Radio. He thus converted the three most troubling words in our police vernacular to three words of profound inspiration.

John Abraham, and a team of volunteer officers, created a program of organized responses to tragedies, involving cops around the world. If those tragedies brought the families to Seattle Washington for the incomparable medical care, John and his team would be there for them. These impassioned, unselfish officers were thus prepared for the following:

In April of 2005 a Coeur d'Alene Idaho officer was shot in the face during an arrest. The bullet pierced the officer's eye socket, severed his carotid artery, and ricocheted in pieces into his spinal cord. He was air-lifted to Sea-Tac Airport, in Seattle. The officer arrived at Sea-Tac airport, in critical condition.

Meanwhile, a devastated family was advised by police commanders that their lives had instantly changed. A citizen of Couer d'Alene volunteered to fly the family to Seattle. Officer Abraham arranged for Port of Seattle Police Department officers to stand by at the airport to escort the ambulance to Harborview Medical Center. He then arranged for motorcycle police escorts from Washington State Patrol and Seattle Police Traffic officers for the myriad of family members arriving in the area at two different airports. He arranged for uniformed Seattle Police guards at the hospital room of the fallen officer.

The family was housed in John's home, while more permanent arrangements could be made. He devoted every spare second of his personal time to transporting the family to and from the hospital, and viewing the painful recovery for the officer himself. He, and his team, forged a lasting bond with the family over the months spent in Seattle that saved the patient's life.

This scene was repeated over nearly twenty years by Officer Abraham. He adopted scores of families. He took them into his home, provided meals and necessities, and showed out-of-staters the most beautiful sights of Seattle Washington. No doubt the most spectacular sight for those so affected was the graying, mustachioed, and ever smiling John Abraham. John is one of the most unselfish and giving persons ever to grace this world. He could often be seen outside of Safeco Field, directing traffic. His smile and laughter was ever present. Passing crowds went by totally unaware of the fact that they were in the presence of greatness. But the nearby men and women in uniform were all aware that they were blessed to work around or near the man known as, "Seattle's Blue Angel." He has recently retired from police-work, but his huge heart will serve mankind for all his life, without doubt.

***

Mr. Dutch Schisler

By age nine, young Dutch Schisler had begun his career of drinking. Having come from a troubled home, he forged age documentation and joined the military. While he would serve our country with distinction, the young man's bout with alcoholism would later become daunting.

For over two decades Dutch's alcoholism descended to the rock bottom of the societal strata. He was a "skid-row" wino. He slept for years on the bitter cold sidewalks of many a large city. His peripatetic slumbering finally landed him on the cold streets of Seattle Washington.

Suddenly, and inexplicably, Dutch finally found an end to his plight. As he would later relate, Dutch finally could not stand his self-imposed suffering another day. He never touched another drink for the remainder of his life. As he often recalled later, "God turned on a light bulb for me... but it was more like a fluorescent... slow and steady."

Dutch Schisler turned his personal suffering into a cause to help others. He founded the first detoxification center in the country. Suddenly, hordes of hopelessly intoxicated individuals could find a home beyond a cold sidewalk, or a jail cell. Dutch obtained federal grants to create a medical facility for the chronic street alcoholics. Vans were purchased to cruise the downtown Seattle environs to locate those collapsed hopelessly on sidewalks and in alleys.

Over the years, Dutch hired and trained dozens of former alcoholics to work within his program. Incredibly filthy, sometimes parasite/ disease-ridden individuals were literally carried into the van by Dutch and his employees. They received medical care at Harborview Medical Center, and subsequent placement for several days in a detoxification center. The brutal "D.T's" were monitored and controlled. Dutch did not preach to his clientele, save for one oft-repeated mantra — "Quit feeling sorry for yourself."

Dutch was a daily companion to the downtown Seattle

street cops. He picked up the down and out and found an appropriate home for them. He often identified dead bodies found in run-down hotels. He had an extraordinary memory for the hundreds of street alcoholics. They were like family to him. He always brought an extraordinary persona of happiness. He knew that he was living on borrowed time, and treasured each additional day that his liver would still function. Occasionally, Dutch would wear his famous three-piece suit on the streets. He had been a guest on the Johnny Carson show due to his extraordinary philanthropy. He wore the suit during that television appearance.

Dutch Schisler was a street version of Will Rogers. He truly never met a man or woman whom he did not like. Years later, the ravages of decades of alcoholism would take Dutch's life, at age 67. His funeral was attended by hundreds. He is dearly missed on the streets by the cops whom called him friend. Yet, his program has increased in effectiveness exponentially since the original days of the founder. It has spread nationwide. Dutch's compassion, toughness, and amazing personality will never be forgotten.

***

Ms. Renee Hopkins

Sitting in a spacious 7th floor office with a view overlooking Elliott Bay is an exceptionally attractive and bright young woman of some thirty-six years of age. She staffs a Seattle Police Foundation Executive position. Her name is Renee Hopkins. She has used her Master's Degree in Public Administration to work a number of jobs. All of such jobs have had the exclusive purpose of helping society. She has worked with the under-privileged and decimated communities in Nicaragua, in order to seek economic and legal justice. She has worked with homeless kids in Spokane Washington. And the Seattle Police Department was fortunate in obtaining her services to work in grant services, and years later, Seattle Police Foundation support for the department's officers. Renee Hopkins used her intellect and experienced to gain vast sums of federal and local grant monies toward efforts for the benefit of Seattle youths and their families.

Ms. Hopkins was instrumental in securing and maintaining years of grant funding efforts for troubled youth, known as "Project Ride." I believe the program held the answers to the majority of America's looming problems. My only wish is that we could have spread word on a national level of how overwhelmingly successful such a program could be. In essence, were America to devote its efforts toward the issues facing our youth, we would have far fewer issues years later with our adults. I will describe the aspects of the program funded by Renee to a vast extent below, in hopes that a version thereof may be revived on a national scale:

The program provided intense interaction with troubled youths, their families, and an impassioned Seattle Police Juvenile Squad which I supervised. Young people whom were committing crimes, failing school, and seeking choices, such as gang involvement, drugs, and prostitution, suddenly received what they needed most--attention.

Overwhelmed parents soon found pairs of detectives in their homes, earnestly seeking to assist in stopping the downward spiraling of the lives of their young. Contracts were written in juvenile courts wherein specific lifestyle rules were agreed upon by the youths, parents, prosecuting attorneys, and defense attorneys. Clear consequences were delineated.

Ultimately, the youths were held to reasonable standards. They were to attend school, avoid anti-social contacts with negative peers, and abide by household rules, such as curfews. The grant allowed for the detectives to become highly involved in the lives of the youths. The outpouring of support by the community, facilitated in part, by Ms. Hopkins, was overwhelming. Churches, schools, businesses, athletic clubs, et al donated time or money toward the program.

Young people with previously low self -esteem were afforded jobs, tutoring, vocational training, and involvement in a myriad of local athletic associations and clubs. They were shown the obvious benefits to positive behaviors. By the same token, were the particular youths to violate curfew, and disappear to whereabouts unknown seeking to commit more crimes, SPD detectives and King County probation officers would immediately begin the search. Very relieved parents would be advised that the searchers quickly located their youths — in the wrong parts of town. Thus, the violators would spend the weekend, or more, in juvenile detention. Excuses were not accepted. The parents would be delighted to learn that the grant allowed for funding of tutors and teachers within the confines of the Youth Service Center. Thus, positive measures were constantly followed.

Through the program the youths experienced the following: Job Placement, Tutoring, Fishing excursions, Boxing club enrollment, celebrity athlete mentoring, mental health services, alcohol/ drug treatment, anger management training, escorts to the funerals of youths whom had made horrible life choices, police ride-alongs, and constant police/probation scrutiny. Often, such scrutiny led to arrests. In short, the kids received both carrots and sticks toward positive life choices. The crimes committed by dozens of chosen kids would ultimately be reduced by 95 per cent over a number of years. There could be no argument that such efforts worked.

Over the years, some of the troubled youths chose to re-offend. Some lost their lives by violent means due to horrible choices. Moreover, the overwhelming majority of kids, who would have gone down the societal toilet, turned their lives around. Countless productive adults returned to our precinct to visit with my extraordinary squad of detectives. They came by with college scholarships in their hands. They wore Marine and Navy uniforms. They had successful corporate business careers. They all wished to point out that they would have otherwise been deceased or imprisoned in their youth, were it not for my group of six- plus extraordinary human beings with badges, whom had made a difference. Sadly, egos, selfishness, department politics, and corruption ultimately brought an end to a program that could revolutionize this country. Many families suffered as a result. Our phones would often ring at the cessation of the program with desperate mothers advising that their kids were missing at night.

Nonetheless, it shall always be remembered that Ms. Hopkins had quietly managed to make this all happen with her work behind the scenes. In addition to Renee Hopkins, my detectives about whom I shall forever hold great pride and admiration for their innovation and dedication to troubled youths were the following: Detective Susan Vijarro, Detective Linda Dolane (now retired), Detective Al Lebar, Detective Tawnia Pfaff, and Detective ("Saint Fred") Villaflor,(also now retired).

Over the years, I have often engaged in heated debate with Renee Hopkins regarding philosophies and politics. We often disagree, while seeking the same goals. I was once arrogant enough to claim Ms. Hopkins lacked any insight into the experiences of victims in our society. Only patiently, over many months, did Renee inform me that she had more intimate knowledge of victimology than I could ever dream of gaining. I was, eventually, embarrassed and humbled to learn that the depths some of Ms. Hopkins's personal tragedies. Some of her experiences had merited national attention. Others were private issues of profound impact. She had seen the ugliest sides of society from the inside out. Yet, she had never shown an instant of anger or self- pity. Instead, she had dedicated her life to the betterment of others. She is yet another quiet hero, surrounded by those mentioned above and those overlooked.

***

And, finally...

When I sought insight into how to construct a non-fiction book, I was told to scribble down ideas for several story lines. I was told to hope for forty to fifty such ideas. I finally stopped writing down ideas when my numbers neared 500. While I am sure many officers shall argue the accuracy of my stories, it is I whom retained copious notes, photographs, press clippings, and police reports during my career. It was rather overwhelming to take a retrospective look at that 32- year adventure. I could have answered in-depth questions about taking the life of another human being. But the issue was too personal. I could have delved much further into the macabre or matters regarding corruption. But I sought to strike a balance. While I belabor how drastically times have changed in recent years, I can still celebrate the roller-coaster ride for which I applied. The vocation lived up to my expectations, and then, so much more.

While some people have traveled the world to see humankind, I stood still and watched it pass before my eyes. The trip for me was an extraordinary education for a naive, skinny kid from Yakima, Washington, who was way too serious in his youth. Even now, I wonder if I was ever cut out for such a difficult line of work. Yet, I believe there will be some peers who might assert that I carried my weight. I will treasure my badges forever, and pass them on to my daughters when my laps around the sun cease. I now have a book of experiences for my granddaughters to someday study. I hope they will be proud of their "Grandpa-Steve." This history is theirs as well.

It is my hope that I have not over-used the words "I" or "Me" throughout this endeavor. I am most assuredly not the star of the show. Humankind has to take the limelight. That includes those amazing people with whom I worked. It is my hope that I have not embarrassed my peers needlessly. But I sought to be truthful. Few have made more mistakes along the way than I.

Above all, it is my hope that I have aptly captured the remarkably unique personalities of those whom have served, and those whom we do serve. They are like an enormous cast of the longest, greatest movie. Many of my peers were bigger than life, and I am not worthy of carrying their shoes.

I now enjoy the times that I so looked toward, when I handed my metaphorical pail to the next recruit. They will take their turn shoveling the sand against the tide. Someday, they will walk away wondering if they made a difference at all. But they made take solace, at least, in the knowing that they took the time to try. It is my hope that they feel great pride and interest in the fact that they were part of a very unique group. Moreover, it is the only such group in society that may travel from mankind's penthouse to the basement, and every floor in between. That group shall always be the cops.

I will forever tip my hat to those whom do not sleep at night, so that others may.

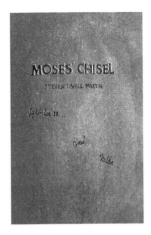

Moses' Chisel

By
Steven Lowell-Martin

They will hear the table conversation of the Last Supper live. Government, academic, and religious leaders convene far beneath the earth's crust in a super-secret catacomb at the invitation of the National Security Agency to be witnesses to the impossible. Suddenly, the world's most advanced listening post is privy to every conversation in history. But some stories are better left alone. The greed-driven corporate ruse that was 9-11, Bin-Laden, and the resultant gulf wars is unexpectedly revealed. A triad of mega-billionaires proves willing to pay with their fortunes or the blood of innocent witnesses in order to conceal their scheme. The full story of the resurrection of Christ and the involvement of Islamic icons is similarly revealed. The Vatican becomes an unwitting participant in the man-hunt for the project's founders. Stanford Physicist Gordon Huard and corrupt NSA Director Michael Portworth are propelled into worldwide exile. They are reunited by the most unlikely of sources and drawn together to bring down the "New World Order," inclusive of a sitting President.

Everlasting Publishing
PO Box 1061
Yakima, Washington 98907
USA

everlastingpublishing.org

Made in the USA
San Bernardino, CA
22 November 2014